Dearest 'Bro,

Mark Twain

+

DAVID LEVY :

2 Great Men = 1 Superlative Book !!

Enjoy ! Happy 61st !!

&

much love,

Mark Twain, 1908. (Photolibrary.com)

David W. Levy

David Ross Boyd Professor
of History, Emeritus
The University of Oklahoma

Mark Twain

The Divided Mind of America's Best-Loved Writer

THE LIBRARY OF AMERICAN BIOGRAPHY

Edited by Mark C. Carnes

Prentice Hall

Boston Columbus Indianapolis New York San Francisco Upper Saddle River Amsterdam
Cape Town Dubai London Madrid Milan Munich Paris Montreal Toronto Delhi
Mexico City São Paulo Sydney Hong Kong Seoul Singapore Taipei Tokyo

For Richard and Linnea

Executive Editor: Ed Parsons
Editorial Assistant: Amanda A. Dykstra
Senior Marketing Manager: Maureen E. Prado Roberts
Marketing Assistant: Marissa O'Brien
Operations Specialist: Renata Butera
Cover Designer: Karen Salzbach
Creative Art Director: Jayne Conte
Manager, Visual Research: Beth Brenzel
Manager, Rights & Permissions: Zina Arabia

Manager, Cover Visual Research & Permissions: Karen Sanatar
Cover Illustration: Mark Twain Memorial House & Museum
Full-Service Project Management: Joseph Barnabas Malcolm, PreMediaGlobal
Composition: PreMediaGlobal
Printer/Binder: Edward Brothers
Cover Printer: Lehigh-Phoenix Color/Hagerstown
Text Font: Sabon

Library of Congress Cataloging-in-Publication Data

Levy, David W.
   Mark Twain: the divided mind of America's best-loved writer / David W. Levy.
      p. cm. — (The library of American biography)
   Includes bibliographical references and index.
   ISBN-13: 978-0-205-55375-4
   ISBN-10: 0-205-55375-3
   1. Twain, Mark, 1835-1910. 2. Authors, American—19th century—Biography.
3. Humorists, American–Biography. I. Title.
   PS1331.L48 2010
   818'.409–dc22

                                                                                                        2010011362

Prentice Hall
is an imprint of

www.pearsonhighered.com

ISBN-10:   0-205-55375-3
ISBN-13: 978-0-205-55375-4

Contents

Editor's Preface

In many respects, Mark Twain is an anomalous figure: a humorist who is among America's first notable writers of "serious" literature; a celebrity in a nation that has rarely made celebrities of its writers; an author whose immense popularity in his own time has been superseded by his posthumous legacy. Indeed, he is the only professional writer to be profiled in the Library of American Biography, a collection that presents the lives of those who best illuminate the American past. Why was Twain the foremost writer of an age that included many literary titans? Why has he grown in stature while most of the others have faded? And why should one seeking to understand America's Gilded Age—a term coined by Twain himself—read a book about Twain rather than his own distinctive words on the subject?

The answer to each of these questions relates to another of Twain's anomalous qualities. Most successful writers are keen observers whose critical faculties are improved by a measure of distance from their subjects: Charles Dickens, writing from his comfortable Victorian study, laid bare the inequities of a British legal and economic system that his peers regarded as the envy of the world; Harriet Beecher Stowe, a comfortable Northerner, rendered the inhumanity of a slave system that white Southerners had accepted as a way of life. Twain, by contrast, made his name with wickedly comic accounts of his own lived experience (*Innocents Abroad*, *Life on the Mississippi*) and propelled it to greatness with fiction that drew heavily on his small-town,

Southern childhood and nomadic young adult years (*Tom Sawyer, Huckleberry Finn*). A journalist by profession and an inveterate traveler by choice, Twain was as sharp an observer as his literary peers. But he often lacked the requisite distance from his subjects to regard them with detachment. In these pages, David W. Levy, a renowned scholar and teacher of American intellectual history, argues that Twain's work reveals intense and conflicting reactions toward the enormous industrial, economic, and social change he witnessed in America during his lifetime.

To be sure, Twain, a born cynic, found plenty to criticize. Indeed, few writers have viewed the failings of their own societies with such bitterness. In the final section of *A Connecticut Yankee in King Arthur's Court,* for example, Twain describes how 25,000 knights in plumed helmets are blasted by dynamite, electrocuted by high-voltage fences, and sliced up by Gatling guns. Their rotting corpses spread disease. This is, quite literally, overkill—a hijacking of a funny novel into dark realms, for Twain was intent on denouncing both the chivalric impulse that led Southerners into the Civil War and the brutal efficiency with which Northern factories crafted the machinery of slaughter.

But Twain's criticism of America's elite and powerful was never that of an outsider. While Twain sniffed at the trappings of social status, he was building a grand house in Hartford and sporting distinctive white suits; while satirizing the restless pursuit of money, he was scheming to get more of it for himself; while poking fun at the mechanical contrivances of the modern age, he was exhausting his savings to invest in dubious new inventions. The American people understood that Twain was one of them: they perceived that he did not so much write about American life as live it.

The publication of this biography coincides with the hundredth anniversary of Twain's death. It is a fitting memorial. With wit, humor, and consummate craftsmanship, Levy illuminates the intersection of an extraordinary writer with extraordinary times—an ideal match of biographer and subject.

MARK C. CARNES
ANN WHITNEY OLIN PROFESSOR OF HISTORY
BARNARD COLLEGE/COLUMBIA UNIVERSITY

Acknowledgments

Over the years, I have had the pleasure of discussing Mark Twain and various of his works with hundreds of undergraduates at the University of Oklahoma. It is a pleasure to acknowledge here the numerous ideas and insights that I have gained from those discussions. Two good friends, Robert Shalhope and Melvin Urofsky, rendered me the generous service of reading through the entire manuscript at an early stage; they will recognize many of their helpful comments and suggestions in this final version. Mark Carnes, the general editor of the Library of American Biography series, has been a model of what an editor should be—a source of very sound advice and generous encouragement. There is scarcely a page in this book that has not been considerably improved by the editorial assistance of Amanda Dykstra. Her sure hand, sharp eye, sympathetic expertise, and steady good sense have made working with her a genuine pleasure. Finally, to my wife Lynne, I owe, as usual, enormous gratitude for her unfailing support and daily help in a thousand ways; I have become accustomed to her sacrifices on my behalf, but hope that I have never taken them for granted.

DAVID W. LEVY
DAVID ROSS BOYD PROFESSOR OF HISTORY, EMERITUS
THE UNIVERSITY OF OKLAHOMA

Prologue

I

Some of the most famous lines ever written by Mark Twain occur near the end of the sixteenth chapter of *Adventures of Huckleberry Finn*. Those who have read and loved that book will probably remember the setting. Young Huck Finn, the escaping white boy, and his companion Jim, the escaping black slave, have been floating down the Mississippi on a raft. Their journey down the mighty river has drawn the two of them into a friendship that could never have blossomed on land. They exult in the freedom and serenity of their time together in the midst of nature. Huck describes their primitive life on the raft in perfectly idyllic terms: "We catched fish, and talked, and we took a swim now and then to keep off sleepiness. It was kind of solemn, drifting down the big still river, laying on our backs looking up at the stars, and we didn't ever feel like talking loud, and it warn't often that we laughed, only a little kind of a low chuckle." Later on Huck says that "other places do seem so cramped up and smothery, but a raft don't. You feel mighty free and easy and comfortable on a raft."

Near the end of Chapter 16, however, it is nighttime, and Huck and Jim hear, coming toward them over the black water, the ominous sound of that prodigious symbol of mid-nineteenth-century industrial technology, a steamboat. "We could hear her pounding along, but we didn't see her good till she was close. She aimed right for us." Huck gives a graphic and horrifying

1

description of the approaching monster: "She was a big one, and she was coming in a hurry, too, looking like a black cloud with rows of glow-worms round it; but all of a sudden she bulged out, big and scary, with a long row of wide-open furnace doors shining like red-hot teeth. . . . There was a yell at us, and a jingling of bells to stop the engines, a pow-wow of cussing, and whistling of steam—and as Jim went overboard on one side and I on the other, she comes smashing straight through the raft." The intensity of Twain's language in that passage, and the fact that shortly after writing it, he put the novel aside for three years, justify a suspicion that he was trying to say something important, something troubling and heartfelt about the encounter between the innocent and vulnerable natural world and the steam-belching, fire-breathing, big and scary mechanized world of American technology—a world that was coming in such a hurry, too.

That moment in *Huckleberry Finn* was not the only time that Twain depicted steamboats as monstrous creatures, frightening in their awesome power, cruel and brutal and heedless of nature and humanity. In his first novel, *The Gilded Age* (written with his friend and neighbor Charles Dudley Warner) a similar collision between the peacefulness of nature and the fury of the steamboat occurs. The Hawkins family, migrating to Missouri in search of new opportunities, finds itself on the east bank of the Mississippi. After supper, Uncle Dan'l and his wife, Aunt Jinny—the family's two gentle slaves—go with the children to view the river. Sitting quietly on a log, they "contemplated the marvelous river and discussed it." The natural setting is quite perfect: "the moon rose and sailed aloft through a maze of shredded cloud-wreaths; the sombre river just perceptibly brightened under the veiled light; a deep silence pervaded the air and was emphasized, at intervals, rather than broken, by the hooting of an owl, the baying of a dog, or the muffled crash of a caving bank in the distance." The little group was "so awed . . . by the grandeur and the solemnity of the scene before them," that—like Huck and Jim on the raft—"their voices were subdued to a low and reverent tone."

But then the peace is shattered. "Suddenly Uncle Dan'l exclaims: 'Chil'en, dah's sumfin a comin'!'" He points down the river.

"A deep coughing sound troubled the stillness. . . . All in an instant a fierce eye of fire shot out from behind the cape and sent a long brilliant pathway quivering athwart the dusky water. The coughing grew louder and louder, the glaring eye grew larger and still larger, glared wilder and still wilder. A huge shape developed itself out of the gloom, and from its tall duplicate horns dense volumes of smoke, starred and spangled with sparks, poured out and went tumbling away into the farther darkness. Nearer and nearer the thing came. . . ." The huddling and terrified observers are convinced that the steamer must be an unfriendly deity. They fall to their knees, and Dan'l offers a frightened prayer for mercy, but then "the flaming and churning steamer was right abreast the party" and "the awful thunder of a mud-valve suddenly burst forth, drowning the prayer." Uncle Dan'l grabs up two of the petrified children and they all flee into the woods.

In the next chapter of *The Gilded Age* Twain gives another vivid description of the destructive potential of those fearful machines. Two proud steamboat pilots find themselves racing side-by-side down the river; neither is willing to concede the contest to his rival; both order more fuel piled into the dangerously overstrained furnaces. "And then there was a booming roar, a thundering crash," as one of the boats explodes. The other one "took off the dead, the wounded and the unhurt—at least all that could be got at, for the whole forward half of the boat was a shapeless ruin, with the great chimneys lying crossed on top of it, and underneath were a dozen victims imprisoned alive and wailing for help." Then, "a new horror presented itself. The wreck took fire from the dismantled furnaces!" The stricken boat "went drifting down the stream an island of wreathing and climbing flame that vomited clouds of smoke from time to time, and glared more fiercely and sent its luminous tongues higher and higher after each emission. A shriek at intervals told of a captive that had met his doom." The survivors and rescuers "saw a pitiful sight and heard a world of pitiful sounds. Eleven poor creatures lay dead and forty more lay moaning, or pleading or screaming. . . ."

When Twain wrote that harrowing description of the explosion of a steamboat, he was almost certainly remembering a real explosion that had occurred more than a dozen years earlier, in 1858. On the morning of June 13, the steamer *Pennsylvania* blew up about sixty miles down river from Memphis, four of its eight boilers erupting and lifting the front third of the boat high into the air and landing it onto the remaining wreckage. Dozens of passengers were hurled into the river and a fire broke out. Some who were not killed immediately suffered terrible injuries or were scalded beyond help and "shrieks and groans filled the air." Many were trapped in the fire and "begging piteously for help." Mark Twain's beloved younger brother Henry was among the casualties on that fearful day. Twain, who had been working on another boat, rushed to the makeshift Memphis hospital in time to watch as his brother slowly died. "Long before this reaches you," the shattered Twain wrote to his sister-in-law from the bedside, "my poor Henry,—my darling, my pride, my glory, my *all*, will have finished his blameless career, and the light of my life will have gone out in utter darkness. O, God! this is hard to bear."

Thus Mark Twain understood very well the fearsome and destructive potential of that marvelous, that awesome, that monstrous creature of American technological and mechanical progress. He knew its darkest side: its enmity to the natural world, its threat to human relationships, its capacity for the merciless devastation of innocence and decency and humanity itself.

II

But that was not the only way that Mark Twain wrote about those monsters. In some moods he loved steamboats. He had, after all, spent four of the most fulfilling years of his life working aboard them. In his classic account, *Life on the Mississippi* (which was published *between* those terrifying descriptions in *The Gilded Age* and *Huckleberry Finn*), he gives readers quite a different perspective. "When I was a boy," Twain tells us, "there was but one permanent ambition among my comrades in our village on the west bank of the Mississippi River. That was, to be a steamboat man. We had transient ambitions of other sorts, but they were only transient. When a circus came and went, it left us all burning to become clowns; the first negro minstrel show that came to our section left us all suffering to try that kind of life; now and then we had a hope that if we lived and were good, God would permit us to be pirates. These ambitions faded out, each in its turn; but the ambition to be a steamboatman always remained." Since boyhood he had admired and envied the god-like heroes who piloted those magnificent machines past his little village, jealous even of the lowly cabin boys and the young-sters from his town who occasionally reappeared as apprentice engineers or deck hands: there he was, Twain remembered one such boy, sitting on that boat, so conspicuous, pretending to be hard at work "where we could all see him and envy him and loathe him."

Twain and his neighbors understood very well what steamboats meant to the nation and particularly what they meant to the Mississippi Valley. Since the first commercially successful one made its appearance, less than thirty years before Twain's birth, steamboats had transformed America. Their ability to navigate upstream as well as downstream made them the chief carriers of goods and passengers on the nation's inland waterways. By the time Twain himself piloted one in the late 1850s, hundreds of them chugged up and down the great river, carrying agricul-tural produce down to New Orleans, bringing manufactured goods from far away, creating villages and towns along the Mississippi's banks. Steamboats were a critical part of the advances in transportation and commerce that revolutionized American economic life in the decades before the Civil War. They were the lifelines of commerce and prosperity, and the pilots who commanded them enjoyed enormous prestige and high wages (a pilot in the late 1850s earned as much money as the vice-president of the United States). Twain loved that life and exulted in its status, its financial rewards, and its power. "A pilot in those days," he thought, "was the only unfettered and entirely independent human being that lived in the earth." And a quarter century after leaving the river, when he was a world-famous author, he could still say of steamboating that "I loved the pro-fession far better than any I have followed since, and I took a measureless pride in it."

In *this* mood Twain gives us a far different picture of those miraculous machines. He could be positively lyrical in describing their beauty, their enormous power, their breathtaking luxury. Of one of the boats on which he worked he writes: "She was a grand affair. When I stood in her pilot-house I was so far above the water that I seemed perched on a mountain. . . . The pilot house was a sumptuous glass temple; room enough to have a dance in; showy red and gold window-curtains; an imposing sofa; leather cushions and a back to the high bench where visiting pilots sit, to spin yarns. . . . The moment we were under way I began to prowl about the great steamer and fill myself with joy. She was as clean and as dainty as a drawing-room . . . she glittered with no end of prism-fringed chandeliers; the clerk's office was elegant, the bar was marvelous. . . ." Twain does not disguise his feelings: "This was unutterable pomp. . . . I had never felt so fine before."

And in *this* mood, Twain gives us a far different picture of the collisions between steamboats and rafts. When these accidents are described from the viewpoint of the pilot house rather than from the viewpoint of Huck and Jim on the raft, Twain appears to abandon one set of sympathies and adopt another. Whenever the river rose, he tells us in *Life on the Mississippi*,

> down came a swarm of prodigious timber-rafts from the head waters of the Mississippi, coal barges from Pittsburgh, little trading scows from everywhere, and broad-horns from "Posey County," Indiana. . . . Pilots bore a mortal hatred to these crafts; and it was returned with usury. . . . Once, at night . . . we should have eaten up a Posey County family, fruit, furniture, and all, but that they happened to be fiddling down below and we just caught the sound of the music in time to sheer off, doing no serious damage, but coming so near it that we had good hopes for a moment.

Is it too much to suggest that Mark Twain's curious ambivalence about steamboats and rafts reflects, in his deepest being, a profound ambivalence about modern industrial technology and traditional, natural American life? Does the fact that he could never quite decide whether it was better to float lazily down the majestic river on the raft or to be the master of the fire-belching machinery from the glory of the pilot house, does that fact indicate a lifelong uncertainty about what was new in America and powerful and coming on in such a hurry and what was traditional and pastoral and disappearing with such speed?

III

In many ways Twain was a full and eager participant in the dynamic age into which he had matured, an age of machinery and cities, of steam and electricity, of big business, big money, and big schemes. All his life he was addicted to money, and he loved to show off with it. He had a keen eye for what would sell, and his uncanny sense of the literary marketplace played a large part in determining what he chose to write about next and where he chose to have his work published. He peddled his work with an expert's sensitivity to its cash value. Charles Gold, who wrote a book about Twain's business ventures, concluded that "there has scarcely ever been an established, critically acclaimed American writer so preoccupied with money and business. . . . Money, perhaps the dominant motif of his life, did as much as anything, even as much as the great river, to shape the man he became." And Justin Kaplan, one of Twain's most perceptive biographers, agreed: "it is hard to think of another writer so obsessed in his life and work by the lure, the rustle and chink and heft of money." There were entire periods of his mature life—and not brief ones either—when his financial affairs were much closer to the center of his mind than was his writing.

His obsession with money was not the only Gilded Age trait that he shared with other flamboyant successes of his time. He enjoyed living extravagantly. He kept servants, sometimes as many as a dozen at a time. When at home, he entertained guests constantly and lavishly. When he went abroad, which was frequently, he took the best staterooms, stayed at the best hotels, dined in the best restaurants. From his earliest days he paid careful attention to his clothes and to the impression they would make. He loved being in the presence of men of wealth and authority. He shared with his age, moreover, a fascination with the newest machinery—it was not only the steamboat that captured his imagination. He was, in 1877, one of the very first Americans to install a telephone in a private home (in his autobiography he proudly claims to have been the first person in the *world* to do so). He was probably the first writer to complete a major manuscript using that new marvel, the typewriter, and the first to try dictating his words into one of Thomas Edison's new phonograph machines for later transcription. At the age of forty-nine he got himself one of those brand new high-wheeled bicycles and set out to master its perils. He loved gadgetry of all kinds and idolized those transcendent heroes of the Gilded Age, the inventors; "an inventor is a poet—a true poet," he told his sister Pamela, "and nothing in any degree less than a high order of poet." With such an admiration for gadgetry and inventors, it is not surprising that he tried his own hand at it, even securing patents for some of his own creations. Perhaps it was natural that he became an inveterate gambler, a high-stakes investor in somebody's new invention or somebody's fresh get-rich-quick project.

In all these ways, then, Mark Twain appeared to be perfectly at home with the other fabled figures of Gilded Age America and perfectly comfortable with the spirit of that boisterous time. Like Carnegie and Edison, like Philip Armour and John D. Rockefeller, he rose from modest circumstances to the height of his profession. He loved money and the luxurious life it could buy for him; he enjoyed rubbing shoulders with the rich and powerful; he was ready, indeed he was eager, to embrace the newest machine, the newest scheme, the newest opportunity to get his hands on legendary wealth.

And yet, when he and his neighbor Charles Dudley Warner bestowed upon their age the name it has carried ever since, they chose the word "gilded," not the word "golden." To "gild" is to apply a thin coating of gold paint over some less attractive reality. To Twain and Warner it meant, in the words of Vernon Parrington, the attempt to cover "the slovenly reality" with "a gaudy exterior." Mark Twain was well aware of the tawdry vulgarity, the grotesque materialism, and the self-centered individualism of late nineteenth-century America. With a part of his being, as we have seen, he was himself a prime exemplar of those very traits. But there was also something about him that recoiled against the spirit of his time and that caused him to recognize its evils and the dangers it posed to treasured American ideals. He was too honest to ignore the peril, and he became the sharpest and most famous critic of his age.

At the same time that he relentlessly pursued riches, he well understood money's seductive and destructive power, its ability to uproot morality and debase individuals and societies. Perhaps he said it most frankly in a letter written in 1905 to his longtime friend, the Hartford minister Joseph Twichell. While admitting that "money-lust has always existed," Twain insisted—in words that sound almost like self-denunciation—that "not in the history of the world was it ever a craze, a madness, until your time and mine." The unrestrained scramble after money has made America (and Europe too) "hard, sordid, ungentle, dishonest, oppressive. . . . All Europe and all America are feverishly scrambling for money. Money is the supreme ideal—all others take tenth place." At the same time that he was yearning to keep company with the rich, he lamented and ridiculed their ostentation and made merciless fun of their hypocrisy, their religiosity, their indifference to the toiling poor. His fiction and his essays are filled with shady businessmen, scoundrels who swindle their trusting friends, who plot against the destitute widow and the helpless orphan, who water the stock and falsify the ledger. At the same time that he sought the friendship of powerful politicians and was thrilled at being allowed to use the office of the Speaker of the House for his lobbying efforts on behalf of copyright reform, he could be perfectly vicious: "Suppose you were an idiot," he once famously said. "And suppose you were a member of Congress. But I repeat myself." At the same time that he was installing a telephone and experimenting with a typewriter and buying a bicycle and investing frantically in one questionable contrivance after another, he knew that machines carried their own perils and that gambling on them was a dubious proposition. To be sure, he declares in his letter to Twichell, "the 19th century made progress—the first progress after 'ages and ages'—colossal progress. In what? Materialities. Prodigious acquisitions were made in things which add to the comfort of many and make life harder for as many more. But the addition to righteousness? Is that discoverable? I think not." And as far as indulging in the sort of wild financial ventures that cost *him* several fortunes was concerned, he knew better and advised against it. "There are two times in a man's life when he should not speculate," he warned. "When he can't afford it, and when he can."

IV

Mark Twain has typically been regarded as the most "American" of all this country's great writers, and there are many reasons why that characterization of him has endured for the hundred years since his death. The bottomless well of his imagination, his flashing and wicked wit, the dexterity and beauty of his language, his common touch and wide sympathies with the poor and oppressed, his ability to unfold a story, his audacious willingness to tell the truth as he saw it—these, and no doubt other attributes, help to account for his persistent popularity and for the deep affection felt for him by millions of American readers over the years. But part of his hold over us certainly has something to do with the universality of the questions he raised both in his writing and in the way he lived his life.

America has been a country characterized by *both* a headlong and heedless scramble after the "American dream" of personal wealth *and* a nagging nervousness about the effects of that scramble on cherished ideals, on the world of nature, on human relationships and community feeling. In evoking these questions, in exploring that relentless tension between the modern and the traditional, Twain tapped into deep regions of the American psyche. Like him, many Americans responded eagerly to the beckoning opportunities offered by a lush continent and a climate of personal freedom, ready to work hard, to exploit, and to enjoy the rewards. Indeed, many would have considered it cowardly and lazy to have *failed* to enter the contest. But like him, surely many of the most thoughtful of his fellow citizens wondered about what it was all costing.

If it is possible to detect this particular double-sided strain in the American mind long before his birth and even easier to find it in the years since his death, the dilemma must have struck many with special force and urgency during Mark Twain's own lifetime. The country was dramatically transformed during those years and almost everything that could be measured increased exponentially. In 1835, the year of his birth, there were 15 million people living in the United States and only about 30 places in the whole country that claimed populations of more than 10,000. By the time he died, in 1910, there were more than 92 million Americans and nearly 600 places that had more than 10,000— and 50 of those were now homes to more than 100,000 souls. When he was born the country operated about 1,100 miles of railroad track; when he died, there were more than 1,300 railroad *companies*, operating more than 240,000 miles of track. The number of factories and inventions and banks and corporations, the number of immigrants and wage-earners, the quantity of dollars invested in manufactures and the value of the nation's manufactured goods—all increased at rates far faster than the increase in the general population. When Twain was sixty-five, Edward Atkinson, a leading economist, observed that "there has never been in the history of civilization, a period, or a place, or a section of the earth in which science and invention have worked such progress or have created such opportunity for material welfare as in these United States in the period since the end of the Civil War." Twain's friend Andrew Carnegie could hardly contain himself: "The old nations of the earth creep at a snail's pace," he exulted. "The Republic thunders past with the rush of the express." In the year of Twain's death, the Kansas journalist William Allen White published a book significantly entitled *The Old Order Changeth*. In it he compared his own America with the country that Alexis deTocqueville had visited at the time of Twain's birth. "The two—politically, economically, and socially—are almost utterly dissimilar," he declared. "Something has intervened."

Mark Twain's ambivalence about what had intervened, his inability finally to decide whether he preferred the steamboat or the raft, must have echoed the ambivalence of numerous other Americans who lived through that transformation. Undoubtedly most of his countrymen were content to carry on their lives holding *both* a faith in progress and the American dream *and* an uneasiness about what it all meant, never troubling themselves much about negotiating the discrepancies and tensions these beliefs entailed. Twain was not so lucky. There were many reasons, as we will see, for the dark despair that marked his final years, that withering cynicism and merciless ridicule of human nature at the end of his life. His financial difficulties, a certain disappointment about his literary work, and a series of crushing family tragedies would have embittered many people. But it is hard to escape the conclusion that his pessimism had social and intellectual dimensions as well. At the end, he was torn by the direction in which he thought his country was heading and appalled at the thoughtlessness of its citizenry. For the important ways in which Mark Twain's life and views mirrored those of his generation and for the important ways in which he differed, his story is fascinating and instructive.

I

Preparation

Literature is an *art*, not an inspiration. It is a *trade*, so to speak & must be *learned*—one cannot "pick it up." Neither can one learn it in a year, nor in five years. And its capital is *experience*. . . . the moment you venture outside your *own* experience, you are in peril—don't ever do it. . . . live within your literary means, & don't borrow. Whatever you have *lived*, you can write—& by hard work & a genuine apprenticeship, you can learn to write well; but what you have not lived you cannot write, you can only pretend to write it. . . .

Mark Twain to a young writer (1885)

1

Growing Up in Hannibal

I

Samuel Langhorne Clemens was born on November 30, 1835, in a tiny Missouri village named Florida. The "Samuel" came from his paternal grandfather; the "Langhorne" is something of a mystery but might have been taken from one of his father's friends. As it happened, Halley's comet, while no longer visible in the night sky, was paying one of its regular visits to the neighborhood of the planet Earth as the infant entered the world. When Clemens (by then universally known as Mark Twain) was an old man of seventy-four, he said "I came in with Halley's comet in 1835. It is coming again next year, and I expect to go out with it. . . . The Almighty has said, no doubt: 'Now here are these two unaccountable freaks; they came in together, they must go out together.'" He insisted that "it will be the greatest disappointment of my life if I don't go out with Halley's comet." It was one disappointment he was destined to be spared.

In 1835 Florida, Missouri, was "nearly invisible." It had two short streets, a number of muddy lanes, a few houses, most of them made of logs, some sawmills, and a church. The town's population was around one hundred, and Twain later boasted that he had increased that total by a full percentage point. "It is more than many of the best men in history could have done for a town," he said. "It may not be modest in me to refer to this but it is true." Like many other towns in the American West, Florida was built on hard work and wildly exaggerated dreams of future prosperity. If only they would dredge the Salt River, the town could connect to the Mississippi and blossom into a thriving commercial center;

if only the railroad would come and connect the town to St. Louis, eighty short miles to the southeast, then riches would surely follow. These were exactly the sort of inflated hopes that were likely to attract and seduce a man like Sam's father.

Except for a certain advantage in education and a religious skepticism that led him to abandon his Presbyterian upbringing, John Marshall Clemens was a typical pioneer. He was a wanderer, always in pursuit of some new opportunity, continually chasing that elusive American dream of getting wealthy by virtue of hard work and a little luck. He had been born in Virginia in 1798, but moved as a child with his widowed mother to Kentucky. He studied law, married a lively local girl named Jane Lampton, and after the birth of their first child, Orion, moved to Tennessee where he tried to make a success practicing law in one Tennessee town after another. He tried his hand at farming, clerking, and running a store; he speculated in land and served as a postmaster; he had carpentry skills and built and sold wagons. And when things were going nowhere in Tennessee, he eagerly grasped at his brother-in-law's glowing reports about the golden opportunities awaiting in Missouri. In June 1835, the family, now numbering five, made the arduous journey. Jane was carrying another child on that trip, and Sam was born, prematurely, six months after arriving at their new home.

One thing that John Marshall Clemens did while still in Tennessee had important implications both for the future of the family and for the mental outlook of his unborn son. The father sunk every dollar he could scrape together into purchasing Tennessee land. Before leaving for Missouri, he had accumulated at least 70,000 acres—perhaps as many as 100,000—and he lived on the faith that this land would someday be worth unimagined millions. Things might be rough for the family right now, but once the Tennessee land was sold, the children would have everything they had ever dreamed of. Along with this mirage came the well-understood admonition that they would be fools to sell those acres too soon, that the land's value would rise inevitably if they could only hold on a little longer. "He had always said that the land would not become valuable in his time," Twain remembered, "but that it would be a commodious provision for his children some day. . . . My father's dying charge was, 'Cling to the land and wait; let nothing beguile it away from you.'" Like everything else into which the father put his hopes, the Tennessee land came to nothing. But for Mark Twain, those acres were symbolic: "With the very kindest intentions in the world toward us he laid the heavy curse of prospective wealth upon our shoulders. He went to his grave in the full belief that he had done us a kindness. It was a woeful mistake but fortunately he never knew it. . . . It is good to begin life poor; it is good to begin life rich—these are wholesome; but to begin it poor and *prospectively* rich! The man who has not experienced it cannot imagine the curse of it." In his first novel, *The Gilded Age*, Twain created a character named Squire Hawkins, who was lured from Tennessee to a forlorn town in Missouri and who spent his days dreaming of the riches his family would someday know because of the large tract of land he had acquired back in Tennessee.

By the time Sam turned four his father had given up on Florida—they were never going to build that railroad or dredge that river—and decided to move to a more promising Missouri village called Hannibal. Thirty miles east of Florida, Hannibal did not require a connection to the Mississippi; it was located between two bluffs and overlooked the magnificent river. In Hannibal, John Clemens achieved a modicum of respectability. He became a justice of the peace and was elected clerk of the Surrogate Court, but he was still dogged by failure. He bought a ramshackle hotel and opened a general store on its first floor, but both the hotel and the store failed and he gave up the place after a couple of years. After guaranteeing a loan to a defaulting acquaintance, he was virtually destitute. His wife took in laundry and cooked for another family; he sold some of the furniture and sent Orion to St. Louis to learn to be a printer; his eldest daughter gave piano lessons.

Twain did not often speak or write about his father, and some critics have noted the absence of fathers in much of his fiction. He remembered him to be distant, unemotional, and stern: "Silent, austere, of perfect probity and high principle; ungentle of manner toward his children . . . [he] never punished them—a look was enough and more than enough." John Clemens influenced his son in both positive and negative ways. The mature

Twain inherited his father's puritanical morality, particularly as regards financial dealings (both father and son had to work their way out of bankruptcy, and both were determined to pay back every penny). Twain also saw, in his father's example, that a rigorous moral code was possible without the benefit of formal religion—even theological skeptics could live upright and honest lives. On the other side, it seems clear that, although the son pursued opportunities with the same eagerness, he resolved to provide for his own family better than his father had provided for his; this compulsion, together with the example of his father's consistent disappointments, inevitably led to his lifelong worrying about money. If the father had failed to achieve the American dream, the son was determined to do better. And when it came to his emotional relations with his own wife and children, Twain—tender, loving, playful, ebullient, generous— could not have rejected more decisively the atmosphere he had known as a boy.

Sam was much closer to his mother, and she was easily the most important presence in his early life. Her own story was not an entirely happy one. She was an attractive and animated young woman with a slender figure and lush red hair (which her son inherited); one observer said she was thought to be "one of the most beautiful women in the state." According to her own account, told many years later, she had been in love, back in Kentucky, with a young medical student: "I loved him with my whole heart, and I knew that he felt the same toward me, though no words had been spoken." Everyone "supposed we were engaged—took it for granted we were—but we were not." After a bizarre misunderstanding, the young man left town, erroneously believing that Jane Lampton did not return his feelings. To silence "the clacking tongues" and show that she didn't care, she married John Clemens, the grim and self-contained young lawyer in town who had business connections to the Lampton family. She later admitted that she never loved him, but married him in a fit of pique.

The pair decided to make the best of it. "All through my boyhood," their son was to recall, "I had noticed that the attitude of my father and mother toward each other was that of courteous, considerate and always respectful, and even deferential friends;

that they were always kind toward each other, but . . . there were no outward and visible demonstrations of affection." He attributed this polite distance to his father's dignity and reserve. His mother, he felt, "was warm hearted, but it seemed to me quite natural that her warm-heartedness should be held in reserve in an atmosphere like my father's." (Orion Clemens could remember seeing his parents kiss only once—when their infant son died and both parents were torn with grief.) Unlike her skeptical husband, Jane Clemens was a faithful churchgoer who sought consolation in the stern tenets of the Presbyterian church. She would need consolation in the years ahead. The unfortunate marriage was the start of a difficult and unhappy life that was punctuated by tragedy. Jane Clemens gave birth to seven children and lived to bury four of them.

Twain was to offer several word-paintings of his mother. He said, for example, that she was the model for Tom Sawyer's Aunt Polly—a tight-lipped disciplinarian, the ruthless enemy of boyish hijinks, a grim believer in the necessity of school and the benefits of church; but underneath that forbidding exterior, loving, sentimental, generous-hearted, and kindly. "She would drown young kittens when necessary," Twain told his biographer, "but warmed the water for the purpose." Unfortunately, recent scholarship has revealed that Twain "borrowed" several incidents from the work of other writers (including that story about warming the water for the doomed cats) and presented them as factual episodes from his own growing up. It is, therefore, difficult to be sure of her actual traits. Twain claimed that she was always a friend to the weak, and he recalled incidents of her brave defense of the helpless. He asserted that "to the very day of her death she felt a strong interest in the whole world and everything and everybody in it," and that when either her pity or her anger was aroused "she was the most eloquent person I have heard speak."

Sammy, born two months prematurely, was such a frail child that his survival was in grave doubt. "When I first saw him," his mother remembered, "I could see no promise in him. But I felt it my duty to do the best I could. To raise him if I could." A neighbor lady took one look at the infant and warned against unrealistic hopes. Perhaps because of the baby's precarious prospects, Jane Clemens felt a special affection for him and labored hard to keep the boy alive. Like many others in ante-bellum America, she believed in the miracles of various medical fads ("there was almost no possible remedy that Jane Clemens would not try," writes biographer Fred Kaplan). She seems to have invested a special hope in hydrotherapy, or the water cure. At the age of eight or nine, "my mother used to stand me up naked in the back yard every morning and throw buckets of cold water on me. . . . And then, when the dousing was over, she would wrap me up in a sheet wet with ice water and then wrap blankets around that and put me into bed." Aunt Polly was to apply precisely the same curative to poor Tom. Only when all the home remedies and unorthodox therapies had proved unavailing was Dr. Meredith called in to see what he could do. Somehow the boy survived these treatments. Once, to illustrate his mother's natural wit, Twain reported a conversation he had with his mother when he was approaching sixty and she was in her late eighties. He asked her about those sickly early years:

> "I suppose that during all that time you were uneasy about me?"
> "Yes, the whole time."
> "Afraid I wouldn't live?"
> After a reflective pause . . . "No—afraid you would."

II

Readers of Mark Twain will already have some idea of what the village of Hannibal was like—at least in the memory of the man who had grown up there, made the place famous, and set so many of his tales in small towns. From the boyhood paradise of Tom Sawyer's St. Petersburg, to Pudd'nhead Wilson's darker village of Dawson's Landing, to the easily corruptible Hadleyburg; from the marvelous description of the drowsy citizenry in *Life on the Mississippi* as they waited for the steamboat to come and break the monotony, even—many would argue—to the village of Eseldorf in sixteenth-century Austria, Twain again and again set out the variety of life in places like Hannibal, Missouri. There was little consistency in these descriptions.

Sometimes he saw such places as vicious and violent, sometimes as free and contented and neighborly. All of these depictions reflected young Sam's varied experiences during his fourteen years as a resident of Hannibal.

When Jane and John Clemens moved there, they were both a good bit older than the town itself. Hannibal was originally settled in 1819, but after its first eleven years it had attracted only thirty residents. Because of its location on the river, however, it had promising commercial prospects. As new settlers poured into the region and the economic life of the Midwest started to quicken in the 1820s and 1830s, the town began to thrive. By the time the Clemens family arrived Hannibal had already grown to a thousand, and before Sam was fifteen its population had doubled. It became a center for the rich agricultural region that surrounded it; wheat and tobacco came to town for shipment to St. Joseph and St. Louis; thousands of pigs arrived each year to be butchered in the two slaughterhouses. Its wharves and whiskey distilleries, its tannery and cigar factory brought a measure of prosperity and a bright promise for the future. In short, Hannibal was a typical western town on the make. It boasted a couple of hotels, three saloons, some general stores and blacksmith shops, two churches, and an equal number of schools. It is a measure of John Clemens's economic ineptitude that he was unable to succeed even in a booming place like Hannibal, Missouri.

A small debate exists about whether growing up in Hannibal was good or bad for the young man destined to become a writer. In *The Ordeal of Mark Twain*, a controversial and influential book of 1920, the prominent literary critic, Van Wyck Brooks, laments the harsh and stultifying environment of the town—its dry and dusty streets, the dreary and draining life exacted by the hard work of pioneering, the absence of books and ideas, the narrow intellectual horizons, the oppressive religion with its confining moralism, the pervasive suspicion of the man or woman of intelligence or sensitivity or specialized skills. According to Brooks, a town like the one Mark Twain knew as a youth was "a desert of human sand!—the barrenest spot in all Christendom, surely, for the seed of genius to fall in." A dozen years later, Bernard DeVoto argued that, on the contrary,

Hannibal was abundant with stimulation and culture, with music and newspapers, with a rich tradition of folktales and folk art, of western literature and western humor. Towns like Hannibal, DeVoto insisted, were refreshingly democratic, free from deadening eastern and European class-consciousness and pretense; they were pervaded by the spirit of good fellowship and a rough equality that nurtured the imagination and inspired youngsters with notions of their own possibilities. And, in the case of Hannibal, there was always the river: "here passed the world," writes DeVoto. Along that great highway "the energy of America boiled violently," and every day it brought to the village hints of romance and adventure, intimations of distant places and unfamiliar ways of life, inspiration enough for any youth's artistic imagination.

Hannibal had its share of frontier violence and other unpleasantness, and young Sam witnessed much of it. There was a good deal of drunkenness in town, and it frequently led to fights, knifings, and gunplay. Sam saw one unarmed man shot down in the street in cold blood (an event he was later to re-create in *Huckleberry Finn*), and he watched as the poor man was carried to the drugstore where, half an hour later, he died. In 1845, when he was nine, he witnessed the murder of a slave who had displeased a white man "for merely doing something awkwardly—as if that were a crime." The victim was struck on the head with a chunk of iron ore and died within an hour. Two years later, Sam and some friends were exploring an island near the Illinois side when they discovered the corpse of an escaped slave who had been murdered and mutilated by white woodcutters, and three years after that he saw a widow gun down the leader of a gang of intruders trying to break into her home.

Missouri was a slave state, and Sam Clemens saw the institution every day of his youth. Although the slavery he witnessed in Hannibal was on a smaller scale and undoubtedly less brutal than in some other parts of the South, nevertheless there was a slave-market in town where regular sales of chained human beings occurred, especially when some owner had died and an estate had to be settled. When he could afford it, John Clemens owned slaves, and Sam sometimes saw his father beat them and sometimes sell them down the river. Jennie had been a slave of the Clemenses since the family lived in Tennessee—Twain remembered her as being "like one of the family." She had helped to nurse the frail child and had once rescued him from the creek. When Sam was seven, his financially desperate father sold Jennie to an especially unsavory slave trader. Sam naturally and thoughtlessly adopted the racial attitudes of the community that surrounded him. "In my schoolboy days I had no aversion to slavery," he writes in his autobiography. "I was not aware that there was anything wrong about it. No one arraigned it in my hearing; the local papers said nothing against it; the local pulpit taught us that God approved it, that it was a holy thing and that the doubter need only look in the Bible if he wished to settle his mind . . . ; if the slaves themselves had an aversion to slavery they were wise and said nothing." He and his white friends played freely with black children. "We were comrades and yet not comrades; color and condition interposed a subtle line which both parties were conscious of and which rendered complete fusion impossible."

Some of the racist views that he imbibed as a youth stayed with Mark Twain for a long time, and, especially by modern standards, his view of African Americans will seem appalling. In private letters and in published writings, he unselfconsciously used the word "nigger"—a word that today marks any speaker who utters it as an ignorant bigot. He would always remember fondly the old minstrel shows ("nigger shows," he called them) where white men blackened their faces with burnt cork, drawled with exaggerated accents, played their banjos, and pretended to be stupid. Even to the end, Twain was capable of speaking of African Americans with cloying sentimentality or obvious condescension. And yet, as we shall see, the remarkable thing about Mark Twain's attitude toward African Americans is the great distance he traveled toward sympathy, tolerance, and outrage at the injustices to which blacks were subjected, both in America and worldwide. Few native white Southerners of his generation harbored more enlightened and generous views of race than he harbored. He claimed Frederick Douglass, the militant defender of black rights, as a "personal friend" and provided scholarship aid to bright African Americans who wanted to go to college. William Dean Howells thought that he "never saw a man more respectful of negroes" than the mature Mark Twain.

Twain began the long journey toward better racial understanding, not in the town of Hannibal, but at the farm of his uncle, John Quarles. Between the ages of seven and eleven or twelve, Sam spent several months each summer there. The 250 acres were located a few miles from the old home in Florida. Twain recalled these summertime vacations with rhapsodic affection—"it was a heavenly place for a boy, that farm of my uncle John's." Even after sixty years, his memories of the Quarles farm were deeply nostalgic and unusually detailed. "I can see the farm yet, with perfect clearness. I can see all its belongings, all its details. . . ." During those golden summers, he romped over the countryside with his numerous cousins and devoured glorious meals—"it makes me cry to think of them," he writes, and he meticulously enumerates three dozen culinary delicacies that he fell upon in that farmhouse. He explored the woods and swam secretly in the forbidden ponds. But part of those idyllic summertime months at the farm were the intimate and memorable contacts with African Americans, adults as well as children. The Quarleses had around a dozen slaves, and on many evenings Sam and his cousins walked through the orchard to visit their cabins. Aunt Hannah, the children thought, was about a thousand years old and had known Moses personally; Uncle Dan'l, six feet tall and charismatic, enthralled them with his ghost stories, his deep voice, and his wonderfully musical dialect. Many of Mark Twain's best known African-American characters were to owe something to Uncle Dan'l. "It was on the farm," Twain remembered, "that I got my strong liking for his race and my appreciation of certain of its fine qualities."

Sam Clemens's childhood was crowded with troubling and traumatic episodes. He must surely have been affected by his own precarious health and his mother's bizarre remedies. He was, as we have seen, no stranger to murder. The economic misadventures of his father, the brief successes and prolonged failures—his mother having to cook for other families and take in boarders, having to watch the pennies and to sell off the slave Jennie—must surely have touched a boy as sensitive and delicate as little Sam. But there were worse things. In August 1839, his big sister Margaret contracted yellow fever and died, and his mother's inconsolable moaning filled the house.

In May 1842, his big brother Benjamin, aged nine, died of the same disease; this time his unstrung mother brought each of the surviving children, one at a time, into the room with the child's corpse and insisted that each of them kneel before the body and touch its face. No one should be surprised that Sam Clemens was subject to terrifying nightmares. He thought that he possessed special psychic powers, and his mother and some of the neighbors agreed. Throughout his childhood he was a sleepwalker and the family was occasionally startled to see him drift in and out of rooms fast asleep.

And yet, despite all of this trouble, this sickness and death and poverty and violence, Mark Twain was often to recall his childhood in Hannibal with affection and joy. He never forgot the unpleasantness and the horror; indeed, we know about these things only because he wrote about them afterward, and in some of his later literary portrayals of village life the unpleasantness is amply revealed. But he had, apparently, a deep need to remember his boyhood and his town in happy and carefree terms. In 1887, when he was a famous writer, he received a letter from a childhood friend of Hannibal days. "You have spirited me back to a vanished world and the companionship of phantoms," he replied. "[I]n thinking of it, dreaming over it, I have seemed like some banished Adam who is revisiting his half-forgotten Paradise and wondering how the arid outside world could ever have seemed green and fair to him."

We can see now that Samuel Clemens lived in two quite distinct kingdoms during these days of his youth. There was the town of Hannibal with its frankly commercial values, with its oppressive and hated school and its boring and hated church, with its violence and slave market and sordid schemes for getting money, with its dismal family failures. And, counterpoised against it, there was the natural world that surrounded the town. Whether in the woods and caves on three sides of Hannibal, or on the forested islands of the river, or on the river itself, or at the farm of his Uncle John, there was another world. It was a world of escape from restraint, a world of boyhood adventure and independence, of old clothes and tobacco and wild escapades. For the rest of his life Mark Twain would frequent both of these worlds. He would be attracted to some of the excitement and glamour of the former and attached nostalgically to memories of the latter.

A goodly part of his best writing would be an attempt, not always successful, to navigate the compelling attractions and insistent contradictions of these two kingdoms.

III

On March 24, 1847, when his son Sam was eleven, John Marshall Clemens, weakened by all those years of hoping, striving, and failing, caught pneumonia and died at the age of forty-nine. On his deathbed, John Clemens called his daughter to him, kissed her, and whispered "let me die." Not having witnessed his parents' embrace at the death of his brother Benjamin five years before, *this*, the son thought, was the only time that he had witnessed any member of his family kissing another. Two events associated with his father's death were to leave lasting impressions on Sam. In a reprise of the scene that followed the death of Benjamin, Jane Clemens—by her own version of the episode published forty years later—"took him by the hand and went with him into the room where the coffin was." With her on one side of the body and the boy on the other, she extracted a promise from Sam, who "turned his streaming eyes upon me," that he would try to be a better boy and grow up to be a respectable man, honorable and moral like his poor father. Van Wyck Brooks argues that this singular moment played a crucial role in restraining the boy's artistic imagination and setting his feet on the road to material success and social acceptance. Other authorities, while not denying the oddity of that weird and memorable event, are unwilling to ascribe to it the same long-term results as Brooks. And if the pledge elicited over the coffin were not sufficient, it seems that later Sam peeked through a keyhole into that room and saw Dr. Meredith use his surgeon's knife to cut into his father's body as he performed, with his mother's approval, an autopsy.

If there were any doubts in Hannibal that Sam Clemens was an unusual boy or that he was haunted by his own peculiar demons, an incident that occurred a few months later probably erased them. In the summer after his father's death* the town was stricken by a severe outbreak of measles—now a harmless

---

*Some authorities, following the account in Twain's autobiography, place this event two years earlier, in 1845. I am following the date he gives in his essay, "The Turning Point of My Life," published in 1910.

childhood disease, but in the nineteenth century a dreaded harbinger of death. "For a time," Twain recalled six decades later, "a child died almost every day." Sam was haunted by the possibility of his own death—every time he shivered he was certain that he would die. Unable to endure the misery of not knowing whether he was among the doomed, he decided to contract the disease "and have it over, one way or the other." He escaped from his mother's watchful quarantine and stole over to the home of his friend Will Bowen, who had come down with the disease and was very ill. Sam crept into Will's room and climbed into bed with him. Will's mother discovered him there and dragged him back home. But he now had the measles and for two weeks "I came near to dying." All of Hannibal was "interested, and anxious, and sent for news of me every day." The aged Mark Twain polished off that ancient story of his boyhood with a flash of his patented self-deprecating humor: "Everybody believed I would die; but on the fourteenth day a change came for the worse and they were disappointed."

Partly because of the economic hardship now confronting the fatherless household (the lovable but hapless Orion, twenty-one years old, living in St. Louis, and possessed of the same, lifelong economic maladroitness as his departed father, was now head of the family), and partly, no doubt, because of the measles episode, Jane Clemens thought it was time for a change. While still in school, Sam had been doing odd jobs around town to help a little with family finances. He worked in a grocery store and a bookstore and had a paper route; he did menial jobs at the office of the *Hannibal Gazette*. But when school was over in June 1848, his mother "was tired of trying to keep me out of mischief, and the adventure of the measles decided her to put me into more masterful hands than hers." She mercifully released Sam from the unbearable imprisonment of school. The boy had always despised that particular institution and evaded it whenever he could. (Fifty years later he wrote: "In the first place God made idiots. This was for practice. Then he made School Boards.") When Joseph Ament came to town, bought the *Gazette,* and changed its name to the *Missouri Courier*, Jane apprenticed her son to him.

For the next five years, Sam Clemens learned about the newspaper business. During the first half of that period, aged thirteen to fifteen, he worked for Ament in the usual apprenticeship arrangement: "that is to say, board and clothes but no money." Although the printing office was only a short walk from home, he usually slept in the Aments' cellar and, in order to save the family some money, usually ate the meager meals at their table. Although Sam liked his coworkers, he grew to despise Ament heartily—the ill-fitting hand-me-down suits he bestowed upon the apprentices, the straw pallet bed on the office floor, and the stingy fare at mealtime. It was probably Joseph Ament whom Sam had in mind when, in an 1852 sketch, he called an unnamed Hannibal editor "this diminutive chunk of human meat." But by that time, Sam had another employer. Toward the end of 1850, Orion had returned from St. Louis to open a rival paper in town, and shortly thereafter, both Sam and young Henry Clemens went to work for their elder brother. Wages were promised, but there was hardly ever enough money to actually pay them.

The five years that Sam worked for Hannibal newspapers were valuable to him in several ways. He had always been a reader; even as a youngster he had taken full advantage of his father's small collection of books. Working as a printer in a newspaper office undoubtedly refined his sensitivity to language, grammar, and the elegance or inelegance of literary style. Printers habitually poured over texts—and not only the texts they were correcting or setting into type. Alert newsmen scoured the productions of their rivals, probing for some weakness, some reprehensible comment that might be righteously and viciously ridiculed in the rough-and-tumble manner of frontier journalism. They daily perused the work of other American papers, looking for material they could steal and pass off as their own. Like Benjamin Franklin, whom he much admired during these years, Samuel Clemens was made a better writer because of his boyhood vocation. In Orion's absence, he tried his hand at producing a few sharp-tongued articles for the paper, and in the spring of 1852, he sent a couple of short and flimsy journalistic pieces to publications in Boston and Philadelphia. Besides the advantages to his writing, his occasional work as a reporter of local stories may have helped to sharpen his powers of observation and memory. And finally, he now knew a real trade; he was equipped with the means of earning his own livelihood, the possessor of a useful skill that was an indispensable part of leaving childhood behind and becoming an adult.

By the time he was seventeen, Samuel Clemens had acquired many of the physical traits and personal proclivities that would remain with him for the rest of his life. Small in stature (about 5'8"), with sharp blue-green eyes, bushy eyebrows, and luxuriant reddish hair (the famous mustache would not appear for another ten years), he was gregarious and popular with his fellows, already an experienced and constant cigar smoker, known for his sparkling conversation and boisterous wit. He had a musical voice and told his amusing, hypnotizing stories with an engaging slow drawl. He was hungry to learn new things from books, but always ready for the next experience, the next adventure.

IV

Then, in June 1853, the seventeen-year-old did a remarkable thing. Armed now with a marketable skill, he left town. When he told his mother he was going, she took out the family Bible and made her boy swear that he would not "throw a card or drink a drop of liquor" while away from home. Partly, we may assume, he was driven to leave Hannibal by that eager pursuit of the next experience; partly, no doubt, he was anxious to get clear of Orion's supervision. His brother's newspaper was tottering on the brink of failure, and Sam probably saw no good reason to stay and witness the final collapse. In his *Autobiography* he makes his departure seem very much like an escape: "I disappeared one night and fled to St. Louis." His sister Pamela had married a prosperous St. Louis merchant, William Moffett, and Sam probably moved in with them and earned money by setting type for various St. Louis newspapers. Then, ten weeks later, Jane Clemens got a letter from New York City. "My Dear Mother," Sam wrote, "you will doubtless be a little surprised and somewhat angry when you receive this, and find me so far from home." Eight weeks after that, he was writing to her from Philadelphia where he was setting type for the *Philadelphia Inquirer*. Soon he was in Washington, D.C., for a few days of sightseeing. He then went back to Philadelphia and from there returned to New York. Although he was never to live in

Hannibal again (except, of course, in his vivid memories of the place), Mark Twain went back for brief visits half-a-dozen times during his life, the last few times greeted as a returning hero covered with glory, the most illustrious and celebrated citizen that the little village ever produced.

Those months in the East were eye-opening for the teenager. If he had heretofore thought of little Hannibal, with its shops and bars, its river commerce and murders, as a sort of metropolis and a metropolis from which one broke away by adventuring off into surrounding forests and caves and at his uncle's farm, he now knew better. He had seen unimaginable wonders and had unimaginable experiences. St. Louis, the first real city he had ever encountered, had a population more than thirty times larger than Hannibal's. There, the shock of strangeness was cushioned by the presence of his relatives. But when he boldly stepped off alone into the unknown, boarding a steamer and crossing the Mississippi into Illinois and then getting on an actual train, he met with what must have seemed marvels. More than a half million souls lived in New York City, nearly seven times the number that called St. Louis home. In that city and in Philadelphia Sam saw strange peoples arriving in increasing numbers—Irish and Chinese, Jews and free blacks. He saw libraries and Broadway shows, palatial homes and ornate churches. He paid homage to a fellow-printer by visiting Ben Franklin's grave; he visited the place where the Founding Fathers declared America's independence and went to look at the Liberty Bell. In Washington, he sat in the Senate gallery and spotted Stephen Douglas, William Seward, and Lewis Cass. It was intoxicating, and Sam was hooked on the color and drama of it. He wrote descriptive letters home that Orion published in his newspaper and began the lifelong habit of writing his observations down in little notebooks.

By the spring of 1854, a little less than a year after he had fled in the night from Hannibal, he rejoined the family, which had moved to Iowa while Sam was gone. Orion had finally failed in Hannibal journalism and was working diligently toward his next failure, as publisher of the *Muscatine Journal*. Sam was probably forced back to the family by a sudden surplus of printers in the East and the resulting scarcity of work, but he did not stay very long. Soon he was back in St. Louis setting type for the *Evening News*. When Orion gave up in Muscatine and started a printing business in Keokuk, Iowa (where his wife's parents lived), Sam joined him and Henry for a short period at Orion's "Ben Franklin Book and Job Office." Naturally, Orion had trouble coming up with the $5 a week he had promised his brother, and Sam was disgusted: with Orion, with typesetting, with life in Keokuk. He then was the beneficiary of a major miracle: while walking down Main Street, the wind blew him a fifty-dollar bill, "the largest assemblage of money I had ever seen in one spot." He promptly bought himself a ticket to Cincinnati, Ohio. After a visit to the family in St. Louis—Jane had moved in with Pamela and her husband again—and producing a little southern-dialect sketch for the *Keokuk Post* (using the pseudonym "Thomas Jefferson Snodgrass"), he finally got to Ohio. It was the beginning of the greatest adventure of his life.

The Great Mississippi

I

It all began strangely enough. While in Iowa, Sam read about the miraculous medicinal properties of coca leaves, the basic ingredient in cocaine. He hatched the harebrained scheme of going to Brazil, setting up shop on the Amazon River, and getting in on the ground floor of the potentially lucrative business. He even approached some possible financial backers in town. Although, as Ron Powers, a recent Twain biographer, puts it, "the idea of Samuel Clemens turning Keokuk, Iowa, into the mid-19th century cocaine capital of America has its irresistible nutty appeal . . . it was not to be." The backers soon lost interest, but Sam did not. In mid-February 1857, after three months of setting type in Cincinnati, he embarked boldly in the general direction of Brazil. This he did by boarding the steamboat *Paul Jones,* heading down the Ohio River to the Mississippi, and then steaming down the Mississippi to New Orleans where he hoped to find transportation to the Amazon. The pilot of the *Paul Jones* was named Horace Bixby.

Sam soon discovered that it was not possible to get to Brazil: "a vessel would not be likely to sail for the mouth of the Amazon under ten or twelve years." After four days in New Orleans, he learned that Bixby, now assigned to the southern-most stretch of the river, was about to start for St. Louis. The old dream of becoming a steamboat pilot, shared by so many boys along the river, was reawakened in Sam Clemens, and he was somehow able to persuade Bixby to take him on as a cub pilot. "He agreed to teach me the Mississippi River from New Orleans to St. Louis for five hundred dollars, payable out of the first wages I should receive after graduating." When the *Paul Jones* docked at St. Louis, Sam hurried to his sister's house and borrowed the $100 down-payment from his brother-in-law. Thus began those four wonderful years working on "the great Mississippi, the majestic, the magnificent Mississippi, rolling its mile-wide tide along, shining in the sun. . . ." He was to describe that experience, two decades later, with such affection, such dashing wit and heartfelt beauty, that many think that certain chapters of his *Life on the Mississippi* contain some of his finest, most moving and engaging writing.

"I entered upon the small enterprise of 'learning' twelve or thirteen hundred miles of the great Mississippi River with the easy confidence of my time of life," he was to write. "If I had really known what I was about to require of my faculties, I should not have had the courage to begin. I supposed that all a pilot had to do was to keep his boat in the river, and I did not consider that that could be much of a trick, since it was so wide." For the next two years, he studied the river's every minute feature with a diligence and concentration that he had never been able to muster at school. "My boy," said Mr. Bixby early in the apprenticeship, "you must get a little memorandum-book, and every time I tell you a thing, put it down right away. There's only one way to be a pilot and that is to get this entire river by heart." The young cub crammed into his notebook and then into his head the name of every point on the shore—every little town, every bend, every island, every bar and chute and reef, every prominent hill along more than a thousand miles. He had to remember where significant landmarks—woodpiles, one-limbed cottonwood trees, lonely plantation houses—indicated the best places to make a crossing. He had to know exactly where the invisible wrecks of less fortunate boats were lying just under the surface, waiting to wreck his. He had to memorize the "shape" of the shore, but he also had to understand that its shape was constantly changing. And then—he could scarcely believe it—he had to remember all of those things *in reverse* for the return trip to New Orleans. He had always vaguely understood that steamboats traveled at night as well as in broad daylight, but he suddenly realized that someone had to actually pilot them through the darkness. Even worse, there were various kinds of darkness. In the pitch black, the shoreline always looked perfectly and deceptively straight; in starlight the shadows were tricky, and starlight shadows were not the same as moonlight shadows. Bluffs in the water that were caused by the wind were harmless and could be driven over with impunity; bluffs caused by a sandbar could mean death to the boat and everyone on it. Piloting upstream, he learned, was a good deal safer than piloting downstream with the swift current pushing the boat from behind. In all these many things—and in myriad others—Sam Clemens, in his early twenties, became an expert.

After two years under the stern tutelage of Horace Bixby ("my gun-powdery chief" who frequently "went off with a bang . . . and then went on loading and firing until he was out of adjectives"), Samuel Clemens received his Pilot's Certificate on April 9, 1859. Before his career on the Mississippi was over, he would serve on almost a score of boats and make at least 120 trips between New Orleans and St. Louis. The experience changed him in a multitude of ways.

He had always been a good observer—those letters he had sent home from New York and Philadelphia reveal his keen eye and his talent for noticing. But his habits of observation were infinitely sharpened by his four years on the river. If the books and essays he was later to write are notable for their attention to the telling detail, the revealing nuance, the subtle change that hinted at volumes, then some of the credit must go to the extraordinary powers of observation that he picked up while learning to navigate the Mississippi River. Along with this enhanced ability for marking detail, moreover, he developed a considerable talent for remembering. He quickly came to believe that memory was the chief trait required of a riverboat pilot. On the river, he later wrote, "I had trained my dull memory to treasure up an endless array of soundings and crossing marks, and keep fast hold of them." His lifelong ability to remember—people, places, events from the distant past—also owed something to his training on the river.

The new abilities to observe and remember were not the only benefits that he derived from those four years. Until this point in his life he had never demonstrated much self-discipline, but he had now entered upon an occupation that demanded it. There was not only the considerable effort needed to learn and memorize, but the discipline required by a pilot's demanding schedule. Pilots normally worked four hours on and four hours off; to arrive at the wheel even a few minutes late to take over from one's co-pilot was regarded as a serious breach of courtesy. Sleep had to be snatched during the four-hour intervals between shifts. No doubt some of Sam's boyhood friends who recalled the carefree, forest-wandering, school-evading lad from Hannibal days would have been surprised to see it, but he somehow mastered the will not merely to manage this rigorous new life but to thrive under it.

There were other changes. For the first time in his life he knew the feeling of affluence and, as it happened, it was a feeling he liked. Early in his new career, he told his brother Orion that he liked letting folks catch a glimpse of the hundred-dollar bill peeking out of his wallet. "You will despise this egotism, but I tell you there is a 'stern joy' in it."[1] Nor did he object to the greatly increased status that attached to the position. By the spring of 1860, Sam informed Orion that he was banking around $100 a month and marveling at "what vast respect Prosperity commands!" He also experienced parts of the world that had been, until now, unknown to him. Both on board the boat and in the streets and rough dives of St. Louis and Memphis and New Orleans, he came into contact with reckless gamblers, painted women, sharp businessmen, slave traders, foreign visitors, workingmen, the whole panoply of Mississippi Valley humanity. He even had the dizzying experience of an ardent and entirely chaste four-day siege of a lovely maiden (only fourteen years old) named Laura Wright; she would haunt his memories and dreams for the rest of his life and now and then turned up in his books. "When I find a well-drawn character in fiction or biography" he later wrote, "I generally take a warm personal interest in him, for the reason that I have known him before—met him on the river."

---

[1]Calculating the value of money during Twain's lifetime and comparing it to early twenty-first-century values is a tricky business, but, in general, readers will not be far off the mark if they multiply the earlier figures by 20–25 to get an idea of what Twain's money might be worth today. Thus, the $100 that he flashed in the late 1850s would be worth between $2,400 and $2,500 now. The words "stern joy" came from Sir Walter Scott's poem of 1810, "Lady of the Lake."

Samuel Clemens took away one other legacy from those days as a pilot. The leadsman is the person on the boat who throws a weighted line into the river in order to measure the water's depth. He then shouts out the number of fathoms so that the pilot can know whether the river at that point is deep enough to ensure the safety of his boat. At one point in *Life on the Mississippi*, the writer describes a particularly harrowing passage near Hat Island, undertaken as night was falling. "The cries of the leadsmen began to rise out of the distance and were gruffly repeated by the word-passers on the hurricane-deck. 'M-a-r-k three! M-a-r-k three! Quarter-less-three! Half twain! Quarter twain! M-a-r-k twain! Quarter less—'" Two fathoms meant twelve feet of water beneath the bottom of the boat, and the leadsman's shout of "mark twain" meant that the water was safe.

II

One of the most remarkable and revealing passages that Mark Twain ever wrote occurs at the very end of the ninth chapter of *Life on the Mississippi*. In four marvelous and lyrical paragraphs, Twain summarized not only what the arduous effort to learn the river meant to him, but also what it cost him. And in those memorable few lines he was somehow able to encapsulate a dilemma that went straight to the heart of his creative life, a dilemma that was to haunt him for the rest of his days.

"The face of the water in time became a wonderful book," he begins. That book was written in a language that could never be read by the unschooled passenger who strolled complacently along the deck or gazed dreamily at the flowing river. But, Twain tells us, it "told its mind to me without reserve delivering its most cherished secrets as clearly as if it uttered them with a voice." It was a book, moreover, that "had a new story to tell every day. Throughout the long twelve hundred miles there was never a page that was void of interest, never one that you could leave unread without loss, never one that you would want to skip. . . ." The ignorant passenger, to whom the language of the water was unreadable, saw only "pretty pictures," but the pilot was not so lucky. What might seem to the passenger like a charming dimple on the surface of the water (if the passenger ever noticed it at all) appeared to the pilot as "an *italicized* passage; indeed it was more than that, it was a legend of the largest capitals with a string of shouting exclamation-points at the end of it, for it meant that a wreck or a rock was buried there that could tear the life out of the strongest vessel that ever floated."

Twain then contrasts the two ways in which he had looked at the Mississippi River. "I still kept in mind," he writes, "a certain wonderful sunset which I witnessed when steamboating was new to me." The sinking sun caused the river to be "turned to blood; in the middle distance the red hue brightened into gold." Here was a conspicuous black log floating along the current; there "a long, slanting mark lay sparkling upon the water"; in another place, "the surface was broken by boiling, tumbling rings, that were as many-tinted as an opal." The shore on the left was forested, and it featured a dead tree that still had one leafy branch that "glowed like a flame in the unobstructed splendor that was flowing from the sun." Everywhere he looked, "there were graceful curves, reflected images, woody heights, soft distances, and over the whole scene far and near, the dissolving lights drifted steadily, enriching it every passing moment with new marvels of coloring." It was a moment of exquisite beauty, unforgettably engraved on the young man's consciousness. "I stood like one bewitched. I drank it in, in a speechless rapture."

But then, Twain continues, he set about studying the river, learning to read its language. "[W]hen I had mastered the language of this water and had come to know every trifling feature that bordered the great river as familiarly as I knew the letters of the alphabet, I had made a valuable acquisition. But I had lost something, too. I had lost something which could never be restored to me while I lived. . . . [A] day came when I began to cease from noting the glories and the charms which the moon and the sun and the twilight wrought upon the river's face; another day came when I ceased altogether to note them." He then looks back at that glorious sunset scene, but now through the eyes of the pilot: that sun means a heavy wind tomorrow; that floating log means a rising river; the tumbling boils mean a dissolving sand bar and a shifting channel; the dead tree, with its one living branch, will not last much longer "and then how is a body ever going to get through this blind place at night without the friendly old landmark?" Now, he laments, "the romance and beauty were all gone from the river. All the value any feature of it had for me now was the amount of usefulness it could furnish toward compassing the safe piloting of a steamboat."

Twain closes this striking passage with a striking analogy. "Since those days, I have pitied doctors from my heart. What does the lovely flush in a beauty's cheek mean to a doctor but a 'break' that ripples above some deadly disease? Are not all her visible charms sown thick with what are to him the signs and symbols of hidden decay? Does he ever see her beauty at all, or doesn't he simply view her professionally and comment upon her unwholesome condition all to himself? And doesn't he sometimes wonder whether he has gained most or lost most by learning his trade?"

For all of his mature life, Mark Twain was torn by this quandary. On the one side, he was constantly solicited by the allure of the modern world: the utility of science, the seductive attractions of progress, professional reputation, business, power, the exercise of influence; it was a world characterized by machinery and technology and specialized knowledge, and it held out before his eyes the prospect of big money and prestige. And he was solicited on the other side by a longing for the beauty, the romance, the unhurried ease and innocence of a simpler, more natural time. He longed for both of these worlds and tried very hard, in his life and his writing, to have them both at the same time.

III

At the same time that Sam Clemens was honing his skills and satisfying his aspirations as a riverboat pilot, history (as usual) was lumbering forward, entirely indifferent to his private ambitions and desires. From the time of his birth in the mid-1830s, sectional feelings in the United States had grown steadily more bitter, and tensions between the North and the South constituted the chief political issues of the day. The war with Mexico, which began as Sam was approaching his tenth birthday, was widely believed in the North to be an undisguised maneuver on the part of southern conspirators to increase the number of slave-holding states and upset the balance in the Senate. When he was fifteen, the famous Compromise of 1850, including its Fugitive Slave Act which many northerners swore to disobey, did little to quiet the suspicions of conspiracy on either side of the Mason-Dixon line. The publication of Harriet Beecher Stowe's *Uncle Tom's Cabin* two years later persuaded thousands of Northerners that their southern fellow-citizens were barbaric tyrants, while convincing almost as many Southerners that any Northerner who subscribed to that depiction of their way of life was an implacable, misguided, and deadly enemy. The furor aroused by whether the territories of Kansas and Nebraska should enter the Union as free states or slave states gave birth to a new political party, the Republicans, who were determined to prevent the spread of slavery into the West. And if the new party infuriated the South, the Dred Scott decision in the Supreme Court, when Sam was twenty-two, infuriated the North. John Brown's raid, praised by many abolitionists, was proof among Southerners that the North was peopled by bloodthirsty fanatics. And if the South required more evidence of northern hostility against its way of life, the election of Abraham Lincoln in November 1860 supplied all the proof that was needed.

These evidences of increasing animosity agitated the entire nation, but they struck with particular force in the state of Missouri. It had been admitted as a slave state under the terms of the great "compromise" of 1820, and by the time Clemens earned his pilot's license, there were more than 140,000 slaves in Missouri in a total population of 1.2 million. White opinion in the state was split. Ambitious settlers from Kentucky, Tennessee, and Virginia came to Missouri in search of better soil, and they brought their slaves with them. Meanwhile, a large population of German immigrants, many of them refugees from the failed liberal European revolutions of 1848 and vehemently opposed to slavery, had settled in St. Louis; they were joined by a sizable number of Mormons who poured into the state from the north. Except for Arkansas to its south and a small piece of Kentucky across the river, Missouri was virtually surrounded by "free soil." Once the Kansas-Nebraska Act left the slavery decision to a vote of the people living in those territories, Missourians watched developments in Kansas carefully. Some Missouri proslavery adherents even entered Kansas to vote, and bloody skirmishes inevitably followed. Finally, Dred Scott, the principal party in that notorious Supreme Court decision of 1857, had been a slave in Missouri before being taken to free territory by his owner. Not surprisingly, therefore, after South Carolina seceded from the Union in December 1860 and was rapidly followed by five other states in January 1861, an emotional debate erupted in Missouri about whether to follow the others. In the end, despite a pro-secessionist governor, an elected assembly voted to keep Missouri in the Union. (Before it was all over, Missouri would send only 30,000 of its sons to fight for the Confederacy, but 109,000 to fight for the Union.) Nevertheless, both the proslavery and the antislavery factions soon raised troops, and a small civil war broke out within the boundaries of the state itself.

Sam Clemens seems to have been almost completely oblivious to these developments. His overwhelming interest in life was his occupation, and he probably weighed each new issue chiefly in terms of its impact on his career as a pilot. That calling naturally brought him into contact and discussion with avid partisans on both sides. Some of his friends and fellow-workers fluctuated wildly, sometimes condemning slavery unconditionally, sometimes defending the rights of the states to make their own decisions in the matter. Several incidents in his own life, during the days preceding the war, show him also to have been genuinely torn between his loyalty to the nation and his loyalty to states' rights and the southern way of life. The views of his family were of no help to him in reaching a firm conclusion. His mother retained her allegiance to the South and her unquestioning belief in slavery, and his brother-in-law William Moffett declared that, should he be drafted, he would rather go to jail than fight against his fellow Southerners. On the other hand, his brother Orion was an abolitionist and courageously campaigned in northern Missouri for the election of Abe Lincoln. Sam probably understood that secession, if it were to come about, would have serious consequences for commerce on the river; he certainly knew that if Missouri left the Union, navigation would be possible only as far north as Cairo, Illinois, and that St. Louis would be cut off. His political preferences are uncertain, but it is likely that in the presidential election of 1860 he voted either for Stephen A. Douglas or John Bell, both of whom were proslavery, but firm advocates of the Union. He did his best, no doubt, to ignore the gathering storm clouds for as long as he could.

Eventually things were decided for him. Lincoln was inaugurated on March 4, 1861, and on April 12, the South Carolinians bombarded Fort Sumter, the federal installation in Charleston harbor. Even Sam Clemens now had to admit that things were serious. The captain of the ship he had been working on, who was an ardent supporter of the Confederacy, now decided to keep his boat on the southernmost part of the river. On May 14, Sam left New Orleans as a passenger aboard the *Nebraska*, determined to find a berth on some other steamer. The *Nebraska*'s pilot was a friend of his named Zeb Leavenworth. They steamed up the river and got past Memphis—it turned out that the *Nebraska* was to be the last civilian boat allowed to pass through the Union blockade. But as they approached St. Louis a couple of days later, with Sam keeping Leavenworth company as he stood at the wheel, federal troops fired an artillery shell as a warning. Then a second shell hit close enough to damage the pilot house where Sam and his friend were standing. Years later, Twain recalled the incident to his biographer:

> Zeb Leavenworth fell back into a corner with a yell.
> "Good Lord Almighty! Sam," he said, "what do they mean by that?"
> Clemens stepped to the wheel and brought the boat around.
> "I guess they want us to wait a minute, Zeb," he said.

When he finally reached St. Louis on May 21, Clemens went into semiseclusion at the home of the Moffetts. He feared that, because of his skill as a pilot, the Union army would press him into service against his will; at least some of the stranded pilots were spreading that rumor down at the headquarters of the Western Boatman's Benevolent Association. But then, in mid-June, an old Hannibal friend came to the Moffett house and invited Sam to join up with some of his boyhood companions who were about to form a unit in the Missouri State Guard. They were responding to the urgent call of Missouri's pro-southern governor, Claiborne Jackson, that the loyal sons of the state arm themselves in order to thwart the designs of the Union army, which had moved into the state. Sam agreed and left St. Louis for Hannibal where he and the others formed a unit that they called the Marion Rangers (named in honor of the county in which Hannibal was located). There were fourteen of them. In accord with the lax and democratic custom of the day, they elected their own officers, and Sam Clemens was chosen second lieutenant.

It didn't really matter, however, because none of the Rangers, being typical products of the American frontier, was about to take actual orders from anybody—and certainly not from some old friend with whom they had grown up and gone to school. They were a ragtag bunch of youngsters out on a camping trip. They had no uniforms. They were armed with whatever they had brought along with them—shotguns, bowie knives, axes, revolvers—but that also didn't matter because they would never have an occasion to employ these instruments of war. The neighborhood where they set up their camps was home to men and women sympathetic to the Confederate cause, and these good-hearted farmers and their wives gladly supplied the boys with mules and horses and barns to sleep in and, best of all, substantial meals of well-cooked food. It is hard to imagine that anyone could have seriously believed that the Marion Rangers were going to play a plausible part in any actual battle they were unlucky enough to be tricked into fighting. Instead, Sam and his friends, regularly assailed by rumors of advancing Union regulars, understood by instinct exactly what to do. "I knew more about retreating than the man that invented retreating." In a supreme understatement, written almost twenty-five years after the event, Mark Twain admitted that "we were hopeless material for war."

That admission came in Twain's charming, but highly fictionalized recollection of 1885, entitled "The Private History of a Campaign that Failed," a reminiscence that Ron Powers considers worthy to stand "alongside Stephen Crane's novel, *The Red Badge of Courage*, as one of the most enduring pieces of literature inspired by the Civil War." Much of Twain's account is the hilarious retelling of the misadventures of that hapless and helpless outfit—the quirky characters who pretended to be soldiers and how this pathetic "herd of cattle started for the war." Twain looks back at them with tolerant bemusement: "What could you expect of them? They did as well as they knew how but really, what was justly to be expected of them? Nothing, I should say. That is what they did." But the writer of that enduring piece of literature had come a long way between the summer of 1861 and his writing of "The Private History." His thinking about war had matured, and he invented for his sketch an incident that abruptly ended the humor of it. One dark night while the Rangers were ensconced in their corncrib of a "camp," a messenger came "with the same old warning, the enemy was hovering in our neighborhood. We all said let him hover." The boys were "having a very jolly time, that was full of horse-play and schoolboy hilarity," when they heard a noise outside in the darkness. They got their guns and crept to the wall of the corncrib. "It was a man on horseback. . . . I got hold of a gun in the dark, and pushed it through a crack between the logs, hardly knowing what I was doing, I was so dazed with fright." Someone yelled "Fire" and "I seemed to see a hundred flashes and hear a hundred reports; then I saw the man fall down out of the saddle." The Rangers left their fortification and gathered around the man. "He was lying on his back with his arms abroad, his mouth was open and his chest heaving with long gasps and his white shirt-front was all splashed with blood." The boys were instantly overcome by remorse. "I was down by him in a moment, helplessly stroking his forehead, and I would have given anything then—my own life freely—to make him again what he had been five minutes before." The dying man "muttered and mumbled like a dreamer in his sleep about his wife and his child," and then he was dead. "The thought of him got to preying upon me every night; I could not get rid of it. I could not drive it away, the taking of that unoffending life seemed such a wanton thing." And then, Twain, looking backward from a quarter-century later, draws the eloquent lesson: that awful incident "seemed an epitome of war; that all war must be just that—the killing of strangers against whom you feel no personal animosity; strangers whom, in other circumstances, you would help if you found them in trouble, and who would help you if you needed it." The conclusion was obvious and inevitable: "my campaign was spoiled."

In another way, Clemens was to undergo a change from his days as a loyal son of the South, a defender of southern civilization. "That part of him that was Western in his Southwestern origin, Clemens kept to the end," wrote his friend William Dean Howells, "but he was the most desouthernized Southerner I ever knew. No man more perfectly sensed and more entirely abhorred slavery, and no one has ever poured such scorn upon the second-hand, Walter-Scotticized, pseudo-chivalry of the Southern ideal." Before long, Sam Clemens was to leave the South forever, first for the West and then for New England and New York and Europe. He was to marry into a family of abolitionists, and he came to revile slavery and to hold himself and his family guilty for having a share in it. He was to do what he could to right that great wrong and much of his fiction can be seen as an implied critique of southern ways. He was, Howells declared, "entirely satisfied with the result of the Civil War."

The last place to which the Rangers retreated, while Sam Clemens was still part of the outfit, happened to be near the village of Florida where Clemens had been born twenty-six years before. There they received another dire warning. The boys were informed that "a Union colonel was sweeping down on us with a whole regiment at his heel." Mark Twain described the dissolution of the Marion Rangers: "This looked decidedly serious. Our boys went apart and consulted; then we went back and told the other companies present that the war was a disappointment to us and we were going to disband." As they rode off toward their homes, they encountered their general, Tom Harris, who ordered them to return at once to their camp, "but we told him there was a Union colonel coming with a whole regiment in his wake and it looked as if there was going to be a disturbance, so we had concluded to go home. He raged a little but it was of no use, our minds were made up." Twain's reasoning was ironclad: "We had done our share, had killed one man . . . ; let him go and kill the rest and that would end the war."

Twain later learned that the Union colonel swooping down to kill him and his friends had been none other than a thirty-nine-year-old West Point graduate named Ulysses S. Grant, who was on the hunt for Tom Harris and the Missouri Guard. Luckily for Sam, he and Grant were not to encounter one another on this occasion. When they finally did meet, they would both be world famous celebrities, devoted admirers of one another, and associates in a historic business venture. For now, Sam Clemens decided that he had enough of military glory and was ready to try something else.

IV

His unlikely deliverer turned out to be his ne'er-do-well brother Orion. Some years earlier, when he was working in St. Louis, Orion had come to the notice of Edward Bates, a prominent lawyer there and a rising force in Missouri Whig politics. Bates took Orion under his wing and served as a mentor to him. When the Whig party was superseded by the Republicans, Bates continued his political ascent, even being mentioned as the new party's candidate for the presidency in 1860. At the Republican convention in Chicago, however, Bates threw his support to Abraham Lincoln, and after Lincoln's victory, Bates was named Attorney General. Shortly after his appointment, Orion Clemens applied to him for a federal position, and Bates—no doubt favorably impressed by Orion's brave willingness to campaign for Lincoln in the hostile territory of northern Missouri—recommended him coolly to Secretary of State William Seward ("Without being very urgent with you, I commend Mr. Clemens to you as a worthy & competent man, who will be grateful for a favor"). Three weeks after Lincoln was inaugurated, Orion got the word he and his wife had been hoping for; he was being appointed as secretary to the Territory of Nevada. It was not a negligible position—easily the most prestigious that Orion would ever have. He was to have many important duties and be second only to the territorial governor himself, and when the governor was absent, he was to be acting governor.

By early July, Orion was packed and ready to head west. He needed money for the overland stagecoach, however, and the government paid no attention to his request for an advance on his salary of $1,800 a year. So Orion did what other members of the family usually did; he went to St. Louis to borrow the price of the stage fare from his prosperous brother-in-law Moffett. Sam happened to be in town. The river was closed; the Rangers had disbanded. The two brothers had a talk and agreed that Sam, who had saved some money from piloting, would pay for the trip and Orion would take his younger brother on as his secretary. On July 11, Orion was sworn in for his new job and one week later, the Clemens boys boarded a steamboat that would take them up the Missouri to St. Joseph. There they were to catch the overland stage for Carson City, Nevada, 1,700 miles away. It was, for Sam, the start of the next new thing.

3

A Young Man Goes West

I

Sam paid for the trip ($300 down, $100 later) and was informed that he and his brother could each take only twenty-five pounds of luggage. They obediently discarded their fancy apparel in favor of the basic necessities—Orion his law books and six-pound dictionary; Sam some rough clothing, his boots, a pouch containing his remaining cash, some pipes, and plenty of tobacco. Both boys carried guns; Sam's was "a pitiful little Smith & Wesson's seven-shooter." He thought the weapon was "grand," but acknowledged that it did have one flaw: "you could not hit anything with it." Next morning at 8 o'clock the adventurers "jumped into the stage, the driver cracked his whip, and we bowled away. . . . It was a superb summer morning, and all the landscape was brilliant with sunshine." From one perspective, of course, the Clemens boys were fleeing from the hardships and perils of a bloody war. But ten years later, when Mark Twain wrote so memorably about that trek in his book *Roughing It*, he chose to picture it as an idyllic and happy escape from the everyday trials of civilization. There was, he wrote, "an exhilarating sense of emancipation from all sorts of cares and responsibilities, that almost made us feel that the years we had spent in the close, hot city, toiling and slaving, had been wasted and thrown away."

The journey into the American West was a plunge into the sparsely peopled world of nature, a world that, to Twain, always symbolized a delicious freedom, being at peace with one's surroundings, a high contentment with life. The coach was filled with mailbags on which the passengers reclined as they watched the scenery zip by at eight or ten miles an hour. "[T]he spinning ground and the waltzing trees appeared to give us a mute hurrah as we went by, and then slack up and look after us with interest, or envy, or something; and as we lay and smoked the pipe of peace and compared all this luxury with the years of tiresome city life that had gone before it, we felt that there was only one complete and satisfying happiness in the world, and we had found it." They absorbed the bleak terrain of the Great Plains, and observed new specimens of plants and animals. On the morning when they saw, looming off in the distance, the Rocky Mountains, they were awestruck by "the first splendor of the rising sun as it swept down the long array of mountain peaks, flushing and gilding crag after crag and summit after summit. . . ." They were astonished to find mountain snow in the middle of a sweltering August. All the while, they drank in the wild tales of bloodthirsty desperados and saw with their own eyes real Pony Express riders.

Sam was also about to encounter actual Native Americans. He could recall only one Indian from his youth, a dissolute, often drunken and homeless wretch who could be seen hanging around the streets of Hannibal, and whom Mark Twain was to immortalize as the cunning and bloodthirsty "Injun Joe" in *The Adventures of Tom Sawyer*. Although he was later able to overcome much of the racial prejudice of his youth, Mark Twain never outgrew the strong dislike of Native Americans that was the standard white attitude of the nineteenth century, particularly on the western frontier where he had grown up. When he and Orion made their trip into the West, of course, Indians (particularly the Sioux on the northern route and the Apache on the southern) occasionally engaged white travelers and skirmishes were not rare—the defeat of Custer on the Little Bighorn still lay fifteen years in the future. In Nevada, Twain would come upon Paiutes, who were sometimes disparagingly called Digger Indians by the whites. Twain gave them the name "Goshutes" in *Roughing It*, and he described them as filthy, treacherous, and savage. These racist attitudes toward Native Americans stayed with him for the rest of his life. And although some of his defenders claim that he was merely ridiculing the ideal of the "noble savage" as portrayed by James Fenimore Cooper, his language in published work and private letters indicate an animosity and contempt that cannot be easily justified. For example, many years later, when he wanted to describe the extreme cruelty and immorality of the French, he could do no better, he thought, than to compare them to the Comanches.

On August 4, the Clemens brothers arrived in Salt Lake City where they found a thriving community of 15,000 Mormons—Orion's superiors had instructed him to sound out their views of the Civil War and assess their loyalty to the Union; Sam was much more interested in hearing about polygamy. Then, two days later, they were back on the coach for the final 430 miles to Carson City. It had been twenty-six days since they had left St. Louis, but Twain insisted that they were not happy to get to Nevada's capital city on August 14. "It had been a fine pleasure trip; we had fed fat on wonders every day; and we were now well accustomed to stage life, and very fond of it; so the idea of coming to a standstill and settling down to a humdrum existence in a village was not agreeable, but on the contrary depressing."

Orion conscientiously set about performing his duties as Secretary of the Nevada Territory—everything from finding a meeting place for the new legislature to buying furniture, keeping the accounts, and standing ready to obey the orders of the New York City politico whom Lincoln had appointed governor. Sam, who quickly discovered that he had few responsibilities, spent his time loafing on street corners and exploring his new home. The village, named for the still-living scout and Indian fighter, Kit Carson, who was, at the moment, off battling the Navajos in New Mexico, was a peculiar place. Only about three years old in 1861, the census of 1860 counted only 714 residents—the entire Nevada Territory that year claimed a population of only 6,857. Within a year or two, however, both the Territory and its capital city experienced an explosion of numbers as thousands of adventurers poured in—Carson City almost tripled in a matter of months. The discovery of an extremely rich quantity of silver ore, the famous Comstock Lode, was the reason for this fabulous growth. Typical of the remote mining regions of the American West, it was largely a male society—the 1860 census could find only 720 women in the Territory and a mere 169 in Carson City—and the mining boom vastly increased the number of single men pouring into the area. Back in 1853, when he was seventeen and leaving home for the first time, Sam had promised his mother not to gamble or drink. Now that he was twenty-five and living in a raw mining town filled with rough men and dozens of bars, he took up both pastimes with enthusiasm.

II

Like most other Americans, including President Lincoln, Sam probably believed that the unpleasantness between the North and the South would be over in a few months and that he would soon be back on the river. Nevertheless, the possibility of becoming fabulously wealthy by finding silver was not lost on him. After only a few weeks lolling about Carson City, he was infected by the craze, and from September 1861 until the summer of 1862, he plunged into the mania with wild abandon. "We were stark mad with excitement—drunk with happiness— smothered under mountains of prospective wealth." It was the latest manifestation of his lifelong pursuit of riches but would certainly not be the last.

Rumors of fresh "strikes" drove men, like frantic schools of minnows, darting first in one direction, then in another. They purchased "feet" of still-unopened mines, usually on credit or with a small down payment. They then speculated on these feet, selling them at a profit if they could or trading them for other feet in grandly named mines that, Twain wrote, "had never been molested by a shovel or scratched by a pick." Sam was not entirely immune from the temptation. Two weeks after arriving in Carson City some of his new friends invited him to come and see for himself. He got a horse and rode about a hundred miles south to the Esmeralda mining district near the California border where he acquired fifty feet of untouched property. Whether he actually paid any of the $10 per foot, or whether his friends bestowed the claim on him in hopes of his contributing later assessments, is unclear. He had not yet been completely hypnotized, however, and he returned to Carson City where he hatched a new scheme.

Initially he thought that the real money lay, not in the back-breaking work of burrowing into the earth for precious metals, but in selling provisions to those who did. One commodity that was much in demand was lumber— not only for building shelters in remote mining outposts but also to shore up tunnels to keep them from collapsing. Timber was not plentiful in the deserts of Nevada, and it therefore brought a handsome price. Sam and another new friend decided to hike the twenty miles to Lake Tahoe and enter a claim for timberland. Like millions of others who have since gazed upon the breathtaking beauty of that place, he was awestruck. The pair had trudged through the rugged wilderness until "at last the Lake burst upon us—a noble sheet of blue water. . . . As it lay there with the shadows of the mountains brilliantly photographed upon its still surface I thought it must surely be the fairest picture the whole earth affords." The two staked out some likely timberland and cut down a few trees to make the "fence" that was needed to establish their legal right to the spot. They cobbled together a "brush house," which was also a requirement for ownership, but they preferred camping out. "If there is any life that is happier than the life we led on our timber ranch for the next two or three weeks, it must be a sort of life which I have not read of in books or experienced in person." That idyll ended abruptly, however, when Sam carelessly let his campfire go out of control. "Within half an hour all before us was a tossing, blinding tempest of flame!" Sam and his partner "stood helpless and watched the devastation." Forced to the safety of their boat, they stared spellbound as the flames roared up the ridges and across the canyons "till as far as the eye could reach the lofty mountain-fronts were webbed as it were with a tangled network of red lava streams . . . and the firmament above was a reflected hell!" Thus ended the lumbering enterprise, and Sam returned to Carson City.

Then, during the last months of 1861 and the first months of 1862, he surrendered to the silver craze. Stories of sudden wealth flooded the town. "Everybody was talking about these marvels. Go where you would, you heard nothing else, from morning till far into the night. . . . I would have been more or less than human if I had not gone mad like the rest. . . . I succumbed and grew as frenzied as the craziest." His first venture was to the Humboldt mining district, about 175 miles northeast of Carson City. He and some friends built a cabin at a little place called Unionville and started exploring. After accumulating thousands of feet of untapped ground, Sam gave up on Humboldt and returned to Carson City, hoping to get some money by trading his holdings. By March 1862, he and Orion had accumulated around 1,400 feet in a dozen locations back in the Esmeralda district, and they hoped to get rich either by a dramatic rise in the price per foot or (even better!) really finding some actual silver. In April, Sam moved down to Esmeralda himself to determine whether it was worth mining some of their holdings. Since the brothers did not have the money to hire laborers, Sam had to do the work himself: "the pick and shovel are the only claims I have any confidence in now," he wrote Orion. "My back is sore and my hands blistered with handling them today. But something must come, you know."

Unfortunately for the Clemens brothers, but luckily for the future of American literature, nothing came. After another brief but doomed experiment—this one involving a milling operation, extracting the valuable minerals from the raw ore that other miners brought in—Sam Clemens decided that he had had enough. By the end of the summer of 1862, he was in serious financial difficulty. "The fact is," he wrote Orion, "I must have something to do, and that *shortly* too." He toyed with the idea of returning to St. Louis but rejected that notion. Not only was the war continuing with unabated fury, but he had also boasted so vociferously in letters to the folks back home about his forthcoming riches that going back defeated and penniless would be too humiliating. He asked Orion to look around for some position on a newspaper, perhaps in Sacramento or San Francisco. And then came an offer from Nevada's oldest newspaper. The *Territorial Enterprise* was published in Virginia City, a mining town about twenty miles north of Carson City. A friend of Sam's, Bill Barstow, worked for the *Enterprise*, and he persuaded the owner and editor, Joseph Goodman, to hire Sam as a reporter at the handsome salary of $25 a week. No doubt the fact that Sam's brother was important in territorial affairs played a part in the arrangement, and it was probably not entirely a coincidence that the *Enterprise* soon became the official printer for the Nevada Territory.

In any case, in August 1862, Sam made his way to Virginia City, appeared at the *Enterprise* office, and introduced himself. He was almost twenty-seven years old, and, in the words of biographer Fred Kaplan, "he had at last discovered a vein that was to prove valuable."

III

Samuel Clemens was no stranger to writing for publication when he took the job at the *Enterprise*. At sixteen, he had published what was probably his first writing in Hannibal's *Western Union*, a paper owned by Orion and about to be merged by him into the *Hannibal Journal*. Sam wrote dozens of pieces while working at the *Journal*, some of them while his brother was off in Tennessee looking after the family's land and Sam was left in charge. Even when he fled from his brother's authority in 1853, he sent his observations of the East back to him for publication. When Orion moved to Iowa and took over the *Muscatine Journal*, Sam sent him half a dozen pieces, and when Orion settled in Keokuk, four of Sam's articles appeared in the *Keokuk Post*. These early works fell generally into two categories, both of which were to serve Mark Twain very well in the years ahead. Some of them were light sketches, detailing the absurd doings of the locals, loaded with slang and dialect, and told in the broad and exaggerated strokes typical of western American humor. Others were travel letters, a popular form of nineteenth-century journalism, in which writers sent back home engaging accounts of the faraway places they were visiting (even today contributors to newspapers are called "correspondents"). Sam signed these sketches and letters with preposterous pseudonyms: "Epaminondas Adrastus Blab," "Thomas Jefferson Snodgrass," "Sergeant Fathom." He had first come to the attention of the owners of the *Territorial Enterprise* for a series of letters from the silver fields that he contributed to the paper under the name "Josh."

The paper had begun its life in the late 1850s, moving its location from town to town until settling in Virginia City in 1859. The discovery of silver made both the town and the newspaper prosperous, at least temporarily. Circulation rose, advertising revenues increased, and the paper was able to purchase modern equipment and hire staff and reporters. There were some talented men working for the *Enterprise*, and Sam Clemens learned a great deal from some of them. The paper's owner, Joseph Goodman, had trained in New York journalism before coming west in 1854; he knew everything about newspapers and a great deal about writing. He recognized talent when he saw it, and he spotted it early in Sam Clemens. Although Goodman was three years younger than Sam, he became his mentor in the art of journalism, and the two remained friends for almost fifty years. Another of Sam's teachers at the *Enterprise* was William Wright, who wrote under the name "Dan De Quille." Like Sam, Wright was a disappointed prospector who turned to journalism. Six years older than Sam and already an experienced writer of comic sketches, he and the new reporter became companions and eventually roomed together. These and a handful of others at the *Territorial Enterprise* comprised a close-knit band of coworkers and friends.

They were, however, a band characterized by wild, unconventional, bohemian behavior. At the office they amused themselves with extravagant practical jokes on one another, followed by inevitable revenge on the part of yesterday's victim. When, late at night, they finished work on the next day's paper, they retreated to some raucous Virginia City bar and drank and smoked and told lies far into the next morning. Sam was an eager participant in these matters, and he possessed such conversational charm, such wonderful storytelling skills and easy gregariousness that he became a local celebrity. His shock of reddish hair, his imposing eyebrows, and sparkling, penetrating blue eyes marked his presence wherever he appeared in town. Virginia City was a rough place—old timers swore that the first two dozen graves in the town's cemetery were inhabited by murder victims. Prostitutes were everywhere, both in the numerous brothels interspersed among the bars and walking the streets, soliciting trade and brawling with one another over customers; drunkards, relaxing from a hard day at some silver mine, were always coming to blows—or worse; gunplay was common. (Once Sam interrupted a letter to his mother because he heard gunshots down on the street. When he came back from investigating the disturbance, he reported to Jane that two of his policeman friends had been shot by some gunman—"both died within three minutes.") Of course the *Enterprise* reporters were above all that physical violence. Their violence was rhetorical, and they indulged themselves, in print, in the most extravagant personal attacks, outlandish tall-tales, and goofy hoaxes. The limits on what got into Virginia City newspapers were set only by the failures of a writer's imagination.

It did not take Sam Clemens long to learn how to play with the best of them. In addition to his daily work of reporting on murders and fires and lawsuits and fresh silver discoveries, he produced comical sketches for the *Enterprise,* including a couple of outrageous hoaxes. In "The Petrified Man," written shortly after joining the paper, he "reported" that a body had been discovered in the mountains, turned to solid rock. Careful readers might have noticed—but apparently there were very few of those—that according to Sam's description of the corpse, loaded with scientific jargon and straight-faced detail, the body was thumbing its nose: one eye was closed, "the right thumb resting against the side of his nose," and so on. A year later, he horrified *Enterprise* readers with an entirely fictitious account of "A Bloody Massacre Near Carson." A distraught fellow named Hopkins, Sam reported, had been cheated by a dishonest San Francisco company. He then killed and scalped his wife, stabbed his nine children, and rode into town carrying the bloody remains of his murdered wife's hair. Poor Hopkins then killed himself at the door of Virginia City's Magnolia Saloon. These hoaxes were widely reprinted in other western newspapers, and, once they were exposed, both (but especially the tasteless "Bloody Massacre") called forth angry denunciations of both the *Enterprise* and the sadistic, irresponsible, and disgusting perpetrator who worked there.

After a couple of months reporting routine stories in Virginia City, Clemens was sent to Carson City in November 1862 to cover the territorial legislature. It was his earliest encounter with the world of politics, and he carried away from it a lifelong contempt for the venality and vulgarity of individual politicians and for the collective silliness and stupidity that these criminals produced when they gathered themselves into legislatures. He soon chanced upon Clement Rice, the capital reporter for the Virginia City *Union*, and his archrival in the business of informing the public of legislative doings. The two immediately embarked, in print, upon a vitriolic and unrestrained competition, jumping on one another's misstatements with ferocious outrage, each accusing his opponent of drunkenness, petty crime, congenital inaccuracy, deliberate lying, mental deficiencies of various sorts, and bad breath. Clemens branded Rice as "The Unreliable" and referred to him constantly by that designation; Rice sarcastically began to call Sam "The Reliable," and Sam started signing his reports with that name. It was a bare-knuckled literary brawl, and readers all over Nevada Territory loved it. Not many of them suspected that Sam and Clement Rice were close friends; they drank together all the time, shared a room in Virginia City for a while, and took vacations with one another (including a two-month debauch in San Francisco).

Once the legislative session ended, Sam grudgingly returned to the tiresome business of reporting daily events in Virginia City. He missed the social life of Carson City, however, and in January 1863, he begged Joe Goodman for some time off. Orion's wife had, by this time, joined her husband and was supervising some happy social gatherings. Sam brought along his fierce rival, Clement Rice, and the two hopped from party to party for about a week. He wrote three "letters" back to the *Enterprise*, roundly denouncing Rice, the Unreliable, for crashing a society party in stolen clothes and eating everything in sight. In tone, the letters were much the same as before, but with one significant difference. He signed the first one, published in the *Enterprise* on February 3, 1863, "Mark Twain." Samuel Langhorne Clemens had found the name he would use—not only in his literary productions, but in countless personal letters to his most intimate friends—for the rest of his life.

IV

When he took off for San Francisco for his two-month spree in the spring of 1863, he found a real city—sophisticated, cultured, interesting, expensive. Already bored with Virginia City, and buoyed by his growing reputation as a wickedly clever, no-holds-barred writer, he was on the lookout for wider opportunities. While in San Francisco, he concluded an arrangement with the *Morning Call* to contribute letters when he returned to Virginia City—just as he was writing letters back to the *Enterprise* while he and Rice were disporting themselves in San Francisco. In July (at the very moment when, back East, young men his age were killing one another with savage abandon at Gettysburg and Vicksburg), he reluctantly prepared to abandon the rapturous orgy of high living—lavish dining, swank hotels, the theater, outlandish hours, and plenty of drinking. He was not happy about going back to the *Enterprise*; "my visit to San F is gradually drawing to a close," he wrote to his mother and sister. Returning to Nevada "seems like going back to prison." Once back, he seized every chance he could find to get out of town—a quick jaunt to Lake Tahoe, a week at Steamboat Springs, Colorado, to cure a bad cold, another brief excursion to San Francisco, later a sojourn in Carson City to report on the constitutional convention.

A high point of his remaining time at the *Enterprise* came during eleven days in December 1863. Charles Farrar Browne— universally known as Artemus Ward, one of the most famous humorists in the United States—arrived in Virginia City to give a couple of lectures. An unconventional free spirit, Ward hung around the *Enterprise* offices, and he and Clemens immediately hit it off. The two were about the same age, and they had both been printers early in life. They shared a raucous sense of humor, a devil-may-care style, and a warm appreciation for one another's talents. Before the visit was over, each of them was indulging in unrestrained praise of the other. Ward suggested that "Mark Twain" send some of his work to the *New York Sunday Mercury* and promised to pave the way by writing to the editors. He hinted that perhaps he might take Sam along on his upcoming tour of Europe.

In his own writing, Artemus Ward specialized in posing as the gullible country rube, holding himself up to the reader's ridicule, spouting exaggerated dialects, absurd misspellings, crazy non-sequiturs, pure nonsense alternating with sound folk wisdom. (Because his "naburs is mourn harf crazy on the new-fangled ideas about Sperrets," Artemus agrees to go to a séance. "Thay axed me if thare was anybody in the Sperret land which I wood like to convarse with. I sed if Bill Tompkins . . . was sober, I should like to converse with him. . . .") It was a gentler humor than the sometimes vicious attacks in which Clemens often indulged, but it was undeniably funny, and before long Twain, who had already experimented with some of those techniques, would be using—and perfecting—some of the others. It was probably as a public speaker, however, that Ward taught Twain the most. Sam had given a speech or two as his celebrity in Virginia City grew, and his efforts won some local praise. But when he sat in the audience for Ward's lecture, "Babes in the Woods," he had the good sense to realize he was observing a genius. The crowd, Sam included, roared with laughter at the deadpan seriousness that slipped easily into some hilarious joke that the speaker apparently never thought was the least amusing. Above all, Artemus Ward was the master of the long pause, the quiet hesitation followed by the joke. Ron Powers gives this example: "I once knew a man in New Zealand who hadn't a tooth in his head [p-a-u-s-e]—and yet that man could beat a drum better than any man I ever saw." It would not be long before Mark Twain would take to the lecture platform himself, packing houses all over the world with howling admirers and earning several fortunes in the process. And everyone who ever tried to analyze his success as a lecturer noted that slow and easy drawl, the hand in the pocket, the dreamy unconcern, the long pause followed by the uproarious stunner.

Ward had something else to teach his new friend. Sam must have been acutely aware that this fellow from the East, so much like himself in years, in style, in attitude and talent, was raking in thousands of dollars a month. It was certainly something worth thinking about. Some scholars of American humor think that Artemus Ward might have eventually towered over all the others, side by side with Mark Twain and, perhaps, almost his equal. Unfortunately, three years after his sensational appearance in Virginia City, Ward died of tuberculosis during a tour of England, just short of his thirty-third birthday.

By May 1864, Mark Twain was more than ready to get out of Nevada. His actual departure, however, was appropriately bizarre. The people of the Territory were raising money for the U.S. Sanitary Commission, the official agency devoted to caring for sick and wounded Union soldiers. Part of the effort was a fancy ball being organized in Carson City by some society women, including Orion's wife, Mollie. Ten days after the dance, Mollie's brother-in-law (perhaps under the influence of alcohol) inserted an inflammatory paragraph in the *Enterprise*, suggesting that the money was going secretly not to the Sanitary Commission but to "a Miscegenation Society somewhere in the East." The idea that their contributions were being diverted to some group devoted to race-mixing did not sit well with the folks in Nevada, and the outcry was thunderous. Twain apologized profusely, calling it a silly joke and claiming that it had never been intended for actual publication and had gotten into the paper accidentally. The embarrassed *Enterprise* hoped the furor would pass; the rival *Daily Union,* hoping that it would not, kept returning to what it was calling "The 'Enterprise' Libel of the Ladies of Carson." Naturally, Orion and Mollie were humiliated by the whole affair. And if this were not enough, another stupid quarrel with the *Daily Union* erupted. Twain accused the paper of failing to fulfill its pledge of $100 to the Sanitary Fund. The *Union* called the charge an outrageous lie. The rhetoric quickly escalated out of control: according to the *Union*, Twain was characterized by "such a groveling disregard for truth, decency and courtesy, as to court the distinction only of being understood as a vulgar liar." Twain challenged the editor to a duel, seconds were appointed, and arrangements made. Meanwhile, he was challenged to another duel by the husband of the woman who headed that fund-raising ball earlier in the month. There was talk that some other Carson City husbands were lining up to do the same.

The duels never occurred. It was against Nevada law to issue challenges, however, and Twain's enemies (who were numerous) might very well have had him arrested, and the punishment was two years in prison. On May 29, he and his friend Steve Gillis, a scrappy *Enterprise* compositor who was to have been his second in the duel, got on a stagecoach and headed to San Francisco. Fred Kaplan's verdict is accurate: "Twain had done well in Nevada, but to some extent he had worn out his welcome. He was not the novelty he once had been. And there were those who did not find him funny as a writer or attractive as a human being."

V

Whether it was ambition, boredom, fear of incarceration, or the dread of death-by-duel that brought him to San Francisco, Mark Twain made himself at home there quickly. Despite the fact that he had little money, he checked in at the expensive Occidental Hotel; it was "Heaven on the half-shell," he wrote in one of his letters back to the *Enterprise* in mid-June. He already had something of a reputation when he arrived—some of his work for the *Enterprise* had been republished in San Francisco, and his letters from Nevada to the *Call* and occasional pieces for the literary journal *Golden Era* were known to local readers. This minor celebrity enabled him to subsist on credit for a few days, and he and Gillis made the most of it. There were parties, high-class restaurants, the theater, and, of course, plenty of liquor. Unfortunately, that carefree life, with its increasing debt, could not last, and Twain took a job as a reporter for the *Call* at forty dollars a week. He and Gillis left the Occidental for more modest quarters, but their noise, their unruly friends, their eccentric behavior and insane hours kept them on the move—they stayed at no fewer than five rooming houses during their first four months in town.

The routine at the *Call* he found oppressive: "it was fearful drudgery—soulless drudgery—and almost destitute of interest. It was an awful slavery for a lazy man." Appearing at the police court at 9 a.m. to report "the squabbles of the night before," he then "raked the town from end to end, gathering such material as we might, wherewith to fill our required columns; and if there were no fires to report, we started some." San Francisco had six theaters. Twain dropped into one each night, stayed for five minutes, "got the merest passing glimpse of play and opera," and wrote a review. It was a different sort of journalism from the easygoing Virginia City *Enterprise*, where he had no real schedule and could write pretty much what he wanted. Three months into the job he bargained for a pay cut and shorter hours, but that was not much better. In October, he quit the paper for good.

One of the reasons he severed his connection with the *Call*, in addition to the intolerable daily grind, was that he had become attached to a clique of artists, poets, and aspiring writers.

San Francisco already had a sizable bohemian community— unconventional, alternately fun-loving and serious, relaxed about orthodox morality, frequenting literary salons, drinking and talking into the night. One of the leaders of the pack was an ambitious young writer named Bret Harte. He had come to California in 1853 at age seventeen, tried various jobs, and had been a part of San Francisco's literary coterie since 1860. His friends, recognizing his talent, had arranged a comfortable job for him at the United States Mint; he had a salary, few duties, and the freedom to write. As it happened, the Mint office was in the same building as the *Call*, and Twain probably met Harte early in his career as a reporter. Harte helped persuade him that he could make a living by continuing to write occasional pieces for the *Golden Era* and becoming a regular contributor to the *Californian*, a new literary journal edited by Harte and a veteran of the *New York Times*, Charles Henry Webb. Both outlets paid Twain twelve dollars for each of his pieces.

Although Bret Harte was a year younger than Twain, he became his literary mentor. "He trimmed and trained and schooled me patiently," Twain told a friend a few years later, "until he changed me from an awkward utterer of coarse grotesquenesses to a writer of paragraphs and chapters. . . ." For a while Harte, on the strength of stories like "The Luck of Roaring Camp" and "The Outcast of Poker Flat," enjoyed a stronger reputation than Twain; he was America's chief literary interpreter of the California mining country. But soon, Harte's reputation was in sharp decline while Twain's continued to grow. The two might have been companions in their San Francisco days, but before long they would be bitter enemies, freely exchanging insults in print. In the meantime, however, Twain eked out a living with his pen. Between the beginning of October 1864, when he left the *Call*, and the end of the year, Harte and Webb published nine of his pieces. In 1865, Twain sent twenty-eight letters to the Virginia City *Enterprise*, twenty more articles to the *Californian*, and almost thirty reviews of plays for the *Dramatic Chronicle*. He was cobbling together a living, but it could not have been easy.

These sketches were, of course, of varying quality. Mostly they were amusing and fanciful productions, long jokes, parodies of other writers and literary styles, obvious fictions parading as news stories. In one, a young woman sits at the bedside of her wounded soldier lover only to exclaim, when the bandages around his head are removed, that she had "fooled away three mortal weeks here, snuffling and slobbering over the wrong soldier!" In another, he parodies American newspapers by giving his version of how they would have reported the assassination of Julius Caesar. A few of his articles reveal an active social conscience, outraged at corruption, angry at injustice, furious at the police treatment of San Francisco's Chinese community. Whatever the caliber of these sketches, they indicate one of Mark Twain's most remarkable traits: he was never at a loss for a topic. The silver mine of his marvelous imagination never ran dry. It was a gift that would last him for the rest of his life.

VI

In December 1864, it became necessary for Twain to absent himself from San Francisco. Steve Gillis had gotten into another bar fight, almost killing the bartender, and Twain had pledged $500 (which he did not have) toward his bond. Both men thought it best to leave town for a while—Gillis returned to Virginia City and his old job at the *Enterprise*. Twain, who had already irritated the police with his stories about their corruption and brutality, headed to a cabin at a remote place called Jackass Hill, a hundred miles east of San Francisco, in Tuolumne County. The cabin belonged to Steve Gillis's two brothers and was a hangout for poets, would-be writers, and other bohemian types who found themselves in the neighborhood; Bret Harte had spent some time there. The area had once been a booming part of the gold rush, but only a few miners were left and they scratched and panned without much success. It was lovely country, an ideal escape from Twain's growing troubles and discontents in the metropolis—one of his periodic retreats from the travails of civilization to the peace and harmony of nature. He stayed away from the city for three happy months. When it was not raining, they would leave the cabin and half-heartedly try their hand at panning for nuggets. When it rained, and in the evenings, they would sit around the fire, drink, smoke, and tell stories. Some of them, including Jim Gillis, were noteworthy storytellers, and Twain jotted down ideas in his notebook.

Then in late January 1865, still not ready to return to San Francisco, Twain and Jim Gillis wandered northeast, up to neighboring Calavaras County, settling in a town called Angel's Camp, where Gillis had some mining property. While they panned for gold there, they encountered in a tavern a local character named Ben Coon, who told them a story about a frog named Dan'l Webster. The frog's owner believed him to be the best jumper in the county and liked to bet on him. The story, it turned out, was an old one, and one version of it had even been printed a dozen years before. But it was new to Twain and he was especially enthralled by the deadpan, serious way Ben Coon told it. Thinking that someday, maybe, something might be done with the tale, Twain picked up his notebook and scribbled a few notes.

4

Making God's Creatures Laugh

I

On February 26, 1865, when Mark Twain returned to San Francisco from his long, bucolic vacation in the California countryside, he found a letter waiting for him. It was from Artemus Ward. Would Mark care to submit a contribution to Ward's forthcoming book on his travels in the American West? The letter, however, had been written four months earlier, and Twain naturally assumed that it was now too late to oblige his friend (and enhance his own reputation). He wrote Ward to express his regret and probably mentioned the story about the jumping frog that he had heard back in January. Then he plunged back into the mundane world of freelance writing, churning out a stream of articles for local periodicals. He concluded an agreement with his old Virginia City paper, the *Territorial Enterprise*: for $100 a month, he agreed to send a daily letter from California.

Typical of his work during this period was a pair of articles published in a new San Francisco periodical, *Youth's Companion*. The pieces appeared in July 1865 and were entitled "Advice for Good Little Boys" and "Advice for Good Little Girls." Satirizing the sentimental moralism of the popular McGuffey school readers and the bland platitudes of pious Sunday school literature, Twain offered young readers more realistic counsel. He told the boys that "You ought never to knock your little sisters down with a club. It is better to use a cat, which is soft. In doing this you must be careful to take the cat by the tail in such a manner that she cannot scratch you." For the girls he had equally practical advice: "If at any time you find it necessary to correct your brother, do not correct him with mud—never on any account throw mud at him, because it will soil his clothes. It is better to scald him a little; for then you attain two desirable results—you secure his immediate attention to the lesson you are inculcating, and, at the same time, your hot water will have a tendency to remove impurities from his person—possibly the skin also, in spots."

With material like this, Mark Twain built a devoted following in the West. If, during the spring and summer of 1865, Californians wanted to learn about the final battles of the Civil War and General Grant's tightening grip on the rebel army, if they wanted somber reflections on the assassination of the president of the United States or the details of the beginnings of Reconstruction, they would have looked in vain at the writings of Mark Twain. He was, apparently, oblivious to these matters. A month before Lee's surrender at Appomattox, he published "An Unbiased Criticism," ostensibly a commentary on a San Francisco art exhibit, but actually a long, humorous digression on everything from the reading habits of Angel Camp miners to an account of a local election and the merits of two competing sewing machines. And a month after Appomattox and the assassination, he wrote "How I Went to the Great Race between Lodi and Norfolk," a two-mile contest between a pair of famous horses; the article turned out to be a hilarious account of the difficulties of getting to the racetrack, without a single word about the race itself.

With his increasing local popularity came an increasing ambition to expand his repute. There had already been a few gratifying notices of his work in eastern periodicals. In a September 1865 article on California humorists, the editor of New York's *Round Table* wrote: "The foremost among the merry gentlemen of the California press, as far as we have been able to judge, is one who signs himself 'Mark Twain.' Of his real name we are ignorant. . . . He is, we believe, quite a young man, and has not written a great deal. Perhaps, if he will husband his resources and not kill with overwork the mental goose that has given us these golden eggs, he may one day rank among the brightest of our wits." These were, undoubtedly, sweet words for Twain to see in print, and they came at a propitious moment. He was a month away from his thirtieth birthday and in an unusually reflective mood. In a remarkably frank letter of October 19, he shared with Orion his thoughts about his past life and future career:

> I never had but two <u>powerful</u> ambitions in my life. One was to be a pilot, & the other a preacher of the gospel. I accomplished the one & failed in the other, <u>because</u> I could not supply myself with the necessary stock in trade—i.e. religion. I have given it up forever. I never had a "call" in that direction, anyhow, & my aspirations were the very ecstasy of presumption. But I *have* had a "call" to literature, of a low order—i.e. humorous. It is nothing to be proud of, but it is my strongest suit, & if I were to listen to that maxim of stern *duty* which says that to do right you <u>must</u> multiply the one or the two or the three talents which the Almighty entrusts to your keeping, I would long ago have ceased to meddle with things for which I was by nature unfitted & turned my attention to seriously scribbling to excite the <u>laughter</u> of God's creatures. Poor pitiful business!

Orion had always recognized his younger brother's talent for humorous writing, but, Sam wrote, "I always regarded it as brotherly partiality on your part, & attached no value to it." However (referring to that praise he had just gotten from the *Round Table*), "it is only now, when editors of standard literary papers in the distant east give me high praise . . . that I really begin to believe there must be something in it."

If Sam's letter to Orion is to be taken seriously, it reveals a good deal about his state of his mind as he entered upon his thirtieth year. His remark about lacking religion is, of course, significant. But what he divulges about his career is even more interesting. He had apparently said goodbye to piloting steamboats (although sometimes, in nostalgic moods, he professed to pine again for that career: "I wish I was back there piloting up & down the river again," he wrote back home only three months later. "Verily, all is vanity and [of] little worth—save piloting."). He had apparently bid farewell to getting rich by extracting precious metals from the earth. The letter might also be read as announcing his readiness to abandon the life of a newspaper reporter. These careers he now seemed willing to forsake in favor of writing humorous literature and bringing laughter to

God's creatures. The self-denigration should also be noted—the conviction that to write jokes is to produce literature "of a low order" and to devote oneself to making people laugh is a "poor, pitiful business." On the other hand, Twain's letter to his brother contains a postscript that, although phrased comically, indicates that, even at twenty-nine, he had his eye on future fame: "P.S. You had better shove this [letter] in the stove—for . . . I don't want any absurd 'literary remains' & 'unpublished letters of Mark Twain' published after I am planted."

If that future renown as a writer of humorous literature was ever to happen, he understood that he would have to make his name as well known in the sophisticated East as it now was in California and Nevada, and for that to happen he would need some sort of a break.

II

The break arrived on the back of that jumping frog of Calavaras County. Artemus Ward replied to Twain's letter of regret, telling him that there was still time to submit the frog story and that Twain should write the piece and send it directly to the publisher in New York. After two unsuccessful drafts, Twain produced a final version in mid-October and sent it off. By that time, it was, in fact, too late. But fortunately for the author, Ward's publisher saw the merit in Twain's story and sent it to the *Saturday Press* where it appeared on November 18, 1865, as "Jim Smiley and His Jumping Frog."

Twain's brilliant stroke was to create a "frame story" out of the tale he had heard in Angel's Camp, a story that gets told *within* an encompassing narrative. The piece begins in the form of a letter to Artemus Ward: "Dear Sir:—Well, I called on good-natured, garrulous old Simon Wheeler, and I inquired after your friend Leonidas W. Smiley, as you requested me to do." Then Twain recounts, ostensibly to Ward, how he found Wheeler in a tavern and asked him about Ward's friend. Wheeler "backed me into a corner and blockaded me there with his chair—and then sat down and reeled off the monotonous narrative which follows this paragraph." It emerges that Wheeler doesn't know any Leonidas Smiley, but that the name reminds him of Jim Smiley, an inveterate gambler ("always betting on anything that turned up you ever see, if he could get anybody to bet on the other side, and if he couldn't he'd change sides . . . just so's he got a bet, *he* was satisfied"). Wheeler then reels off a rambling, disconnected string of stories about Smiley's crazy gambling exploits, but remarks that he was particularly proud of the jumping ability of his frog, Dan'l Webster. Well one day, Wheeler continues, a stranger comes to town, takes one look at the frog, and confesses that he sees nothing all that special about him. "I'm only a stranger here, and I ain't got no frog—but if I had a frog I'd bet you." Smiley, smelling easy money, heads off to the swamp to find the stranger a frog. But while he is gone, the stranger crams pellets of quail shot into Dan'l ("filled him pretty near up to his chin"). When Smiley returns with a new frog for the stranger, the contest begins. Of course, poor Dan'l can scarcely move, much less jump, and the stranger takes the $40 bet and leaves. At that point, Twain resumes the narrative, telling Artemus Ward how he finally escaped the jabbering Wheeler and fled the bar.

"Jim Smiley and His Jumping Frog" (republished two years later as "The Celebrated Jumping Frog of Calavaras County" in a book of Twain's sketches) was probably the best thing he had written up until that point. By adopting the framing mechanism, Twain invited readers to have a chuckle at his own predicament—trapped by a chattering bore from whom he wanted only to escape and vaguely suspecting that Ward had intentionally placed him into this trap as a wicked practical joke. They could also laugh at Simon Wheeler, the deadly serious narrator who had no earthly idea, Twain tells us, that "there was anything ridiculous or funny about his story." Poor Wheeler "never smiled, he never frowned, he never changed his voice from the quiet, gently-flowing key to which he tuned the initial sentence, he never betrayed the slightest suspicion of enthusiasm." And finally, of course, readers could chortle over the frog-story itself, the old tale of the sharp stranger who outsmarts the local rube.

The story created a sensation. Within three weeks of its publication, newspapers up and down the east coast had reprinted it, and the New York correspondent for San Francisco's *Alta California* sent back an ecstatic report. Mark Twain's sketch, he wrote, "has set all New York in a roar, and he may be said to have made his mark. I have been asked fifty times about it and its author, and the papers are copying it far and near. It is voted the best thing of the day." Twain, who had enjoyed a growing, if sometimes notorious fame in the West, now had the satisfaction of seeing his reputation beginning to take root in the East. He began to think cautiously about trying his hand at writing books.

III

In March 1866, while his country struggled with the twin problems of reintegrating the defeated South back into the Union and of what to do about the increasingly unpopular presidency of Andrew Johnson, Mark Twain made a visit to the Hawaiian Islands. Excursions from San Francisco to the Islands, 2,400 miles away, were just beginning; he had declined an invitation in January to join an elite company of California dignitaries on the *Ajax*'s maiden voyage to Honolulu, but he eagerly climbed aboard the steamer for its next trip out. The Sacramento *Union* contracted with Twain (whose stature in California had risen with the approval he was now receiving from the East) to write letters from Hawaii. The paper agreed to pay for the trip and give him $20 for each letter he sent back. He eventually wrote twenty-five letters for the *Union* describing his stay in the Islands, eventually boiling them down into sixteen chapters in his book, *Roughing It*.

The voyage—the first time the former riverboat pilot had been on the sea, but very far from being the last—took twelve days, and on March 18, the *Ajax* docked at Honolulu, a town of around 15,000, but the most populous place on the seven Hawaiian Islands. Twain threw himself into the history, the culture, the geology, the folklore, and the economic, social, and religious life of this new and strange place with exuberant curiosity. His friend and first biographer, Albert Bigelow Paine, explained that Twain was "an insatiable sight-seer then, and a persevering one. The very name of a new point of interest filled him with an eager enthusiasm to be off. No discomfort or risk or distance discouraged him." Not satisfied with remaining on Oahu, he sailed to the other islands and explored and reported on everything he saw: plantations, food, volcanoes and jungles, the free and carefree life of the natives, the "dusky maidens." He was especially charmed by the dusky maidens, whose near-nudity and sexual freedom fascinated him: "At noon I observed a bevy of nude native young ladies bathing in the sea, and went and sat down on their clothes to keep them from being stolen. I begged them to come out, for the sea was rising and I was satisfied that they were running some risk. But they were not afraid. . . ."

He had originally planned to stay for a month, but he stayed four. His California friends had supplied him with "letters of introduction to everyone down there worth knowing," but he probably had no need for them; his own sparkling personality, unorthodox habits, flashing wit, and natural sociability won him entry and friendships everywhere he went. He soon knew every important American businessman and missionary in the Islands (and was kinder, in print, to the missionaries than he would later be to that class). He mingled with the natives and slept in their huts. But he also dined with Hawaiian officials, reported on the doings of the legislature, and met King Kamehameha V. Two American ambassadors, heading for China and Japan, stopped in Hawaii on the way to their posts, and Twain instantly won their friendship. Anson Burlingame, returning to China, was captivated by the ebullient humorist (his son had loved the jumping frog story), and the two shared a lively sense of humor and a love of conversation. Before they parted, Burlingame, fifteen years older than Twain, invited him to come to China and gave him some fatherly encouragement and counsel: "You have great ability; I believe you have genius. What you need now is the refinement of association. Seek companionship among men of superior intellect and character. Refine yourself and your work. Never affiliate with inferiors; always climb." It was sound advice for the coarse, somewhat undisciplined, sometimes badly behaved writer, and Twain was to remember it always.

But what most beguiled him was the ravishing beauty of Hawaii. The glorious colors, the exotic vegetation, the majestic mountains and boundless ocean views enthralled him in the same way he had always been enthralled by his escapes into nature. Like his uncle's farm in contrast to Hannibal, like the peacefulness of the great river in contrast to New Orleans or

Memphis or St. Louis, like the stagecoach across the plains or Lake Tahoe in contrast to Virginia City, Hawaii was a welcome relief from the commotion and commercialism of the city he had left: "instead of the combined stenches of Chinadom and Brannan street slaughterhouses, I breathed the balmy fragrance of jessamine, oleander, and the Pride of India; in place of the hurry and bustle and noisy confusion of San Francisco, I moved in the midst of a summer calm as tranquil as dawn in the Garden of Eden. . . ." He thought that "Californians ought to come here twice a year to soothe down their harassing business cares," and he was impressed that in "these enchanted islands" he encountered "no care-worn or eager, anxious faces in the land of happy contentment—God! What a contrast with California & [Nevada]." He was to retain these glorious memories of Hawaii for the rest of his life, and a quarter century later still spoke of "that peaceful land, that beautiful land, that far-off home of profound repose, and soft indolence, and dreamy solitude. . . . " The good people who die in Hawaii, he said, "experience no change, for they but fall asleep in one heaven and wake up in another." He always hoped someday to return, but he never did.

While in Honolulu he became the unexpected beneficiary of a maritime tragedy. The clipper ship *Hornet*, on a voyage from New York to San Francisco, around the Cape of Good Hope, caught fire off the western coast of South America. The passengers and crew abandoned ship in three longboats. Two of the boats were lost at sea, but on June 15, after forty-three days on the open waters of the Pacific, the third, carrying fifteen starving and weather-beaten sailors, reached land a couple hundred miles south of Honolulu. A few days later, they were brought to the city. Twain, who had already sent a brief account of the tragedy to Sacramento, went to the hospital and, with the help of Burlingame, interviewed the survivors, spent the night writing the tale of their ordeal, and next morning sent his story to the *Union* on a departing ship. On July 19, the paper was the first in the nation to reveal the tragedy, a sensational exclusive. (When Twain returned to California, he went to the *Union* office and demanded an additional $300 for the *Hornet* scoop!)

On the same day that the Sacramento *Union* published the *Hornet* story, its author started back to California, the delightful interlude in the Islands over. On the boat with him were the captain of the *Hornet* and several others from that doomed ship. They shared their experiences with Twain and allowed him to copy their diaries, and the writer sold a fuller account of the disaster to the prestigious *Harper's Monthly*. After idling on board for two weeks when their ship lost its favorable winds and lay becalmed, the passengers finally arrived in San Francisco. Twain was not happy to be back. "Home again," he confided to his notebook. "No—not home again—in prison again, and all the wild sense of freedom gone. The city seems so cramped and so dreary with toil and care and business anxiety. God help me, I wish I were at sea again!"

IV

There was an extremely important by-product of Mark Twain's "luxurious vagrancy in the islands." Returning "without means and without employment," and getting a little desperate about money, he got the idea of presenting a public lecture. At least since the Lyceum Movement of the 1820s, the appearance of public speakers in towns and cities across the country had been an important aspect of the American scene, part of the process of democratizing culture by bring it within the reach of thousands of everyday citizens. In the early days, lecturers ascended the platform to impart instruction to their hearers or to exhort them to moral behavior. By the time Twain was ready to enter the field, however, professional lecturers like Artemus Ward were as much sought after for their ability to entertain as for their ability to instruct. Twain considered that perhaps his adventures in Hawaii might be of interest to San Franciscans. Although some of his friends (including Bret Harte) advised him not to go through with it, arguing that it would damage his reputation as a writer, he nonetheless determined to give it a try.

He agreed to pay $50 (on credit) to rent the city's biggest opera house, seating more than fifteen hundred, and even more boldly, set the ticket price at a dollar. He scraped up another

$150 for publicity. The date was fixed for October 2, 1866, and for the occasion, he composed an advertisement that soon became famous:

A SPLENDID ORCHESTRA
Is in town, but has not been engaged.
ALSO
A DEN OF FEROCIOUS WILD BEASTS
Will be on exhibition in the next Block.
MAGNIFICENT FIREWORKS
Were in contemplation for this occasion,
but the idea has been abandoned.
A GRAND TORCHLIGHT PROCESSION
May be expected; in fact, the public are privileged
to expect whatever they please.

Dress Circle........$1   Family Circle............50 cts.
Doors open at 7 o'clock.   The Trouble to begin at 8 o'clock

Sam had, of course, always been an engaging talker, captivating and mesmerizing his friends with tales he had picked up during his youth and his days on the Mississippi. On three or four occasions, he had even stood on his feet and spoken more formally to actual audiences—mostly after-dinner remarks in front of people that he knew. This, however, was something quite different, and in later life he confessed (perhaps with some exaggeration) to have been petrified at the prospect. For the three days before the performance, he remembered, he was "the most distressed and frightened creature on the Pacific coast. I could not sleep. . . . I grew more and more unhappy. I had sold two hundred tickets among my personal friends, but I feared they might not come. My lecture, which had seemed 'humorous' to me, at first, grew steadily more and more dreary, till not a vestige of fun seemed left. . . ." He claimed to have planted in the audience some loyal friends who agreed to laugh uproariously. "I ate nothing on the last of the three eventful days—I only suffered."

At last the fateful hour arrived. "I thought of suicide, pretended illness, flight." Ninety minutes before the talk was to begin, Twain arrived at the theater, looked out at the empty seats, and skulked backstage "miserable and scared." But all the worry was wasted. He walked onto the stage, "quaking in every limb with a terror that seemed like to take my life away," and stared into a sea of faces. "The house was full, aisles and all!"—and some who wanted to be there were turned away. Momentarily blinded by the stage lights, unable to "gain any command over myself" he stood silent for a full minute. "Then I recognized the charity and friendliness in the faces before me, and little by little my fright melted away, and I began to talk." Within a few minutes he was "comfortable, and even content." The crowd roared with laughter, the newspapers were filled with compliments (Bret Harte wrote that Mark Twain was even funnier than Artemus Ward), and Twain, who brought in $1,200 that night, emerged with a clear profit of $400. He immediately got himself a manager—an old friend from the *Territorial Enterprise*—and arranged a tour. Soon he was lecturing about Hawaii in places named Red Dog, Marysville, and You Bet. Then he crossed over into Nevada and was talking on familiar ground. In Virginia City eight hundred people turned out to greet their former neighbor, and Steve Gillis, reported that "when he appeared on the platform he was greeted with a hurricane of applause."

Thus began what amounted to a second vocation for Mark Twain, a "parallel career" as he himself called it. Whenever he needed money and could not help himself, he ascended the stage, scheduling extensive, grueling tours, giving his famously amusing talks. It paid well enough, but he quickly came to detest the life it forced on him—the daily travel to get to that evening's performance, the inconvenient train connections and cramped hotel rooms and awful food. "I most cordially hate the lecture field," he wrote to his mother, "And, after all, I shudder to think that I may never get out of it." But as much as he disliked the whole business, he was very good at it. Everywhere he appeared, anywhere in the world, the houses were full, the laughter was hearty, and the purse was substantial. Until the joke got stale, he would walk out onto the darkened stage and introduce himself:

I have the pleasure of introducing to you Mr. Samuel Clemens, otherwise Mark Twain, a gentleman whose high character and unimpeachable veracity are only surpassed by his personal comeliness and native modesty. I am the gentleman referred to. I suppose I ought to ask pardon for breaking the usual custom on such occasions and introducing myself, but it could not be avoided, as the gentleman who was to introduce me did not know my real name, hence I relieved him of his duties.

The crowd would laugh, and then off he would go. Slowly, nonchalantly, running his fingers through his abundant red hair, entirely relaxed, with that easy conversational drawl and those long, long pauses and that infectious apparent rambling. "These islands are situated some twenty-one hundred miles southwest from San Francisco. The prevailing opinion—that they are in South America—is a mistake. They are situated in the Pacific Ocean. . . ." Straight-faced, never cracking a smile, with none of those flights of lavish rhetoric or extravagantly theatrical gestures that were the stock of other platform personalities, seeming not to be aware that he was saying anything particularly amusing, making himself, often, the chief object of the humor—for the next three decades, when he had to, he would swallow his dislike of the whole process, regale adoring audiences, and rake in the cash.

V

On December 15, 1866, Mark Twain boarded the steamship *America* and left California. After more than five eventful years in the American West, he was ready to move on to other things, bigger things than he had any reason to hope for. An incident that occurred a month before his departure, while he was out on his lecture tour, illustrates how much he had changed. Some of his old newspaper pals from the *Territorial Enterprise* decided to play a practical joke on him; they dressed up as outlaws, stopped the stagecoach that was carrying him back to Virginia City, and "robbed" him at gunpoint of $100 and a watch. Two days later, they revealed the joke and handed back his money. Although he never much liked jokes where *he* was the victim, in the old days he probably would have chuckled good naturedly, plotted some counter-outrage against the rascals, and taken them all out for dinner and a few drinks. This time he got miffed; he abruptly cancelled the lecture scheduled for the next day, huffed angrily out of Virginia City, and returned to San Francisco. He was no longer, it appeared, one of that fraternity of hard-drinking, late-night-carousing, tall-tale-swapping, devil-may-care boys. Somehow, in those five years, he had grown more mature, less rambunctious, more conscious of his own growing reputation as a respectable professional writer, even more conscious, perhaps, of his potential to become a famous national figure. In a sense, Sam Clemens had begun the process of growing up.

The trip from California to New York was a nightmare. Steaming southward to Nicaragua, crossing the narrow isthmus, and boarding another steamer for New York on the Atlantic side, the voyage took nearly a month. Shortly after leaving California, the passengers experienced a terrifying storm that threatened the ship itself—the lifeboats were readied in case the *America* could not withstand the terrible tempest, and many on board started praying. After that, a small child died and was buried at sea, and then, in Nicaragua, the ill-fated travelers encountered an outbreak of cholera. Before it was over eight of them had died, and with two of those, Twain had become friendly during the voyage. When they reached the Atlantic, their steamer first encountered paralyzing tropical heat and then freezing cold, high waves, and repeated difficulties with the machinery. Many deserted the ship as soon as it docked in Florida. Those who stuck it out, like Twain, steamed into New York harbor on January 12, 1867. There was only one good thing that could be said about the entire ordeal: a wonderfully colorful chap named Ned Wakeman captained the first leg of the trip, from San Francisco to Nicaragua. He was seventeen years older than Twain and something of a legendary figure on the California waterfront. Big, blustery, unschooled, irreverent, Wakeman had sailed everywhere in the world and was every bit as good a story-teller as Twain himself. The two men hit it off at once and spent the time swapping tall tales. Mark Twain was to "use" Ned Wakeman in half a dozen novels and short sketches, most notoriously as "Captain Elias Stormfield," whose memorable voyage to heaven was, after long delays and many attempts, chronicled by Twain and published forty years after the encounter with the man who inspired it.

VI

Mark Twain was thirty-one years and two months old when he stepped off the ship in New York Harbor in January 1867. If, as a boy, he had said to himself, "I am destined to become a writer of books; therefore I must store up as many experiences as I can so as to have ammunition for the stories I will someday tell," he could not have lived the first thirty-one years of his life more fittingly. He had grown up in the rural Midwest and had come to know there both the ways of the small town and the life of the forested countryside and the farm. From an early age he was intimately acquainted with his country's greatest river and the colorful men and women who traveled it. He had seen slavery and had known slaves. He had experienced poverty and had witnessed more than his share of violence and death. He knew the printer's trade and the steamboat pilot's trade and the miner's trade and the reporter's trade. He had lived in New York and Cincinnati, in Philadelphia and St. Louis and Virginia City and San Francisco and Honolulu; he knew the streets of Memphis and New Orleans and Salt Lake City. He had soldiered haphazardly for a few weeks and ridden a bumpy stagecoach into the wilds of the American West. He had seen the boundless landscape of the Great Plains and had drunk in the beauties of Lake Tahoe and Hawaii. He witnessed the flawed work of legislation and the hard life of the mining camps and the uproarious life of the newspaper office and the life aboard ship. He had already met and charmed powerful and famous men: Anson Burlingame, Bret Harte, Artemus Ward. And he combined with this varied experience a remarkable memory for detail, the sharp eye of an inveterate observer, a wondrous wit and an unparalleled dexterity with the English language. It would be difficult to think of any other American writer who, at the age of thirty-one, had compiled so diverse a set of experiences and who had been blessed with so notable a set of talents for exploiting them.

Before leaving San Francisco, Mark Twain made an arrangement with the *Alta California*. He was to be the paper's roving correspondent, "not stinted as to time, place or direction." And wherever he traveled he was to report whatever he observed in his marvelous letters.

5

A Cynic Among
the Pilgrims

I

For six months after landing in New York City, Mark Twain kept himself busy frantically promoting his career. He earned enough to stay alive by pouring out more than two dozen short pieces and letters between January and June of 1867. Most went back to the *Alta California*; others appeared in two or three more obscure papers. Upon arriving, Twain called on his former employer at the *Californian*, Charles Henry Webb, who had also returned to New York. Twain had toyed with the idea of a book about his Hawaiian adventures, but Webb suggested that he try instead a collection of his California sketches, leading off, naturally, with the one about the frog. Webb arranged an appointment for Twain with George Carleton, the publisher to whom Twain had sent the frog story too late to be published in Artemus Ward's book, but who had sent it on to the *Saturday Press*. The interview with Carleton was memorable and jarring. The publisher, perhaps irritated by Twain's slovenly appearance, threw a tantrum, lectured him about all the books people were begging him to publish, unceremoniously rejected Twain's idea, and dismissed him from his presence. (Twenty-one years later, in one of life's rare but satisfying moments, Carleton again encountered Twain, by then one of the best-selling writers in history. The publisher approached him and said: "I have a couple of such colossal distinctions to my credit that I am entitled to immortality—to wit: I refused a book of yours, and for this I stand without competitor as the prize ass of the nineteenth century." Twain then confessed to Carleton that since that interview he had, in his imagination, "taken his life several times every year and always in new and increasingly cruel and inhuman ways," but now, in view of the apology, he would regard Carleton as a "true and valued friend and never kill him again.")

In the end, it was Webb who grabbed the opportunity of publishing Twain's book, offering to help with the editing and agreeing to pay the author ten percent of the sales. On May 1, 1867, Mark Twain's first book, *The Celebrated Jumping Frog of Calaveras County, and Other Sketches* appeared. Priced at $1.25, it contained twenty-seven of his better California sketches. Twain had carefully toned down his language (changing "hell" to "hades," for example, and softening references to alcohol, sex, and death). He undertook this surgery in the belief that eastern audiences were more genteel than western ones. Ron Powers observes that "these edits marked the beginning of an acute self-refining process that would consume him, to a considerable extent, for the rest of his life: a process of tempering his more atavistic impulses to satisfy the decorous tastes of . . . just about everyone. . . . The entire English-speaking world, it must have seemed to him sometimes, was preoccupied with making Mark Twain watch his mouth."

For the occasion, Twain composed a clever dedication:

TO
JOHN SMITH
WHOM I HAVE KNOWN IN DIVERS AND SUNDRY
PLACES ABOUT THE WORLD, AND WHOSE
MANY AND MANIFOLD VIRTUES DID
ALWAYS COMMAND MY ESTEEM,
I DEDICATE THIS BOOK
It is said that the man to whom a volume is dedicated
always buys a copy. If this prove true in the present in-
stance, a princely affluence is about to burst upon

THE AUTHOR

Despite a nice review in the *New York Times* ("there is a great deal of quaint humor and much pithy wisdom in his writings"), the project was a failure. Webb was unable to promote the book adequately and sold only 4,000 copies (the author had hoped for 50,000). Later Twain professed to be ashamed of the book's crudity ("I hate to hear that infamous volume mentioned. I would be glad to know that every copy of it was burned, & gone forever"), but soon after, seeing a chance to make some money, he readily swallowed his embarrassment and agreed to its republication.

After giving Webb the materials for the book, Twain reacquainted himself with New York, a city that had changed, as he had, since his earlier visit fourteen years before. He attended lectures, including one on women's suffrage, saw Broadway plays, mingled with authors, actors, and artists at the Century Club, and explored the possibility of giving a lecture or two himself in the city. On February 3, he crossed the East River to Brooklyn to hear the most famous clergyman in the United States. Henry Ward Beecher was a leading Christian reformer, a veteran of the antislavery crusade and, after the war, active in the women's suffrage and temperance movements and an early defender of Charles Darwin's theory of evolution. It may be assumed that Twain came not as a devout Christian seeking the inspiration of the Gospel, but as a platform speaker looking over the technique of a celebrated fellow professional. He sent the *Alta California* a graphic description of Beecher's preaching: "marching up and down his stage, sawing his arms in the air, howling sarcasms this way and that, discharging rockets of poetry and exploding mines of eloquence, halting now and then to stamp his foot three times in succession to emphasize a point."

Twain was to have a long history with Beecher and members of his illustrious family, including the minister's renowned half-sister Harriet Stowe. But nothing was to be more important for his life and career than the intriguing project that Beecher's church was planning for the coming spring and summer.

II

Two days before Twain went to hear Beecher preach, the minister and his church announced sponsorship of a cruise to Europe and the Holy Land—perhaps America's very first such luxury excursion and an indication of the general prosperity being enjoyed by the upper-middle class in the North immediately following the Civil War. The promoters' eighteen-paragraph advertisement trumpeted the interesting places and pleasurable amenities that were in store for the passengers. "A first-class steamer . . . capable of accommodating at least one hundred and fifty cabin passengers, will be selected," but, prospective applicants were assured, the ship would only be booked to three-quarters of its capacity, insuring plenty of elbow-room. There was to be "every necessary comfort, including library and musical instruments." The sponsors promised that "the ship will at all times be a home, where the excursionists, if sick, will be surrounded by kind friends, and have all possible comfort and sympathy." Naturally, "an experienced physician" was to be on board. The bulk of the advertisement was a detailed itinerary of the marvelous cities and historic sites to be visited. It would not be cheap, of course—no doubt that was one of its chief attractions. "The price of passage is fixed at $1,250, currency, for each adult passenger [roughly $18,000 in today's terms]. . . . Five dollars per day, in gold [more than $70 today], it is believed, will be a fair calculation to make for *all* traveling expenses on shore, and at the various points where passengers may wish to leave the steamer." In case the enterprise's exclusivity was not obvious enough, the advertisement warned that "applications for passage must be approved by the committee before tickets are issued. . . ." It was rumored that dignitaries might be on board; perhaps Reverend Beecher himself, possibly General William Tecumseh Sherman, who had marched so famously from Atlanta to the sea in the late war.

Could anyone who knew Mark Twain doubt that he would have found the whole idea irresistible? Was there another person in America more addicted to travel, readier for the next new thing? He was, after all, that "insatiable sight-seer . . . the very name of a new point of interest filled him with an eager enthusiasm to be off." And the place-names on the itinerary would have been seductive to men and women much less adventurous than he: the Azores, Gibraltar, Naples, Athens, Constantinople, Smyrna, Jerusalem, Beirut, Bermuda, and two dozen other exotic locations. Was there anybody more eager to mingle with and make his way among the respectable? Hadn't Ambassador Burlingame advised him to seek "the refinement of association," to "never affiliate with inferiors; always climb"? And was there anyone else with so sharp an eye for potential targets for satire? No, to Mark Twain it must have seemed that the trip was designed with him in mind. There was, of course, the little matter of paying for it, but that was solved simply enough. He sent a magisterial telegram to the *Alta California*: "Send me $1200 at once. I want to go abroad." After some discussion in the editorial offices, the paper agreed, providing another $500 for expenses. In exchange, Twain promised two letters a week describing the wonderful things he would see.

He turned the act of signing up for the voyage into an occasion for one of his outlandish jokes. He and a friend from the New York *Tribune* appeared at the Wall Street office of Charles Duncan, the man who was to lead the excursion. Duncan later claimed that both of them were unkempt and a little drunk. The friend introduced Twain as a Baptist minister who hoped to share the on-board preaching duties with Rev. Beecher—he hoped the fact that these two men of God were of different denominations would not pose a problem. Duncan, an ardent prohibitionist, dismissed the upstart with a sneer: "You don't look like a Baptist minister and . . . you don't smell like one either!" Next day Twain returned sober, handed over the down-payment, and was readily accepted. Even better, subsequent publicity was soon mentioning that when the steamer left New York in early June, Mr. Mark Twain, the noted humorist from the West, would be among the celebrities on board.

There were still some months before departure, and Twain wanted to put the time to good use. In March, he boarded a train for St. Louis. He had not seen his mother for six years. She was sixty-four now and living with Pamela Moffett and her two children; William Moffett, the benefactor of Sam's youth, had died in August 1865. Brother Orion—having returned from Nevada, having abandoned the idea of becoming a minister, and having failed as a lawyer in Keokuk—also was in St. Louis for the reunion. Twain's anger at his brother's failure to unload the cursed Tennessee land had cooled, and he offered to find Orion a political appointment if he could. He spent about three weeks with the family, roaming around St. Louis, writing letters to the *Alta* describing life in Missouri, renewing his acquaintance with steamboat men, going reluctantly to church with the family ("I don't think I can stand it much longer. I never could bear to be respectable long at a stretch."). One Sabbath, the Sunday school superintendent approached to ask him if he had much experience in instructing little children. "My son," Twain replied, "it is my strong suit." He ascended the pulpit and "told that admiring multitude all about Jim Smiley's Jumping Frog." If there was a worthy moral to that tale, Twain assumed that the children could figure it out for themselves. By the end of March, he was giving lectures at places where he had once lived. The Keokuk paper hailed him as a former printer who "returns to us now, a famous man." The crowd that turned out to hear him lecture in Hannibal on April 2 was the largest in the town's history. In mid-April, Sam said goodbye to his family and climbed aboard the train for the two-day trip back to New York City.

He had thought about trying his luck at lecturing in New York since he first arrived in January and was encouraged by a sizable group of Californians now residing in the city. One of them, Frank Fuller, now a well-established businessman, agreed to manage the enterprise, and a date was fixed for May 6. The promoter laid out $500 of his own money to rent Cooper Union, the large and historic auditorium where Abraham Lincoln had spoken six years before. Fuller also paid $100 for advertising and traveled to Washington to enlist James W. Nye, formerly Nevada's governor and Orion's boss and now Nevada's senator, to introduce the speaker on the big night. Fuller's ambitious plans quickly outran Twain's self-confidence, and he was soon suffering the same doubts that had unnerved him before his first lecture in San Francisco. Ticket sales were worse than slow; he was to appear in competition with enticing attractions and illustrious speakers (among others, the Speaker of the House of Representatives would be lecturing that night); and this was New York, not Hannibal or Keokuk or San Francisco. What if no one came? In desperation, Twain and Fuller began to distribute free tickets to New York schoolteachers. The nervous lecturer wrote to Bret Harte: "Pray for me."

On the night of the talk the house was full; two thousand men and women were seated and at least that number, perhaps attracted by a burst of last minute publicity, were turned away. Senator Nye never showed up; some think it was a deliberate snub because Nye had been a firm Unionist and Sam had been a rebel. Twain, who had been persuaded to wear a tuxedo for the first time in his life, watched from backstage as the crowd filed in. He began to calm down. At the proper moment, he walked out onto the platform. He said nothing. He appeared to wander around the stage looking for something. Finally he turned to the audience and explained that there was to have been a piano and a senator here. The audience began to laugh. He introduced himself in the usual extravagant way. Then he spent a few minutes taking care of the missing Senator—those New Yorkers in the audience who had known Nye from his Tammany Hall days and those Californians who remembered him from his long vacations there, when he had left Orion in charge in Carson City, were soon beside themselves and howling. And then, Mark Twain, in his inimitable, relaxed, informal way began to talk about Hawaii.

As in San Francisco, the New York lecture was a triumph. The *New York Times* thought that "seldom has so large an audience been so uniformly pleased as the one that listened to Mark Twain's quaint remarks last evening." Artemus Ward, who had meant so much to Twain, had died in England only sixty days before and comparisons were inevitable. "The mantle of the lamented Artemus Ward seems to have fallen on the shoulders of Mark Twain," wrote Twain's friend at the *Tribune*, "and worthily does he wear it." The expenses rendered the monetary take negligible, but Twain and Fuller were satisfied; they knew that the acclaim received that night would pay rich dividends in future appearances, and they quickly booked two more lectures in New York.

As the great excursion drew near, Twain was content with his time in America's largest city and ready to go. "I have a large share of curiosity," he wrote in his final New York letter to the *Alta*, "but I believe it is satisfied for the present." He recounted for his California readers the many things he had seen and reported—everything from dens of poverty to magnificent architecture, from stirring pulpit oratory to Barnum's circus, from Central Park to the ethnic neighborhoods. But, he confessed, "there has been a sense of something lacking, something wanting, every time—and I guess that something was the provincial quietness I am used to. I have had enough of sights and shows, and noise and bustle, and confusion. . . ." It was that old tension in him between the excitement and profitability of the city and the repose and contentment that he knew when away from the city. He could never be permanently happy in either setting because he loved them both. It is not surprising, therefore, that he so often seemed a rootless, restless, turbulent soul.

That restlessness was apparent in a letter he wrote to his family on June 1. The departure for Europe and the Middle East had been delayed, and he was unhappy. "How do I know she will ever sail?" he complained to the folks back home. "My passage is paid, & if the ship sails, I sail in her—but I make no calculations, have bought no cigars, no sea-going clothing,—have made no preparation whatever. . . . All I do know or feel, is, that I am wild with impatience to move—move—*Move*! . . . . Curse the endless delays! They always kill me. . . . I wish I never had to stop *any*where a month." Five days later, on June 6, he got together with the editors of the New York *Tribune*. He had concluded an arrangement to send some letters to that paper as well as to the *California Alta*, and their celebration lasted into the early hours of the next morning. The ship was to depart at 2:00 P.M. the next day.

III

When the steamer *Quaker City* finally embarked on the afternoon of June 8, neither Henry Ward Beecher, the man of God, nor William Tecumseh Sherman, the man of war, was on board. The former had elected to stay home and work on his novel; the latter decided to head west and fight Indians. In their absence, the humorist's status was suddenly elevated, and he was awarded General Sherman's deluxe cabin on the upper deck. The other "pilgrims" (as Twain would soon be calling them) were a mixed lot. Depending on how one counted, there were around seventy of them—the hoped-for 110 failed to materialize once Beecher and Sherman dropped out. The nature of the trip, its association with Beecher's church, and its price tag tended to restrict the participants to prosperous Americans of genteel opinion, sincere piety, and a certain level of education and cultural aspiration. There was, on board the *Quaker City*, a serious religious atmosphere. Early in the voyage, one particularly devout passenger proposed that on every Sabbath day the vessel cut its engines and drift quietly, making for a genuine day of rest. The captain quickly vetoed that suggestion, but the ship did boast an organ and there were daily services and plenty of Bible study. There was no shortage of ministers and deacons and their godly wives, eagerly anticipating the sacred sites of the Holy Land, which for them were to be the culmination of the trip. There were also businessmen, doctors, and journalists (among them, would-be correspondents who, like Twain, intended to send letters back to hometown newspapers—although it is likely that they meant their letters to be more earnest and instructive than what he had in mind).

There was also, however, a small number of somewhat less solemn travelers, mostly males and generally younger than the others. They were inclined to gather in Cabin 10, home to Mark Twain and his cabinmate, Dan Slote. In a letter to his mother and sister, Twain described his new friend as "a splendid, immoral, tobacco-smoking, wine-drinking, godless roommate who is as good & true & right-minded a man as ever lived." Among the others who filled Twain's cabin with laughter, questionable language, and heavy cigar smoke were the ship's co-owner, who suggested that if all the religion was to continue he might be tempted to cause an accident to the organ; a Chicago gynecologist; the son of a railroad owner; and a couple of young men from New York. One of these was seventeen-year-old Charles Langdon, whose father was a wealthy lumber and coal dealer from Elmira. His parents, who hoped that the trip would help Charley become more serious, might have thought twice if they had known what was going on in Cabin 10. As it happened, nobody on board was to play a more important role in the future life of Mark Twain than the youngster from Elmira.

One other passenger would seriously impact Twain. She was Mary Mason Fairbanks, seven years older than he and married to the owner of the Cleveland *Herald*. She was also a writer and had signed up for the trip as a correspondent for her husband's newspaper. In one of her letters back home, she drew a classic portrait of Twain as a lively presence on the *Quaker City*:

> There is one table from which is sure to come a peal of contagious laughter, and all eyes are turned toward "Mark Twain," whose face is perfectly mirth provoking. Sitting lazily at the table, scarcely genteel in his appearance, there is nevertheless a something, I know not what, that interests and attracts. I saw today at dinner, venerable divines and sage looking men, convulsed with laughter at his drolleries and quaint original manners.

The feeling was mutual. Twain was drawn to Mrs. Fairbanks, who had a winning way of being decorous, religious, and cultured without being stuffy about it. "She was the most refined, intelligent, and cultivated lady in the ship, and altogether the kindest and best. She sewed my buttons on, kept my clothes in presentable trim . . . lectured me awfully on the quarter-deck on moonlit promenading evenings, and cured me of several bad habits. I am under lasting obligations to her." Their entirely platonic relationship fell into an elaborate sort of role playing. He called her "Mother Fairbanks" and referred to himself as her "cub." He read her the drafts of his letters to the *Alta*, and she criticized them, measuring his rough genius against her inflexible standards of polite propriety and the avoidance of vulgarity. For some reason, he took her suggestions seriously. On at least one occasion, he threw an entire day's work overboard because she did not approve of it. The friendship between Mark Twain and Mary Fairbanks lasted for thirty years and was carried on in dozens of letters, Twain always writing as the rambunctious naughty boy, asking forgiveness for some transgression, Mother Fairbanks sympathizing, forgiving, imparting wise counsel.

Not everyone on board the *Quaker City* regarded Mark Twain as a salutary influence. Some thought he was crude, that he paid scant attention to the religious purpose of the trip, that he drank and swore and played cards and used slang and was the ringleader of the other young delinquents. But whether drawn in by his charm, wit, and conversation, or repulsed by his crudity and bad habits, all of the voyagers had one thing in common. They were about to be rendered immortal, whether they liked it or not, by the irrepressible and irreverent rascal that fate had thrown into their midst. Even before the ship left New York, Twain was jotting into his notebook some fairly blunt observations about them.

IV

The trip itself is easily summarized. Rough weather forced the ship to anchor in the safety of New York harbor that first night. When the weather cleared, the pilgrims journeyed 2,400 miles in ten days and landed in the Azores. After a few days exploring the islands, it was back on the ship, and six days later on June 30, docking at Gibraltar. From there, Twain and a few others crossed to Tangier, Morocco, to explore that Islamic North African town for a day. After reboarding, they cruised up the east coast of Spain, 860 miles to Marseilles, France—patriotically celebrating July 4th aboard ship. Twain and his friends then took a train to Paris and Versailles, rejoining the party at Marseilles on July 13, and voyaging through the night to Genoa, Italy. With his roommate Dan Slote, and Abraham Jackson, the ship's surgeon, Twain spent a month exploring a half dozen of the leading cities and sites of Italy. On August 11, the pilgrims reunited at Naples and lifted anchor for the three-day trip eastward to Greece. The passengers were quarantined and forbidden to enter Athens because of a cholera scare, but at midnight Twain and three other adventuresome lawbreakers sneaked off in a rowboat and risking imprisonment if caught, stole into the city for a glimpse of the Acropolis and the Parthenon by moonlight.

The pilgrims then crossed the Aegean, made their way through the Dardanelles, spent a day in Constantinople, and proceeded into the Black Sea, visiting the resort cities of Sevastopol, Odessa, and Yalta, where, on August 26, they had an unexpected experience. They were entertained by Czar Alexander II, his family, and a group of Russian nobility at the Czar's summer palace. Then it was back to Constantinople for a few days, stopping at Smyrna, the ancient Greek city of Ephesus in Turkey, and, on September 10, Beirut, the entrance to the Holy Land. From there, Twain and seven other ambitious pilgrims, guides, and some servants, journeyed overland on horseback. Across barren dessert and through stifling heat, the party made their way fifty miles to Damascus and then another 150 to Jerusalem. They visited the holy sites—Galilee and Bethlehem, Beersheba and the Dead Sea. On September 30, the passengers again came together, in Jaffa, and the captain pointed the *Quaker City* westward toward home.

They stopped in Alexandria and went ashore to view the pyramids and the sphinx. On October 7, they began the voyage across the Mediterranean, back to Gibraltar and a five-day exploration of southern Spain. On October 25, at Cadiz, they all climbed onboard again and headed into the Atlantic. They spent four days relaxing in the paradise of Bermuda, and finally reached New York on November 19. They had spent a little more than five months together, and many of them were more than ready to depart from one another's company. Mark Twain was desperate to do so.

V

Twain published fifty-eight letters about that excursion—fifty for the *Alta*, another six in the New York *Tribune*, and two others in the New York *Herald* (including the last one, a 2,500-word summary of the trip, written late into the night once the ship docked and he found a hotel). From the beginning, he knew that these letters contained more than enough material for a book, and for the next year-and-a-half, he worked hard, revising, elaborating here and eliminating there, occasionally softening the tone of the original letters. *The Innocents Abroad; or The New Pilgrims Progress* was eventually to appear on August 15, 1869. Throughout both the book and the letters on which it was based, Mark Twain leveled his heavy artillery, with devastating effect, on two targets.

First, he took aim at the things he had seen and the foreigners he had encountered. He was capable, now and then, of putting into striking words the typical traveler's reaction of awe and respect and praise—as, for example, his moving description of the Egyptian sphinx: "The great face was so sad, so earnest, so longing, so patient. . . . If ever image of stone thought, it was thinking. . . . It was thinking of the wars of departed ages; of the empires it had seen created and destroyed; of the nations whose birth it had witnessed, whose progress it had watched, whose annihilation it had noted. . . . The sphinx is grand in its loneliness; it is imposing in its magnitude; it is impressive in the mystery that hangs over its story. And there is that in the overshadowing majesty of this eternal figure of stone . . . which reveals to one something of what he shall feel when he shall stand at last in the awful presence of God." He also said appreciative things about Paris and Athens in the moonlight. But if at times Twain could wonderfully express the admiration and reverence that so many others have felt and voiced over the long history of travel-writing, that was not his distinctive characteristic; nor was it what the readers of his letters and book noted and roared over and remembered.

It was, rather, Twain's defiance of the conventions of such writing that set his book apart—his utter contempt for what other writers had fallen down and worshiped, his boredom with what they had always found so exciting, his ridicule of what they had admired. Other writers had politely praised the people of the countries they visited and found them quaint, picturesque, and admirable; Twain more often found them backward, ignorant, unclean, and dishonest. His first encounter with foreigners, in the Azores, was typical: "A swarm of swarthy, noisy, lying, shoulder-shrugging gesticulating Portuguese boatmen, with brass rings in their ears and fraud in their hearts, climbed the ship's sides." When the pilgrims went ashore to explore the city of Fayal, they found "men and women, and boys and girls, all ragged and barefoot, uncombed and unclean and by instinct, education, and profession beggars. . . . [T]hese vermin surrounded us on all sides and glared upon us." The people of the Azores, Twain reported, "lie, and cheat the stranger, and are desperately ignorant. . . . [They are] little better than the donkeys they eat and sleep with."

And so it went. The women of Morocco? "I have caught a glimpse of the faces of several Moorish women . . . and am full of veneration for the wisdom that leads them to cover up such atrocious ugliness." The rural Italians? "We were in the heart and home of priestcraft—of a happy, cheerful, contented ignorance, unaspiring worthlessness." The bazaar at Constantinople? "the only solitary thing one does not smell . . . is something which smells good." Muslims? "The Koran does not permit Muhammadans to drink. Their natural instincts do not permit them to be moral. They say the Sultan has eight hundred wives. This almost amounts to bigamy." The morals of Mediterranean Christians? "Greek, Turkish, and Armenian morals consist only in attending church regularly on the appointed Sabbaths and in breaking the Ten Commandments all the balance of the week. It comes natural to them to lie and cheat in the first place, and then they go on and improve on nature until they arrive at perfection." The Arabs of Palestine? "The ring of [our] horses' hoofs roused the stupid population, and they all came trooping out—old men and old women, boys and girls, the blind, the crazy, and the crippled, all in ragged, soiled, and scanty raiment, and all abject beggars by nature, instinct, and education. How the vermin-tortured vagabonds did swarm! How they showed their scars and sores, and piteously pointed to their maimed and crooked limbs, and begged with their pleading eyes for charity." In his notebook he remarked that the Jews of Palestine were "like any other savages." At one point, while viewing a group of Arabs gathered around an ancient well, Twain recalled seeing a similar scene back home in an engraving. "But in the engraving there was no desolation; no dirt; no rags; no fleas; no ugly features; no sore eyes; no feasting flies; no besotted ignorance in the countenances; no raw places on the donkeys' backs; no disagreeable jabbering in unknown tongues; no stench of camels; no suggestion that a couple of tons of powder placed under the party and touched off would . . . give to the scene a genuine interest and a charm which it would always be pleasant to recall, even though a man lived a thousand years."

If Twain was unkind to the people he encountered, he was also cynical and sarcastic about the attractions that other travelers had professed to admire. For a long time, European visitors to the United States had pointed out the weaknesses (even the entire absence) of American culture—the artistic and literary poverty, the unbridled materialism and obsessive practicality, the lack of ennobling tradition, the stubborn enmity to beauty, sophistication, and subtlety. Mark Twain was about to even the score a little, to give the Europeans back a bit of their own—and Americans, even some who suspected that those critics might have been right and who suffered at the allegations of American inferiority, loved his brash attacks, and they loved him for voicing them.

The innumerable paintings of those he contemptuously called "the Old Masters," he found, after a while, wearying. He ridiculed the tourists who groveled over them: "I envy them their honest admiration, if it be honest," but he wondered how those fawning sycophants could see beauties that were not visible. DaVinci's "Last Supper" was especially disappointing and Twain reported that the crowd of amateurs making copies of the masterpiece were producing better work than the faded original. He was similarly bored by the endless parade of decrepit churches and dusty cathedrals. Of Notre Dame in Paris: "It was like the pictures." Of Venice: "She sits among her stagnant lagoons, forlorn and beggared, forgotten of the world." When he got to the Roman Coliseum, he emphasized the barbarities that occurred within its confines: "A matinee for the little folks is promised for this afternoon, on which occasion several martyrs will be eaten by the tigers." Lake Como was pretty enough, but it was no Tahoe. Constantinople was "the very heart and home of cripples and human monsters." He scorned what he regarded as the outright worship of barbaric relics, the body parts of saints, the hundreds of pieces of the original Cross, the "kegs" of crucifixion nails, the half dozen authentic Crowns of Thorns he saw on display and being venerated. He came to detest the guides who led them through these wonders; as a little private joke, he and his friends began calling all of them "Ferguson." For another amusement they—with pretended wide-eyed innocence—asked the same question about every personage that any of the Fergusons mentioned (Columbus, Michelangelo, DaVinci, who-ever): "Is he dead?" In short, the Europe that Twain presented to his readers and held up to derision was degenerate, superstitious, degraded, and filthy; its best days were behind it. Americans had no cause to drop their eyes and blush at comparisons between their country and the Old World.

When it came to the Holy Land, Twain was, if possible, even more scathing. To begin with, he was surprised at how tiny it was compared to the vast size it occupied in his boyhood imagination ("The state of Missouri could be split into three Palestines and there would then be enough material left for part of another.") Its villages were squalid. The Sea of Galilee was "dismal and repellant." The land where Jesus walked was "desolate and unlovely." The "celebrated Scriptural localities" were invariably broken-down and disappointing. The holy city of Jerusalem was nothing more than "rags, wretchedness, poverty, and dirt. . . . Lepers, cripples, the blind, and the idi-otic assail you on every hand." The Pool of Bethesda, in that city, was "a slimy cesspool." Everywhere there was barren soil, rocky landscapes, raw desert wind, and suffocating heat. It was not, however, in his published descriptions that he made his most acerbic comment about the place. In his notebook, he wrote: "No second Advent. Christ been here once—will never come again."

VI

Twain's second target was the group of pilgrims with whom he traveled. He found them hypocritical, sanctimonious, over-bearing, and uninteresting, and he did not conceal their unpleasant traits from his readers. He discovered what *their* sort of religion was when the *Quaker City* first headed east toward the Azores, but he put his complaint in the mouth of the ship's executive officer. "There they are, down there every night at eight bells, praying for fair winds—when they know as well as I do that this is the only ship going east this time of the year, but there's a thousand coming west—what's a fair wind for us is a *head* wind to them—the Almighty's blowing a fair wind for a thousand vessels, and this tribe wants him to turn it clear around so as to accommodate *one*—and she a steamship at that! It ain't good sense, it ain't good reason, it ain't good Christianity, it ain't common human charity." Another irritating example of self-centered piety occurred near the end of the trip. Twain's party had to make the overland journey to Damascus in three days. This schedule would be hard enough on the poor horses in that sweltering heat. It was rendered excruciating for the beasts when three of the group announced that they could not possibly travel on Sunday. "We pleaded for the tired, ill-treated horses, and tried to show that their faithful service deserved kindness in return and their hard lot compassion. But when did ever self-righteousness know the sentiment of pity?"

Beside their ostentatious and inconsiderate religiosity, the pilgrims had other annoying habits. They were habitual vandals of the places they visited, defacing and pillaging sacred sites, stealing souvenirs to take back home as trophies. While contemplating the eternal majesty of the sphinx, for example, "we heard the familiar clink of a hammer and understood the case at once. One of our well-meaning reptiles—I mean relic-hunters—had crawled up there and was trying to break a 'specimen' from the face of this, the most majestic creation the hand of man has wrought." Twain reported additional disagreeable traits. Among these was their apparent inability to resist lecturing the handful of sinners on board—those who tended to gather in Cabin 10—about their moral shortcomings and how much happier they might be if they would only reform themselves. But juxtaposed with that evangelical impulse was their tendency to quarrel endlessly with one another about everything from points of doctrine to the ship's itinerary. Twain summed up his disgust with them in one of his wonderfully understated sentences: "It was not the most promising party to travel with and hope to gain a higher veneration for religion through the example of its devotees."

Then on the way home, while docked at Gibraltar, the pilgrims found their mail waiting for them. Some friends and family had courteously sent them copies of the letters that their traveling companion had been publishing in the *Alta* and other papers, and the pilgrims discovered what Mark Twain had been saying about them. Not surprisingly, the atmosphere aboard the *Quaker City* became chilly during the last days of the expedition, and Twain spent a lot of time in his cabin. But the poor souls were aware only of his relatively polite, published views. Privately he was less restrained. To his California friend, Joe Goodman, he wrote: "Between you and I . . . this pleasure party of ours is composed of the d——dest, rustiest, [most] ignorant, vulgar, slimy, psalm-singing cattle that could be scraped up in seventeen states."

The final letter to the *Herald*, written the day the journey ended, was certainly rushed into print by Twain for the sole purpose of annoying the pilgrims. Twain wanted them to read his comments before they departed New York for their homes across the country: when he finished the piece at 10 P.M., he wrote to his mother and sister that he had just written "a long article that will make the Quakers get up & howl in the morning." Over breakfast next morning, his erstwhile companions picked up the *Herald* and read that, although the enterprise was advertised as a pleasure excursion, "it did not act like one." The passengers were too old. "The pleasure ship was a synagogue, and the pleasure trip was a funeral excursion without a corpse. . . ." The passengers, he charged, were devoted to playing harmless games of dominoes. "[T]hey played dominoes till they were rested, and then they blackguarded each other privately till prayer time." "Such was our daily life on board the ship—solemnity, decorum, dinner, dominoes, devotions, slander."

Thus ended the great *Quaker City* expedition of 1867. For all the bitter humor and unrestrained sarcasm Mark Twain unleashed, the trip had been good for him. Not counting the jaunt to Hawaii, it was his first extended overseas adventure. It turned out that he loved it and very soon would be addicted. The delicious letters he wrote were very widely read and by the time he landed his name was more generally known than ever before. It was a dead certainty that the book he was going to write about the trip would be extremely popular. These were not inconsiderable benefits from that five-month junket. But there was also another life-changing gain, and until the end of his life he would always believe that all the other benefits were as nothing by comparison.

Olivia Langdon Clemens, c. 1872. (Reprinted with permission of
The Mark Twain House, Hartford, Connecticut)

Livy

I

Charley Langdon was thirteen years younger than Twain, but the Elmira teenager found the writer to be one of the few congenial spirits on the *Quaker City*. Young Langdon was soon one of that clique of unconventional passengers who gathered in Cabin 10 to smoke, drink, and scandalize the orthodox. He was one of those to whom Twain read drafts of his letters, and in October, as the ship was returning home, Charley wrote his folks in Elmira, "I have been hearing Clemens['] Holy Land letters. I do wish you could hear them, they are characteristic of him[.] I do not like them as a whole but he says some good things." His parents probably paid little attention to Charley's evaluation of Twain. But they had no way of knowing that he was telling them about the man who was going to be their son-in-law.

Charley had a twenty-two-year-old sister named Olivia (but everyone called her Livy). According to a story Twain was to tell so many times that he probably came to believe it himself, one day while the *Quaker City* was anchored in Smyrna Bay, he wandered into Charley's cabin. In the course of an idle conversation, Charley showed him an ivory miniature portrait of his sister. Twain always insisted that from that moment on he was hopelessly in love with the girl in the picture. Sadly, scholars have since thrown doubt on the tale, attributing it to Twain's incorrigible habit of mythologizing and embroidering. No such portrait was ever discovered, probably none actually existed. Moreover, for weeks after that supposedly magical moment, Twain never mentioned any new infatuation in his notebook or his letters to friends and family. Indeed, even after first meeting Livy Langdon, he let half a year pass before actively pursuing a courtship. He was certainly going to be smitten by her, but that moment was not in the Bay of Smyrna.

The Langdons were a wealthy and prominent family—cultured, intelligent, well connected, and respected members of the local aristocracy. Livy's father, Jervis Langdon, was a living embodiment of the American dream, enjoying a life far different from the one that Twain's own father had struggled through. He had made some money in the lumber business in New York, moved to Elmira in 1845 (the year of Livy's birth), and garnered a large fortune by shrewd investments in railroads and coal. He was active in the antislavery movement, and when his church broke apart over that issue, he helped to start a new church and to persuade Thomas Beecher, Henry and Harriet's brother, to become its minister. Jervis Langdon was almost certainly a participant in the "underground railroad," secretly spiriting escaping slaves to safety, and both Frederick Douglass and William Lloyd Garrison had been guests in the Langdon home. Livy's father also enlisted in the cause of temperance and, in 1855, helped to found Elmira College, a pioneering institution for the education of women. He was, in short, in active sympathy with much of that wave of social reform sentiment that swept over New England and western New York in the decades before the Civil War. In his business dealings and reform work, Langdon had earned a reputation for integrity, morality, and benevolence. He and his wife were affectionate and nurturing parents, and they raised children (in addition to Livy and Charles there was an adopted older daughter named Susan) with these values.

A pampered and treasured child, Livy grew up in one of the most elegant houses in town and was well educated, intelligent, serious, and devout. "If I only grow in Grace and in the knowledge of our Lord and Savior I am content," she wrote to a friend in the same month that Twain returned from abroad. When she was sixteen she had fallen on the ice and became an invalid, confined to her bed in a dark room, unable to walk or sit up without assistance. Although she slowly recovered, she was always delicate and on the frail side, prone to illnesses and easily tired. While not ravishingly beautiful, she was decidedly attractive.

Twain's future friend, William Dean Howells, was to describe her as "classically regular in features, with black hair smooth over her forehead, and with tenderly peering, myopic eyes, always behind glasses, and a smile of angelic kindness."

Twain was susceptible to attractive women and had been in love more than once. There had been that bewitching fascination with fourteen-year-old Laura Wright, back on the river ("I was not four inches from that girl's elbow during our waking hours for the next three days"), but there were other women as well. And although nobody has been able to uncover an intimate sexual relationship with any of his infatuations and some believe that he was a virgin when he married, Twain was undeniably drawn to women. He was particularly vulnerable before women of a certain type: intelligent and cultured, properly Victorian—respectable, delicate, modest, and pure. Livy Langdon was all of those things. Moreover, Twain was now more than ready to get married and settled. Two weeks after his thirty-second birthday, he quipped to his shipboard counselor, Mother Fairbanks, "I want a good wife— I want a couple of them if they are particularly good. . . ."

But even if he had the audacity to imagine courting Olivia Langdon—a woman whom he had yet to meet—what were the chances? Even he, with all his impetuous vivacity and bold self-assurance, must have realized that invading the Langdon family (and to the Langdons, when the time came, it must have seemed very much like an invasion) would not be easy. He was the son of a frontier slaveholder and had briefly enlisted on the side of the Confederacy; she was the daughter of an ardent abolitionist. He was an unkempt comic from the wild West, the epitome of bad habits, skeptical of religion, and prone to drink; she was from a family of exemplary moral behavior, anti-alcohol sentiments, and deep devotion to the church. When he did set his heart on her, even he must have known that it was going to be an uphill climb. In the meantime, he had other possibilities to pursue.

II

One of those possibilities involved Senator William Stewart of Nevada. Like so many others, Stewart had hurried to the gold fields of California in 1850. Two years later, at twenty-five, he gave up on digging in the earth and became a lawyer. In 1860, he moved to Virginia City, where he was to meet the young reporter who came to town two years later. Stewart was soon a prominent figure in Nevada politics, and in 1864 was elected to the U.S. Senate. One day, while aboard the *Quaker City* near Naples, Twain got a letter from Stewart offering him a job as his private secretary. Even before formally accepting, Twain fired off a letter to Frank Fuller, who was setting up lecture dates: "Don't make any arrangements about lecturing for me. I have got a better thing, in Washington." Two days after landing in New York, Mark Twain caught the night train to the nation's capital.

He probably hoped the job would be like the one Bret Harte held at the San Francisco mint—a steady salary and duties light enough to permit him to concentrate on writing. Ten days after he arrived in Washington, he opened an encouraging letter from Elisha Bliss of the American Publishing Company in Hartford, Connecticut: "We are desirous of obtaining from you a work of some kind, perhaps compiled from your letters from the East. . . . If you have any thought of writing a book, or could be induced to do so, we should be pleased to see you." Besides needing time to work on his travel book, Twain had also arranged with the *Herald* and the *Tribune* in New York City, and the *Enterprise* and *Alta* in Nevada and California to serve as their Washington correspondent and provide letters describing life in the capital. Twain had also promised to look around for a political job for Orion. Meanwhile, he would room with Senator Stewart and tend to chores which he hoped would be minimal.

Forty years later, Stewart published his *Reminiscences* and treated readers to a rather uncomplimentary, and probably exaggerated, picture of his new secretary. "I was seated at my window one morning when a very disreputable-looking person slouched into the room. He was arrayed in a seedy suit, which hung upon his lean frame in bunches with no style worth mentioning. A sheaf of scraggy black hair leaked out of a battered old slouch hat . . . an evil-smelling cigar butt, very much frazzled, protruded from the corner of his mouth. He had a very sinister appearance." Stewart then proceeded to roast his slovenly clerk for his outrageous hours, his habit of smoking cigars in bed, and his merciless harassment of their prim landlady. "Her timid, aristocratic nature shrank from him, and I think she was half afraid of him. He did not overlook any opportunities to make her life miserable." One of his favorite gags was to pretend to be drunk and to stagger through the house scaring the life out of poor "Miss Virginia." It was obvious that sharing living quarters could not last very long and the Senator threw him out. (Four years later, Twain took his revenge. In Chapter 44 of *Roughing It*, he accused Stewart of going back on a mining deal with him back in Virginia City and putting "the guilty proceeds in his own pocket." So that no one would miss his point, Twain illustrated the text with a "Portrait of Mr. Stewart," showing him with the black eye-patch of a buccaneer over one eye!)

Twain had come to Washington at an exciting time. Congress was debating three questions heavy with historic implications. The first was what to do about the South. A fierce debate erupted between those who favored a relatively painless route to reunion for the former Confederate states and those who believed that harsher measures were needed to change southern attitudes and democratize southern traditions. The Radical Republicans who controlled Congress had imposed a mild military government on the South only eight months before, and the former Confederate states were now writing new constitutions preparatory to applying for readmission. The second question facing Congress concerned the treatment of the former slaves. Most white Southerners, forced to accept the abolition of slavery, favored a sort of second-class citizenship for African Americans, institutionalizing their subordination to whites and imposing restrictions on them through so-called Black Codes. They insisted that the management of race relations be left to state governments and local authorities. Many Northerners, including the Radical Republicans, thought the former slaves were entitled to full citizenship and federal protection from the schemes of their former masters. Finally, Congress was locked in a bitter struggle with President Andrew Johnson, a Tennessean who favored lenient terms for the South and was no friend of black Americans. He persistently vetoed the Radicals' legislation and the Radicals persistently overrode his vetoes. Things were coming to a head between the two branches and Johnson's testy annual message on December 2, which Twain was there to report, increased the tension. Even before Twain's arrival, the House Judiciary Committee had recommended impeachment (the entire House would not vote for impeachment for another three months). On each of these large questions, Senator Stewart took the position of the Radical Republicans, and some of the animosity between Stewart and his secretary might well have been caused by Twain's southern origins and lingering sympathies.

In any case, Twain dutifully sent his letters to the newspapers that had enlisted his services, wrote little word-sketches of Washington figures into his notebook for future use, and hobnobbed with important people in the press and Congress. Especially noteworthy was a brief (and awkward) interview with Ulysses Grant, the man who had struck terror into the hearts of the Marion Rangers in 1861; it was the start of an acquaintanceship that would prove important to both men. Above all, Twain renewed and multiplied that intense contempt for politics and politicians that he had felt in Carson City. "There are lots of folks in Washington who need vilifying," he wrote Mother Fairbanks. He was appalled by the rampant corruption, bribery, speculation, and job-selling that he saw everywhere; he was disgusted by the smallness of the men who governed the nation; he was shocked by the way private interests consistently overrode the public good. Typical was a letter that Twain sent to the *Territorial Enterprise* in February 1868: "Right here in this heart and home and fountain-head of law— in this great factory where are forged those rules that create good order and compel virtue and honesty in the other communities of the land, rascality achieves its highest perfection."

Unsurprisingly, Twain soon got bored with Washington—not even outrage could hold his interest for very long. Severing his connection with Stewart (or having it severed for him) and devoting himself entirely to writing did little to relieve his restlessness. After only three weeks in the city, he asked Fuller to arrange a lecture tour, claiming that he was "already dead tired of being in one place so long." One of the ways he amused himself was to take frequent jaunts to New York City to visit friends, including that small handful of former *Quaker City* shipmates he had *not* irretrievably alienated. One of those jaunts, taken over Christmas 1867, was to prove particularly significant.

III

Charley Langdon had been eager to introduce his family to Mark Twain, and for the holiday, the Langdons had also come to the city. Two days after Christmas, the family and the writer came together for dinner at the exclusive St. Nicholas Hotel on Broadway. Suddenly Twain was face-to-face with Olivia Langdon. Dixon Wecter, a pioneering Twain scholar and editor of *The Love Letters of Mark Twain*, describes what that meeting must have been like:

> Here was "the wild humorist of the Sage Brush hills". . . this ex-printer and steamboat pilot now rising in the world by his quick wit and slow drawl, with piercing blue-green eyes under brows so thick and fierce that to one observer they resembled 'a sort of plumage,' russet hair and mustache, hawk nose, and sensitive nervous hands missing the perennial cigar they dared not bring forth in the presence of unfamiliar ladies. And facing him in the parlors of the St. Nicholas was the wealthy coal dealer's only daughter, a slender figure, pale and lovely, with great sweetness and dignity, her eyes peering with a tender myopic vagueness, her black tresses combed severely back from a high white forehead.

In his *Autobiography*, Twain declared, "It was forty years ago; from that day to this the sister has never been out of my mind nor heart."

The next few days had all the marks of a serious infatuation. On New Year's Eve, Twain and the Langdons went together to hear the renowned British novelist, Charles Dickens, read from his *David Copperfield*. Next morning, Twain set out to make his New Year's Day calls—there were thirty-four places he hoped to visit. When he arrived at the first house on his list, who should he discover but Miss Langdon and her friend, Alice Hooker (daughter of the suffragist crusader, Isabella Beecher Hooker, a niece in that omnipresent Beecher family). A week later he wrote his mother about it: "I started to make calls, New Year's Day, but I anchored for the day at the first house I came to—Charlie Langdon's sister was there (beautiful girl,) & Miss Alice Hooker, another beautiful girl. . . . then I just staid there & deviled the life out of those girls. I am going to spend a few days with the Langdon's, in Elmira, New York, as soon as I get time. . . ." Yet, despite this spirited beginning, and despite his later claim that he was instantly captivated by Livy, it would not be until mid-August, seven months later, that he finally showed up in Elmira and began his campaign. For the present, he seemed more interested in following up the suggestion of the Hartford publisher Elisha Bliss for a book to be fashioned out of his *Quaker City* letters. He returned to Washington, moved in and out of a series of rooming houses, and worked night and day on his writing. He still owed the *Alta California* some letters describing the great excursion and, in order to eat, continued his correspondence to several newspapers. In the evenings and far into the night he worked on the book. In mid-January he decided to go up to Hartford to negotiate with Bliss face-to-face. On his way, he stopped in Brooklyn to consult Henry Ward Beecher about how to bargain—the minister had just concluded a lucrative deal for his forthcoming biography of Jesus. Twain told his mother—perhaps embroidering the conversation for her benefit—that the famous minister told him: "You are one of the talented men of the age—nobody is going to deny that—but in matters of business, I don't suppose you know more than enough to come in when it rains; I'll tell you what to do, & how to do it."

The American Publishing Company was a "subscription" publisher. It did not produce books to sell to bookstores in the hope that customers would wander in and buy their new title. Instead, subscription publishers used door-to-door canvassers, who worked on commission and signed up purchasers ahead of a book's publication. Enticed by the salesperson's prospectuses, buyers agreed to take a copy once the volume was published. Subscription publishers had long specialized in selling Bibles, other inspirational works, and medical compendiums, but they were gradually expanding to include the sort of popular literature that Twain was writing. The conventional wisdom in the trade was that the books had to have no fewer than five hundred pages before purchasers thought they were getting their money's worth. With most Americans having no access to bookstores, subscription publishing was a profitable business. Always interested in making a profit, Twain published his books that way into the 1890s, even after greatly increased access to urban bookstores cut into the business drastically—as he was to discover to his dismay. In Hartford, Bliss offered Twain a choice: either $10,000 immediately or five percent on each copy sold. It was a measure of Bliss's confidence in the project that he offered Twain a higher percentage than he was paying his other authors; it was a measure of the writer's confidence that, despite his urgent need for cash, he chose (wisely) the second option. He promised to hand over a 500- to 600-page manuscript within six months and plunged into work with prodigious energy.

There was one last obstacle to overcome. The folks at the *Alta California* got wind of Twain's plan, and they did not like it one bit. The letters upon which Twain was going to base his book, they argued, belonged to them. They had, after all, paid good money for them, to say nothing of their having paid for the trip itself. They hinted that they themselves might very well issue the letters in book form. After an exchange of testy telegrams, Twain determined that it might be advisable to go to California and hash things out. On March 11, he caught a steamer to Panama, crossed the isthmus, boarded another steamer and landed in San Francisco on April 2. He immediately began negotiating with his old friends at the *Alta*, and, astonishingly, they gave in on every point. They agreed not to publish his letters themselves (after he rejected their offer of ten percent), and they settled for him merely "acknowledging" the paper's release of their rights—Twain stoutly refused to "thank" them. When the book appeared, its preface read: "I have used portions of letters which I wrote for the *Daily Alta California*, of San Francisco, the proprietors of that journal having waived their rights and given me the necessary permission." He wrote to Bliss triumphantly on May 5, exulting in his success and adding "I am steadily at work, & shall start east with the completed manuscript about the middle of June."

Having decided to work on the book in San Francisco, he saw no reason not to earn a little extra money by giving a few lectures. His appearances around San Francisco were packed, despite some critical comments from the local press and pulpit. Some in the press found his humor mindless and vulgar; some in the pulpit found his descriptions of the Holy Land irreverent, even sacrilegious. One called him "this son of the Devil" and another denounced his ridicule of "subjects that are dear to every Christian heart." Twain took these accusations as good advertising and booked additional appearances across the Nevada border at Carson City and Virginia City. Despite the distractions of lecturing, on June 17, he was able to inform Mrs. Fairbanks that he had accumulated 2,343 pages of material. He asked his friend Bret Harte to read the manuscript critically, which Harte generously agreed to do. Harte "told me what passages, paragraphs & chapters to leave out—& I followed orders strictly." Twain stayed in California longer than he had planned, but on July 6, he retraced his path across Panama and arrived in New York on July 29.

Six months earlier, while he was concluding his agreement with the American Publishing Company and staying with the Hooker family, Mark Twain described to his mother and sister the attitude he carried into the negotiations: "But I had my mind made up to *one* thing—I wasn't going to touch a book unless there was *money* in it, & a good deal of it. I told them so." Regarding the terms he had wrung out of the company, he remarked smugly that "Beecher will be surprised, I guess, when he hears this." It would be another five years before Twain and his future neighbor, Charles Dudley Warner, bestowed upon the Gilded Age the name it was always thereafter to bear and applied to it their withering criticism of its sordid and grasping ways. But it is clear that the young man from the Missouri frontier—the man who had loved wandering the forests and caves of Hannibal and lamented the disappearance of the romance of the great river and was spellbound by the majesty of the western prairies and the beauties of Tahoe and Hawaii—it is clear that this deeply divided spirit understood the ethos of his time and was perfectly at home with it.

IV

On August 4, 1868, Twain arrived in Hartford to deliver his manuscript, and for the next two weeks he remained there, trimming down the book and participating in editorial decisions regarding its publication. He also explored the town and was impressed by it. Back in January, when he had first come to bargain with Bliss, he had also been attracted to the city and his letter to the *Alta* told why: "This is the center of Connecticut wealth," he reported. "Hartford dollars have a place in half the great moneyed enterprises of the union." Now, six months later in another letter to the *Alta*, he again stressed Hartford's prosperity. "Where are the poor in Hartford? I confess I do not know." A thriving insurance industry and a tradition of arms manufacturing underwrote the community's financial health. Hartford, moreover, was the state's capital and, with around forty thousand residents, boasted a vibrant cultural life and was home to some fairly well known intellectuals and writers, including the world famous author of *Uncle Tom's Cabin*, Harriet Beecher Stowe. He liked the town and could imagine himself settling down there.

Meanwhile there was some unfinished business involving Charley Langdon's sister. Twain got back to New York on August 17, 1868, waited three days, and headed to Elmira. His young friend met the train, was dismayed at Twain's ragged appearance, and brought him surreptitiously into the house so he could change into decent attire before greeting the family. He spent the next two weeks with the Langdons, going for walks or rides around town, chatting pleasantly at the dinner table or in the Langdon gardens. They sang together at the piano. ("Mr C. had a very sweet tenor voice," reported Livy's cousin Hattie, who was staying with her Langdon relatives at the time.) Near the end of his visit, Twain proposed marriage, and Livy promptly declined the offer. The rejected suitor, however, was able to extract one concession. He asked permission to write letters to her as a fond brother to a young sister. She said yes. Before he left the house on September 8, he wrote the first, addressing it to "My Honored 'Sister.'" She had dashed his hopes, he told her, but he had no regrets. "It is better to have loved & lost you than that my life should have remained forever the blank it was before." From now on, he promised to write only with "the sacred love a brother bears to a sister." It was the start of a long campaign of conquest.

While visiting his mother and sister in St. Louis a few weeks later, however, he received a letter from Livy, and best of all, she enclosed a photograph of herself. He must have sensed victory, but he also understood exactly what notes to strike. Livy had promised to pray for him. "Not any words that ever were spoken to me have touched me like these," wrote the religious skeptic. He begged her to continue her praying "for I have a vague, far-away sort of idea that it may not be wholly in vain." Then he offered up the ultimate bait. "I will so mend my conduct," he pledged, "that I shall grow *worthier* of your prayers, & your good will & your sisterly solicitude" and even though "it has taken me long to make up my mind to say these grave words, which, once said, cannot be recalled," but "I *will* 'pray with you' as you ask."

On his way back from St. Louis, at the end of September, he stopped for a night at Elmira. Next morning he and Charley climbed onto a wagon that was to take them to the train, but their bench was poorly attached, and when the horse lurched forward, both of them fell backwards onto the pavement. It was, for Twain, "a fortunate fall," but not in exactly the same sense John Milton had meant at the end of *Paradise Lost*, when he described Adam and Eve's exile *from* paradise. The horrified Langdons rushed to the curb and carried the pair back to the house. Although Twain was not seriously hurt, he took full advantage of Livy's nursing and stayed another couple of days. Soon thereafter he again overplayed his hand, impetuously casting aside the brother-sister charade and expressing his ardor in a passionate letter. For that slip he earned himself a stern rebuke. By this time he was out on his lecture tour and relied on his long and eloquent letters. Then, in late November, he returned to Elmira for a scheduled lecture, an especially nerve-wracking performance because the entire Langdon family was sitting in the audience. To Fairbanks he reported important progress: "She felt the first faint symptom *Sunday*, & the lecture *Monday* night brought the disease to the surface."

By Wednesday he had won: "She said over & over & over again that she loved me but was sorry she did & hoped it would yet pass away." On Friday he left the house "to save her sacred name from the tongues of the gossips," but he wrote her that night. "I am blessed above all other men that live; I have known supreme happiness for two whole days. . . . I do love, love, *love* you, Livy! My whole being is permeated, is renewed, is leavened with this love, & with every breath I draw its noble influence makes of me a better man." At Christmas, 1868, he gave up drinking—for a while.

He had won her partly by his charm and wit, by his persistence and matchless skill with the written word. But he had also prevailed by shrewdly adopting the pose of a helpless sinner, ashamed of his reckless past, yearning for a better life, in desperate need of the support of a pure spirit who might save him from his wretched and purposeless existence. To an earnest, devout, generous-hearted Victorian like Livy Langdon it was an irresistible appeal. Like countless educated and intelligent young American women of her class, she was well-equipped to play some worthy role in society, to make her life count for something. Unfortunately, the gender stereotypes and prejudices of her age confined her, and thousands like her, to a narrow range of possibilities. It was probably outside the reach of her imagination to have pictured herself as a physician or an attorney or a college professor, even if her delicate health would have permitted her to indulge such improbable fantasies. Both Livy and her suitor had admired and discussed Coventry Patmore's "The Angel in the House" (1854), an enormously popular poem which set forth the image of the submissive, but ennobling Victorian woman. The ideal woman was gentle, sympathetic, modest, and devoted to her home, her husband, her children. At the same time, she taught her family, by her shining example, important lessons about religious faith, a life of purity and morality, the need to avoid bad habits, dangerous temptations, and vulgarity. That Livy Langdon felt limitless and passionate affection for Twain cannot be doubted; those feelings would grow steadily in the years ahead. But she must also have been drawn, initially at least, by the prospect of devoting her life to the noble purpose of reforming this untamed genius whom all

America had begun to notice and who fate had thrown across her path. He was smart enough to present himself, perhaps even sincerely, as being open to that mission, even eager for her to work her magic on him.

So much for the maiden. There still remained the maiden's family. At the end of November, Livy's mother wrote to Mary Fairbanks: "I cannot, and need not, detail to you the utter surprise and almost astonishment with which Mr. Langdon and myself listened to Mr. Clemens' declaration to us of his love for our precious child, and how at first our parental hearts said no. . . ." She felt that she had to ask Fairbanks what this Mark Twain fellow was really like. On the same day, the suitor himself wrote to his real sister in St. Louis: "When I am a Christian—& when I have *demonstrated* that I have a good steady reliable character, her parents will withdraw their objections, & she *may* marry me." The Langdons, he ventured to believe, "are not *very* much concerned about my past, but they simply demand that I shall prove my *future* before I take the sunshine out of their house." Sometime in December 1868, they asked Twain for a list of acquaintances so that they could request assessments of his character from them. By mid-January, the replies started arriving, and they were more frank about his wild life and disreputable habits in the West than Twain would have wished. One San Francisco clergyman predicted that the rascal would end in a drunkard's grave. Another told Mr. Langdon that he would rather bury his daughter than have her marry a man like Twain. There were other denunciations. Later, Twain claimed that he was not unduly upset by them because he had himself frankly confessed his past delinquencies to the Langdons.

In early February 1869, while lecturing in Illinois, he was summoned to Elmira for an excruciating private talk with Jervis Langdon. While the victim stood silent, Langdon read him the evaluations he had received. "The results were not promising," Twain wrote a third of a century later. "All those men were frank to a fault. They not only spoke in disapproval of me but they were quite unnecessarily and exaggeratedly enthusiastic about it." Twain could think of nothing to say. "Mr. Langdon was apparently in the same condition. Finally he raised his handsome head, fixed his clear and candid eye upon me and said: '. . . . Haven't you a friend in the world'? I said, 'Apparently not.' Then he said: 'I'll be your friend myself. Take the girl. I know you better than they do.'" On February 4, 1869, Samuel Clemens and Livy Langdon announced their engagement.

The couple agreed to wait a full year before marrying. In the intervening months, Twain visited Elmira whenever he could and sent long and fervent letters when he could not. ("To think that within the last twenty-four hours I should have written fifty mortal pages of manuscript to you," he wrote a month after the announcement.) They discussed what they were reading and marked particular passages for one another's edification. Mostly, Twain poured out his love and his anticipation of their life together: "Livy, you are so interwoven with the very fibres of my being that if I were to lose you it seems to me that to lose memory & reason at the same time would be a blessing to me." At the same time that he was nursing and solidifying their relationship, Twain was belabored by three other matters as he counted the days to the wedding.

Perhaps most annoying was the interminable delay in getting his travel book out. Bliss, at the American Publishing Company, kept explaining that the proofs were not yet ready to review and that preparing over two hundred illustrations was not a simple matter. Then the Company's directors developed reservations about the irreverent tone of the work and about the title—Twain wanted to call it *The New Pilgrim's Progress*, but some pious directors thought it almost blasphemous to allude to John Bunyan's revered seventeenth-century masterpiece. The board's chair even tried to talk Twain into releasing the Company from its contract. Twain refused, but was willing to change his title to *The Innocents Abroad*. By March 1869, the proof sheets began to arrive. He had them sent to Elmira, where he and Livy went over them together. It was their first venture in a lifelong collaboration in which she advised and sometimes censored him in the direction of respectability. Finally, in late July, the book appeared, a year later than originally planned.

His second concern was to regularize the business of his lecturing. Although he detested the hectic scheduling, the erratic train connections, the second-rate hotels and abominable food, the inevitable welcoming committees that dragged him off to admire the local attractions, he knew he was good at it and he needed the money. In the spring of 1869, Twain began a collaboration with James Redpath, founder of the Boston Lyceum Bureau, one of the most prestigious of the booking agencies that had sprung up to manage the burgeoning lecturing business. Redpath, who himself had a colorful career as a reporter, writer, and abolitionist, organized his agency shortly after the Civil War. Many of his star attractions were veterans of the antislavery crusade: Frederick Douglass, Henry Ward Beecher, Charles Sumner, Wendell Phillips. Soon he was arranging tours for musicians, magic acts, and theatrical troupes. He specialized in humorists, including Josh Billings and David Locke, another strong advocate of African American rights, who wrote and lectured as "Petroleum Vesuvius Nasby." Twain and Nasby became close friends once they met as Redpath lecturers. "Nasby called at my room at 10 last night," Twain wrote Livy, "& we sat up & talked until 5 minutes past 6 this morning." Redpath and Twain also struck up an immediate friendship, and Twain toured for the Boston Lyceum every season from 1869 to 1873.

Finally, in view of his new responsibilities, Twain had to give serious thought to acquiring a steady occupation. Naturally, he turned first to the newspaper business, the field he knew best. He hoped to purchase a substantial interest in some promising paper, which he would edit and manage and to which he would occasionally contribute. The *Cleveland Herald*, owned by Mary Fairbanks's husband, was a possibility, but Twain did not much like Mr. Fairbanks and when he raised the price for taking him on, Twain broke off the negotiations. He also tried the *Hartford Courant*, which had the merit of publishing in the town that he was growing increasingly fond of and where the Langdon family had social connections. The editors of the *Courant*, however, seemed lukewarm to the idea and nothing came of Twain's overtures. In the end, Jervis Langdon came to the rescue. In August 1869, he loaned his future son-in-law $12,500 to buy a one-third interest in the Buffalo, New York, *Express*. Both Livy and her family were eager to stay as close as possible, and Buffalo was only 120 miles from Elmira and connected by train.

On August 15, Twain became the managing editor of the *Express* and quickly began to make changes and write sketches and editorials. On weekends he caught the train to Elmira.

At last, on February 2, 1870, the couple was married at the Langdon home. Most of the guests, of course, were from Livy's side, but Twain's sister Pamela Moffet and her teenage daughter Annie made the trip. The Fairbankses came from Cleveland, and Petroleum Nasby was there. From Hartford came a new friend, one of the closest Twain was ever to have, a minister named Joseph Twichell. Notably absent were, on the groom's side, his mother Jane, now sixty-seven, and on the bride's side, her brother Charley, off on another tour that his parents hoped would transform him into a responsible adult. The ceremony was performed by the Langdons' minister, Thomas Beecher, with Twichell assisting. Livy's father, who by this time was suffering terribly with stomach cancer, had one more surprise up his sleeve. The morning after the wedding, a happy party boarded the train for Buffalo—in a private car provided by some of Mr. Langdon's railroad friends. Twain expected to be taken to a boarding house. Instead, their driver carried them to an attractive two-story house with a balcony. It was a $43,000 gift from the Langdons, and it came complete with three servants, a stable, a horse and carriage, and handsome furniture that had been chosen by Livy, who had known about the surprise. Friends and relatives poured out of the rooms to greet the couple and welcome them to their new home. Twain choked up as his father-in-law handed him the deed and a check to help with the maintenance. But he could not resist a wisecrack. Turning to his benefactor he said "Mr. Langdon, whenever you are in Buffalo, [even] if it's twice a year, come right up here, and bring your bag with you. You may stay overnight if you want to. *It shant cost you a cent.*"

He was now nearly thirty-five years old. One part of his life was coming to an end and another beginning. Behind him were all those years of gadding about, all those experiences and adventures and boyhood friends, all those jobs and all that rootless travel. He had a wife now and a big house and a profession. He was already well known and becoming better known every day. Four days after the wedding he wrote a long nostalgic letter to his oldest friend of all, Will Bowen, the Hannibal lad into whose bed he had climbed in order to end the suspense about whether he would die of the measles. "It took me many a year to work up to where I can put on style," he told his old companion, "but now I'll do it." The lad from the Missouri frontier had set his feet on the road to fame and respectability. Even he, with all his buoyant optimism and all his boundless self-confidence, would have been surprised if he had known how very far along that road he was destined to travel.

Fame

Robert Louis Stevenson and I, sitting in Union Square and Washington Square a great many years ago [1888], tried to find a name for the submerged fame, that fame that permeates the great crowd of people you never see and never mingle with; people with whom you have no speech, but who read your books and become admirers of your work and have an affection for you. . . . They have nothing but compliments, they never see the criticisms, they never hear any disparagement of you, and you will remain in the home of their hearts' affection forever and ever. And Louis Stevenson and I decided that of all fame, that was the best, the very best.

Mark Twain in a speech, January 11, 1908

7

Hartford

I

Twain had little interest in running the *Buffalo Express* and avoided the office as much as he could—he was, after all, part owner of the enterprise, not some lowly and enslaved reporter. He improved the paper's format and shifted its editorial slant, making it more sympathetic to his businessman father-in-law and less sympathetic to the labor unions that were giving Jervis Langdon trouble. He wrote occasional pieces, producing more than four dozen sketches and thirty editorials during his tenure at the paper. No doubt a good number of unsigned items in the *Express* also rolled off his tireless pen. He also edited the work of the other writers ("I simply want to educate them to modify the adjectives, curtail their philosophical reflections & leave out the slang."). But his heart was not in it. A week after the wedding he told one correspondent, "I write sketches for it, & occasional squibs & editorials—that is all. I don't go to the office." Nine months later, in November 1870, he told another: "I do not see the office oftener than once a week, & do not stay there an hour at any time. . . ."

There were several reasons for his waning interest. In the first place, his mind was gravitating toward the writing of books. He was percolating ideas for two projects: an account of his life in the West and an exposé of the political misbehavior he had witnessed in Washington, D.C. He was greatly encouraged in this ambition to turn from journalism to literature by the enthusiastic reviews that *Innocents Abroad* was receiving across the country and by the gratifying sales figures. During the first part of

1870, the book sold around 7,000 copies a month, and Elisha Bliss was sending him monthly checks of around $1,300. (During Twain's lifetime, *Innocents Abroad* sold more copies than any of his other books; his gamble to take the royalties rather than Bliss's offer of $10,000 paid off handsomely.) Twain enjoyed a couple of other sources of income, which also reduced the need to devote himself to his newspaper. He earned good money lecturing for Redpath—$100 or $150 a night, with ten percent going to Redpath for making the arrangements—and he knew he could count on those fees for as long as he had the fortitude to submit himself to the ordeal. Finally, in early 1870, he agreed to supervise a humor department for the popular *Galaxy* magazine, producing ten pages each month. The *Galaxy* offered him $2,400 a month, but he agreed to take $2,000, with the proviso that he retain ownership of his contributions—another sign that he was thinking about future books instead of the daily grind of the newspaper business. Eventually, he wrote nearly ninety pieces for the magazine.

Perhaps most of all, his thoughts were drifting away from Buffalo (a shabby and frigid metropolis of 118,000 people) and toward the pleasant city of Hartford (with a population of 40,000). That was the home of the American Publishing Company, of course, and Twain's chief financial interests centered there, but both Twain and his wife also had friends in Hartford. One of Livy's favorite companions, Alice Beecher Hooker, lived there, and she and her parents urged the couple to move. Well aware of the town's economic prosperity and literary culture, the editor of the *Buffalo Express* was more than ready to locate there, build a house, give up journalism, and write his books. It is one indication of his eagerness that when the time came, in March 1871, he willingly took losses in selling both the Buffalo house and his interest in the *Express*. He and Livy stayed in Elmira for the summer, and in October they relocated to Hartford at last.

II

The newlyweds' home life, meanwhile, was a strange mixture of bliss and tragedy. For the first months after the wedding they were ecstatically happy. The pair delighted in one another, and one of the reasons Twain spent so little time at the office was so that he could spend more with his new wife. In that reminiscing letter he wrote to Will Bowen a few days after they were married, Twain tried to describe his bride: "I have at this moment the only sweetheart I ever loved, & bless her old heart she is lying asleep upstairs in a bed that I sleep in every night. . . . & she is much the most beautiful girl I ever saw . . . & she is the *best* girl, & the sweetest, & the gentlest, & the daintiest, & the most modest & unpretentious, & the wisest in all things she should be wise in & the most ignorant in all matters it would not grace her to know, & she is sensible & quick, & loving & faithful, forgiving, full of charity." Nor was the ecstasy one-sided. Livy told her parents she was "happy as a queen." She apologized to them for not feeling more homesick and tried to describe to them her husband's playfulness and wit: "If I could write you a reem [*sic*] of paper I could not begin to tell you half that I want to tell you—I wish that I could remember some of the funny things that Mr Clemens says and does—and besides these funny things, he is so tender and considerate in every way." He was thirty-four and she was twenty-four, but she bestowed on him a nickname that she used for the rest of her life—she would always call him "Youth." Twain's premarital sexual history is unknowable, and it is a virtual certainty that Livy had none, but there was clearly a healthy element of discovery and intimacy between the two. Twain told the Langdons about their rapturous life: "She pulls & hauls me around, & claws my hair, & bites my fingers, & laughs so that you might hear her across the street; & it does appear to me that I never saw anybody so happy as she is in all my life—except myself." By the end of the first month of their marriage Livy was pregnant.

The Clemens family experienced other pleasant things as well. In April, Jane came to Buffalo to appraise her new daughter-in-law and the visit went well enough. Then, at sixty-seven, after a third of a century in Missouri, Twain's mother decided to move to Fredonia, New York (forty miles from Buffalo), joining Twain's widowed sister Pamela and her two children who were already living there. Twain was also able to get Orion a job with Elisha Bliss in Hartford. A few months earlier, the old wound between the brothers had been reopened when

Orion once again bungled the chance to dump those Tennessee acres ("that doubly & trebly hated & accursed land," as Twain called it in an angry letter to his brother in August 1870). Twain was desperate to unload it at virtually any price. Back in April, he had warned his older brother that if he were foolish enough to let the new opportunity fall through, "Providence will not deliver another lunatic into our hands. . . ." Then, on August 1, when Orion confessed that he had once again failed to sell, his brother exploded: "I have tried for 24 hours to write, but I am too infernally angry & out of patience to write civilly." Nevertheless, when Twain learned that Bliss was starting a new periodical, *American Publisher*, to promote the company's new books, he went out on a limb and recommended Orion for the job. "I have told Bliss *positively* that you are *an able editor*," the younger brother warned the older brother, "& I don't want you by word or gesture to show any lack of confidence about assuming responsibility." Suddenly the entire Clemens family had abandoned the Midwest and was settled in New York and Connecticut.

This idyll of familial happiness was shattered in mid-summer, less than half a year after the wedding. News arrived that Jervis Langdon was dying. Twain and Livy sped to the Langdon house. To Mother Fairbanks in Cleveland, Twain wrote, "All of us are in deep grief, this morning, for death seems nearer at hand than at any time before. . . . It is the saddest, saddest time. There is no sound in the house. . . . Blinds are down & [there is] gloom in the hearts of the household. . . ." Langdon, who had been at least as much a father to Twain as John Marshall Clemens, died in terrible pain on August 6, 1870. Twain wrote a heartfelt eulogy: He was "a very pure, & good, & noble Christian gentleman. All that knew him will grieve for his loss. The friendless & the forsaken will miss him." Langdon's will left around a million dollars to his wife and two natural children, Charley and Livy. The Langdons' adopted daughter, Susan, had married his business partner, Theodore Crane, and to the Cranes, Langdon left a charming farm just outside of Elmira. Twain did not know it yet, but Quarry Farm, named for a stone quarry on the premises, would play an important part in his future. Livy's share of her father's fortune was $300,000 (almost $5 million in today's money).

Her husband resolved to regard it always as *her* money and never to touch it himself. This was a resolution that he would not be able to keep.

The death of Jervis Langdon was not the only catastrophe that befell the newlyweds in 1870. Livy, whose health was always precarious, had a difficult pregnancy. The nervous exhaustion caused by nursing her father's last weeks did not help; nor did the inconsolable grief she experienced after his death. She had trouble sleeping. Finally, a close friend named Emma Nye came to Buffalo to help her get through the trouble. Then the unthinkable happened: Emma herself contracted typhoid fever, and Livy, despite her own weakness and mourning, once again assumed the duties of a nurse. For days she attended her young friend, who was now lying in their own marriage bed. By the end of September, Emma became delirious and on September 29, she died. Livy, who was to give birth in December, was devastated by this second death in two months and almost miscarried in October. The couple's first child, a son, was born prematurely in November, and they named him Langdon.

The child was as frail and sickly and hopeless as his father had been thirty-five years earlier in Florida, Missouri. The infant was born with typhoid fever, but somehow survived. He cried constantly, was unable to gain weight, and slow to develop. Livy, unable to nurse him and still depressed over the loss of her father and her friend, fell into a grave illness. "Sometimes I have hope for my wife," a despairing Twain wrote to Bliss in February 1871, ". . . but most of the time it seems to me impossible that she can get well." Eventually, Livy recovered, but Langdon did not. In early June 1872, at nineteen months, he died of diphtheria. In his *Autobiography*, Twain blames himself for the infant's death. He recalled taking him for a carriage ride on a cold morning, dropping into a reverie, and forgetting about the baby. "The furs fell away and exposed his bare legs . . . the child was almost frozen. I was aghast at what I had done. . . ." No one but himself ever blamed Twain for the death of the child; at the time, Livy's friend Susan Warner reported that "everybody thinks what a mercy that he is at rest." Twain had a proclivity to blame himself for calamities for which no reasonable person could have accused him—causing the death of his brother Henry on the Mississippi was an early example, but there were others.

III

By the time little Langdon died, Mark and Livy were living in Hartford. While their own house was being built, they rented the home of John and Isabella Beecher Hooker—the place where Twain had been a guest during his first visit to Hartford in 1868, when he had come to negotiate with Bliss over *Innocents Abroad.* The Hooker home, as well as the site for their own place, was in a neighborhood on the western side of Hartford called Nook Farm. It was a snug and elite residential community that had been developed by Hooker himself. He had purchased the 140 acres in the early 1850s, and began selling lots to carefully selected friends and relatives. He wanted to create an exclusive and congenial community of lively writers and artists, prosperous businessmen, and learned college professors. The five acres that Twain purchased—ultimately he would own eight—shared a property line with Mrs. Hooker's sister, the renowned Harriet Beecher Stowe; other neighbors were Charles Dudley Warner and his wife Susan; Warner's brother George, related through marriage to the Hookers; and a few blocks away, Reverend Twichell. It was a cozy neighborhood of much back-and-forth visiting, musical evenings and theatricals, pleasant dinner parties, earnest discussions, and leisurely, genteel hospitality.

The house Twain constructed was elaborate, expensive, and pretentious. Counting the land and the furniture, it ran to more than $130,000 (around $2.2 million in today's dollars). It occupied three stories and was replete with balconies, turrets, generous overhangs, and chimneys. Some in that decorous neighborhood must have considered the structure—with its octagonal tower, its furbished timber and decorative brick, its huge veranda—just a tad on the garish side, maybe even a bit vulgar. The place had nineteen rooms and five baths. There was a library and a conservatory on the first floor, a study on the second, and a large room on the third devoted to Twain's newest passion, billiards.

Every floor had guest rooms. There was a servants' wing on the second floor, and there were always servants, sometimes a dozen of them—cooks and nursemaids, butlers and maids, coachmen and governesses. The house was built to entertain and, over the years, there were to be countless overnight and dinner guests—relatives from both their families, world-famous artists and intellectuals, lively young people whom Twain found promising, slightly uncouth old pals from California. Twain loved the sociability and was a marvelous host, striding up and down the huge dining room, enthralling the diners with his conversation, reading to them from his new work, mesmerizing them with his charm. For the next twenty years that big house in Nook Farm would be filled with laughter, late night talk, cigar smoke, and billiards.

It would also be the scene of the family's happiest and most fulfilling times together. After the ill-fated Langdon, Livy gave birth to three daughters. The first was christened Olivia Susan, but was always called Susy so she would not be confused with her mother. She was born in April 1872, while the family was living in Hartford, but before the death of her brother and before they were to move into the house. She was always to be her father's favorite child, perhaps because she was so much like him in energy, intelligence, thoughtfulness, and sensitivity. Slim and pretty, her tastes running, like his, to the literary, Susy and her father were unusually devoted to one another. Two years later, in June 1874, a second daughter, Clara, was born, and six years after that, in July 1880, the final addition to the family, Jane—named after Twain's mother, but always called Jean. Clara was to grow into a headstrong and independent young woman, interested in philosophy, religion, and particularly drawn to music. Jean was the least intellectual of the girls and the least accomplished. In the years ahead, all three were to suffer serious health problems, and Twain would not be spared the intense pain of seeing two of the three die before he did; only Clara survived him. But that anguish lay in the future; during the twenty years that they lived in the Hartford home, they were a joyous, close, loving family. He was a watchful and attentive father, full of games and stories and adventures. Probably the two younger girls sensed his obvious partiality for Susy, but he also cared deeply for each of them and worried about their health, their education, and their happiness.

The Clemens family on the porch of their home in Hartford, Connecticut. *Clockwise from left:* Clara, Livy, Jean, Sam, Susy, and Hash the dog. (The Mark Twain House. Hartford, CT)

IV

All his life, Mark Twain possessed a wonderful talent for friendship. Whether as a boy in Hannibal or a pilot on the Mississippi, whether in some mining camp or some smoky bar in Virginia City or a dingy newspaper office in San Francisco, Twain collected friends wherever he went. It was not merely that people were drawn to him because of his magnetism and affability; he was also drawn to them. He loved the companionship, the intimacy, the give and take of lively conversation with bright and interesting men and women.

True, if he ever came to suspect that some former friend was dishonest or bent on doing him harm, Twain was capable of unleashing all the viciousness and vitriol which had characterized him in the rough world of Nevada journalism. He could be brutal, shedding all of that polite respectability that people like his wife and Mother Fairbanks were trying so hard to inculcate, getting down in the gutter and clawing away like some street brawler. His onetime California mentor, drinking companion, and writing instructor, Bret Harte, for example, fell afoul of Twain in the mid-1870s. Harte came to Hartford and stayed with Mark and Livy for two weeks in 1876 while the two collaborated on writing a play. The visit did not go all that well. Harte was sarcastic about everything in Twain's new house, drank to excess, and let slip a remark that appeared to Twain to be insulting to Livy. By 1878, Twain was describing his old friend as "a liar, a thief, a swindler, a snob, a sot, a sponge, a coward. . . . How do I know? By the best of all evidence, personal observation." Twain's *Autobiography* offered the chance for one last whack at the dead Harte: "He was bad, distinctly bad; he had no feeling and he had no conscience," Twain began; that remark was the prelude to nine pages of fervent and withering denunciation. Similarly, somewhere along the way, Twain became convinced that for years his publisher, Elisha Bliss, had "handsomely swindled" him out of his royalties. Twain blasted the man without mercy: "Bliss told the truth once, to see how it would taste, but it overstrained him and he died." Then one last, vicious jab: "Well, Bliss was dead and I couldn't settle with him for his ten years of swindling. . . . My bitterness against him has faded away and disappeared. I feel only compassion for him and if I could send him a fan I would." There were other examples of Twain's thirst for vengeance on disloyal former friends. When he heard a rumor that another erstwhile friend, Whitelaw Reid, editor of the *Tribune,* was engaged in a campaign to slander him, Twain devoted an entire month to collecting damaging material about Reid for a full-length "biography" of the villain. The rumor proved false, cooler heads, including Livy's, prevailed, and the project was fortunately abandoned.

These, however, were exceptions. In general, Twain kept his friends, enjoying sympathetic, loyal, and generous relationships with them until their deaths or his own. And two particular friendships made in his mid-thirties were probably the closest, the most intimate and rewarding, of any of them. One was occasioned by an unusually perceptive review of *Innocents Abroad* that appeared in the nation's most prestigious periodical, Boston's *Atlantic Monthly.* In November 1869, Twain, in Boston for a lecture, walked over to the *Atlantic* offices to meet and thank the anonymous reviewer. It was William Dean Howells, fifteen months younger than Twain, still relatively unknown, but about to emerge as one of the most prolific writers and easily the most influential critic and arbiter of literary tastes of any person of his generation. The two became friends instantly. They were both Midwesterners (Howells was from eastern Ohio); they both had grown up in print shops and journalism; they were both on the verge of illustrious literary careers. Soon they were comparing their views, testing out their ideas for new books on one another, reading each other's rough drafts. The two couples exchanged frequent visits—Howells's wife was as frail as Twain's, another bond of sympathy between the men. When they could not get together, they wrote letters—hundreds of them—and Twain found himself relying on his friend's exquisite taste and good judgment. When Twain died in 1910, it was Howells who wrote the first book about him, an affectionate and incisive volume called *My Mark Twain*. Howells ended that reminiscence with a memorable and often-quoted sentence: "Emerson, Longfellow, Lowell, Holmes—I knew them all and all the rest of our sages, poets, seers, critics, humorists; they were like one another and like other literary men; but Clemens was sole, incomparable, the Lincoln of our literature."

Twain's other new and lasting friendship was with Joe Twichell. During one of his early visits to Hartford, he wrote to Livy: "Set a white stone—for I have made a friend. . . . I have only known him a week, & yet I believe I think almost as much of him as I do of Charlie [Langdon]. I could hardly find words strong enough to tell how much I *do* think of that man." Two weeks later, he elaborated: "Twichell is splendid. And he has one rare faculty—he is thoughtful & considerate. He lends me his overcoat when I go there without one, lends me his umbrella, lends me his slippers. . . . These are small things, but they show the man—he thinks of other people's comfort before his own." Those early impressions bloomed into a lifelong companionship. Joseph Hopkins Twichell, two-and-a-half years younger than Twain, had graduated from Yale, but interrupted his ministerial studies to serve as a chaplain during the Civil War. As soon as the war ended, he finished his training and, with his new bride, moved to Hartford to take up his duties as minister of the Asylum Hill Congregational Church in Nook Farm. He remained a central figure in the life of that notable community until he retired in 1910. Joe Twichell was big, handsome, athletic, and gregarious; he was also highly intelligent and reflective. He had a lively and engaging sense of humor, entirely compatible with Twain's; the scandalous writings of Twain's later career did not bother Joe Twichell (although they bothered William Dean Howells almost as much as they upset poor Livy).

Twain—who, it will be recalled, once told Orion that he had thought about becoming a preacher but felt handicapped because he lacked religion—was drawn to clergymen and counted several of them among his friends. But they were clergymen of a certain sort. He had no patience for those who brooded on unanswerable theological questions or engaged in unending doctrinal disputes or spent their time scolding poor sinners or threatening them with eternal torment; for missionaries he had nothing but contempt. Twain was attracted to ministers whose own lives exemplified Christian concern for others, generosity, social reform on behalf of the downtrodden, and open-minded tolerance. Twain could talk to a man like Twichell, and Twichell listened and sympathized and gave counsel and comfort; he never rebuked Twain's skepticism or his criticism of religion. Twichell didn't even seem to mind it when Twain called his prosperous congregation "the Church of the Holy Speculators." The two families (Twichell and his wife, Harmony, had nine children) were extremely close, and the men took numberless walks together around town and out into the Connecticut countryside. Once they walked the hundred miles between Hartford and Boston. In fact, Twain loved hiking and talking with Twichell so much that he paid his friend's way for a walking tour of Bermuda and a six-week European jaunt in 1878. "You have something divine in you that is not in other men," Twain once wrote to him. "You have the touch that heals, not lacerates." Twichell reciprocated the sentiment: "I love you, old fellow, in spite of all your bad behavior, very, very dearly."

V

All writing is some combination of inspiration and technique, a joining of spontaneous flights of imagination or reflection with the effort to put those flights into sentences and paragraphs. Beginning long before he decided to abandon journalism for book-writing, Twain, like every other writer, had to find ways to produce writing by negotiating, somehow, between his ideas and the best way to express them. In the process, he developed, by the early 1870s, habits and methods of composition that would, in general, govern his practice for the rest of his life.

When Twain got an idea for an article, a sketch, a short story, or a book, he deposited it into one of those notebooks he had been keeping for years—he did this in the same spirit in which other people deposit money into banks to draw upon when needed. Into his notebooks he wrote word-portraits of memorable characters or memorable landscapes, even sketchy outlines for stories. It is possible to see, by comparing an original notebook entry with the final piece of published writing, that often months or even years elapsed before the original inspiration was "withdrawn" and transformed into a finished piece of work. In the case of one famous work, eventually called *Extract from Captain Stormfield's Visit to Heaven*, decades passed, and Twain attempted many drafts before the final version of the work actually appeared. When Orion sounded him out on an idea he had for writing a book, Twain wrote back a revealing description of his own method, using his "Stormfield" idea as an example:

> Nine years ago, I mapped out my "Journey in Heaven." I discussed it with literary friends who I could trust to keep it to themselves. I gave it a deal of thought, from time to time. After a year or more, I wrote it up. It was not a success. Five years ago, I wrote it again, altering the plan. That [manuscript] is at my elbow now. It was a considerable improvement on the first attempt, but still it wouldn't do.—Last year & year before I talked frequently with Howells about the subject, & he kept urging me to do it again. So I thought & thought, at odd moments, & at last I struck what I considered to be the right plan! Mind, I have never altered the *ideas*, from the first—the *plan* was the difficulty.

That letter to Orion was written in March 1879. "Captain Stormfield" would not make its entry into print for another thirty years!

Twain believed that he required the proper inspiration before he could write. Inspiration, of course, could be notoriously fickle and might sometimes disappear (he referred to this as his "tank running dry" and his needing to wait until it was refilled). This led to one of his most distinctive traits as a writer. Almost always, he had more than one project going. When the tank ran dry on one of them, he simply put it aside and worked on another ("It is my habit to keep four or five books in the process of erection all the time," he once explained.) Thus in the case of some of his books, sections would be written, but other parts left unfinished and the project abandoned until the moment when he felt ready to resume. Sometimes he was not quite sure which of his manuscripts to attend to until the time when his feelings caused him to decide between the possibilities. On the other hand, when the inspiration came, he could compose with a maniacal frenzy. His standard practice was to write in ink on separate sheets of 4 × 8-inch paper. When the fury was on him, he could fill fifty such pages a day in a strong and legible handwriting. He liked to keep count of the words he produced, and 2,000 a day was fairly typical for him. As he finished a page, he dropped it to the floor, and at the end of the day he gathered up the pages, put them in order, and headed off to find an audience of family and friends.

When at home in Hartford, he retreated to the billiard room on the third floor for the privacy he needed for serious work. But his best writing was not done in Hartford—he was often too absorbed in business affairs or socializing or walking with Twichell to concentrate properly on literature. He had another place. Livy's adopted older sister, Susan Crane, and her husband Theodore were extremely close to the Twain family—Susan was at Livy's bedside for every childbirth and every illness, and Twain grew very fond of her and her husband (some believed that it had been Theodore's intercession that had led Jervis Langdon to consent to Twain's courtship of Livy). The middle name of their first child, Olivia Susan ("Susy"), was chosen to honor that friendship. While Mark and Livy's own place was being built in Hartford, the Cranes invited them to spend some time at Quarry Farm. Twain talked books and ideas with Susan and, especially, with her husband, and the congeniality led to a standing invitation to spend each summer together at the farm. Then, in the summer of 1874, Susan gave her brother-in-law a marvelous gift. She had a small octagonal retreat built, about a hundred yards from the house, on top of a beautiful hill over-looking the town and the river and a landscape of hills and fields. Inside was a writing table and chair, a sofa and a coal-burning grate for chilly mornings. There were windows on all sides. It was there, in that wonderful hideaway at Quarry Farm, sitting hour after hour in his straight-backed chair, bent over his paper with pen in hand, that Mark Twain produced his best work.

On the basis of critiques from friends and family, but mostly on the basis of his own second and third thoughts, Twain set about revising, rigorously applying the techniques and skills he had mastered over the years, combining in his own unique way inspiration and workmanship. His manuscripts are filled with words added and others crossed out, getting some character's dialect exactly right, refining some description of an event or a landscape to make it more colorful, more accurate or interesting, re-working an idea to make it clearer and sharper. He had no hesitation about throwing away whole chapters of work that he found unsatisfactory. From time to time he experimented with dictation, both early in his book-writing career and, increasingly, at the end of it—his *Autobiography*, in fact, was compiled from a series of dictations he made near the end of his life. He also tried that new invention called the "typewriter"—additional evidence of his fascination with the latest machinery. A practical version of the device was first patented in June 1868; he purchased one in 1874, and tried hard to learn to use it. In the end, while acknowledging its superiority for making his revisions, he went back to the old method. He did eventually move to the practice of having typists convert his handwritten sheets into clean copy, and his book *Life on the Mississippi* (1882) was perhaps the first American manuscript to be sent to a publisher in that form.

One of the oldest debates about Mark Twain's writing is related to the extent to which he allowed his wife to edit his work and the degree to which her influence stifled his robust natural genius. Starting with Van Wyck Brooks's *The Ordeal of Mark Twain* (1920), some scholars have seen Livy's influence—always exerted in the direction of decorum, politeness, and respectability—as censoring and taming the boisterous and lovable devilishness, the earthy virility of her husband's writing. To Brooks, Livy was a pampered and sheltered rich girl of "infantile" tastes and social ambitions, who "chloroformed" her husband's natural talents in her nervous, timid pursuit of social standing. Today, most critics consider the charge to be greatly exaggerated.

While acknowledging that Livy closely critiqued and advised her husband, they insist that she was highly intelligent, well-read, and sensitive to modern tastes and modern limits. Her comments on his rough drafts were thoughtful and sophisticated, and her influence—while definitely present—was, on the whole, minimal, judicious, and not nearly as pernicious as Brooks and others have maintained. It will be remembered, of course, that even before meeting her, Twain himself carefully toned down his rambunctious prose as he transformed his California letters into words that he thought suitable for more genteel eastern readers. The view that Livy exercised excessive censorship on him, moreover, came from Twain himself. He liked to adopt the playful pose, in letters to Howells and others, of the helpless, henpecked, browbeaten slave to his wife's imperious tyranny. For years, he played the role for humor, a little running joke that Brooks and other scholars have taken too seriously.

VI

In general, then, things looked promising for Mark Twain as he passed into his late thirties. His fame was increasing with every year. With *Innocents Abroad* selling well, and his articles in demand and fetching handsome prices, with his lecture tours consistently drawing large crowds and earning good money, with his wife's considerable fortune in reserve, it appeared that his financial worries were over at long last. He was happily married to a woman who was as devoted to him as he was to her. He had built a palatial home in a city he loved and was raising a family that would bring him enormous satisfaction in the years ahead. He enjoyed the friendship of famous and fascinating men and women. He had developed the discipline and techniques required by the writer's calling. He must have felt at the height of his creative power. There were dark spots, of course—the death of his son, the passing of his father-in-law, the periodic illnesses of Livy—but there was something in Twain's makeup (which he himself recognized and commented upon) that enabled him to absorb even serious reversals and rebound quickly into his normal exuberance. All in all, he seemed well fixed for a spurt into a period of genuine creativity.

A Writer of Remarkable Books

I

Between 1870, the year of his marriage, and 1885, when he turned fifty, Mark Twain took full advantage of the relatively favorable situation in which good fortune and his own talent and hard work had placed him, and he produced a string of striking books. He wrote these works with one eye fixed firmly on their marketability and in that respect proved himself an uncanny observer of American popular tastes. But the books he wrote during those fifteen years were so highly regarded by the millions of people who bought and read them that he became securely and permanently embedded in the affections of the American people. No doubt the readers who devoured his books fell in love with them primarily for their entertainment value: the ability of his words to make them laugh, or to transport them back to half-forgotten memories of growing up, or to carry them to fascinating new places or fascinating old times. At the same time, however, each of those books contained deeper meanings, revealing some of the author's most persistent beliefs and, often, some of his most troubling anxieties. At some level, these more provocative aspects of Twain's work must also have touched many of his readers. Perhaps one reason for his abiding popularity and relevance was the fact that he could be read on several levels. His books were entertaining, but they were also more than that.

II

Twain had wanted to write about his experiences in the West for a long time. In some ways, of course, the project was a natural after the phenomenal success of *Innocents Abroad*—the first book describing the writer's excursion to the east, the second, his excursion in the opposite direction. Elisha Bliss was eager for another book from Twain, and in July 1870, the writer signed a contract, promising to deliver a manuscript in about five months. Thus the book was undertaken even before Twain was to know the relative freedom from care that he was later to realize. He had not yet settled in Hartford and was still haphazardly managing the *Buffalo Express*. Moreover, it was a time of considerable travail for him and his bride. When he agreed to write the book, he was in Elmira because Livy's father was dying. In the next months, while he was expected to produce a manuscript (and a humorous one at that!), he had to help his wife not only through the death of her father, but through that of her friend Emma Nye, her own debilitating pregnancy, and the premature birth of their frail son. How he managed, in this atmosphere, to write a book so filled with raucous humor is hard to fathom. On the other hand, the money was attractive: "I suppose I am to get the biggest copyright . . . ever paid on a subscription book in this country," he boasted to his brother. Bliss was offering 7.5 percent royalties.

Roughing It appeared in February 1872. It tells the story of the stagecoach trip to Nevada, life in Carson City, the brief career in silver mining, the resort to journalism in Virginia City and San Francisco, and the time in Hawaii. The book ends with Twain's first public lecture, departure from California, and return to the East. Like *Innocents Abroad*, the work is a series of episodes rather than a sustained and fully developed narrative with a recognizable plot. Twain embellished his pages (partly to produce the bulk that subscription publishing required) with long digressions, tall tales, amusing incidents, and material borrowed from previously published sketches from his journalist days. He was helped along by the recollections of his brother; the moment he began work, he pleaded with Orion, "Do you remember any of the scenes, names, incidents or adventures of

the coach trip?—for I remember next to *nothing* about the matter."
He was also aided by his old California editor and friend, Joe
Goodman, who happened to be visiting while Twain was writing,
reawakening memories, and, as always, giving sound literary
advice. Subscriptions for the book, gathered door-to-door in
1871 and 1872, went well at first. While its sales never surpassed
Innocents Abroad, the book sold more than 75,000 copies in its
first year. Then, probably because of a nationwide depression
that began in 1873, sales plummeted, reaching only around
7,800 copies in 1873, and 5,100 in 1874.

Much has been made of the fact that Twain begins *Roughing
It* with an outright falsehood. He writes, "I was young and
ignorant. . . . I never had been away from home, and that word
'travel' had a seductive charm for me." This, of course, from a
man who had worked in New York, Philadelphia, and Washington,
who had lived for a time in Cincinnati and St. Louis, and who
had piloted a steamboat up and down the Mississippi from New
Orleans to St. Louis. Some critics suggest that the narrator in the
book is "Mark Twain," a semifictional character created by
Samuel Clemens to distance the naive, carefree, slightly disreputable person who goes West from the respectable man of letters
who had married into the aristocracy and was eager to behave
appropriately. Others, particularly the great Twain authority,
Henry Nash Smith, have seen in this opening-paragraph decep-
tion a theme that governs the book: the growth of the narrator—
purposely introduced as an innocent adolescent—through stages
as a primitive miner and a somewhat dissolute town idler, into
an eventually respectable journalist who returns to the East
mature, responsible, and grown-up. Smith calls this process "the
transformation of a tenderfoot." One thing is certain: Twain
knew what he was doing. In the middle of writing the book, he
told Orion that he would soon be sending Bliss some manuscript, "but right in the first chapter I have got to alter the whole
style of one of my characters & re-write him clear through to
where I am now. It is no fool of a job I can tell you, but the book
will be greatly bettered by it."

Twain reveals two major preoccupations in *Roughing It* so
clearly that even casual readers could not have missed them. The
first is that old contrast between the beauty, harmony, freedom,

and peace of nature, and the turmoil, corruption, violence, and loose morals of civilization. His rhapsodic descriptions of the majestic prairies and lofty mountains, of the quiet loveliness of Lake Tahoe, of the natural life at Jim Gillis's shack in Tuolumne County or the beauty and freedom of the Hawaiian Islands—these are set in sharp opposition to the tawdry towns and cities of Nevada and California. There the emphasis is on strong drink and late hours, dishonest speculation, gunplay in the streets, the inconvenience and restraints that come with having to work. This contrast—which Twain had earlier experienced in a less obvious way growing up in Hannibal, and which he had marked more clearly as he meditated on that sunset on the river—is presented forcefully in his descriptions of the West. The second preoccupation that *Roughing It* presents very clearly is Twain's concern about the debilitating effects of unrestrained greed—the addictive and contagious fever of the mining craze, the swindling ways of the speculators, the blind materialism and avarice, the fierce lawlessness of ambitious men guarding their own claims or poaching on the claims of others. Twain understood the seductive nature of that impulse (the narrator is hardly immune from the disease). With his own bargaining over royalties, his own hopes for cashing in on the Tennessee land, his own grandiose plans for the mansion in Hartford—he must surely have been aware that he himself was far from being inoculated against the malady. In post–Civil War America, however, the lure of wealth was not confined to the West. The mad pursuit of money was a national obsession, and he would turn to it in his next book.

III

According to a story that Twain told Albert Bigelow Paine many years later, one evening in late 1872 or early 1873, Susan and Charles Dudley Warner, Nook Farm neighbors, came over for dinner. The two men got on the topic of how awful modern novels were, and their wives challenged them to either produce a better one or stop their complaining. The husbands set to work at once and in three months finished *The Gilded Age: A Tale of Today*, Twain's first novel and the book that was to give a permanent name to an era of American history.

Like Twain, Warner was a man of wide experience. He had gone to college and law school, done some railroad surveying in Missouri, practiced a little law in Chicago, and dabbled in New York real estate before finally becoming editor of the influential *Hartford Courant*. Warner was a steady and prolific writer, widely traveled, knowledgeable about literature and politics. All of these traits and many of these experiences found their way into *The Gilded Age*. In fact, part of the problem with the novel was the complications caused by knitting together two such sets of expertise as Twain and Warner brought to the project.

It is, actually, two novels—two rather separate plot lines only superficially linked. Warner's chapters tell the story of an ambitious and hard-working hero named Philip Sterling and his relations with the upright New England Bolton family, and especially with the spirited and attractive Ruth Bolton. Twain's contribution, on the other hand, was based on his own family history, and his characters were transparently modeled after his relatives. The Hawkinses, as he names them, journey from Tennessee to Missouri. The father, an unsuccessful storekeeper and businessman, has pinned his hopes on a vast quantity of Tennessee land that he acquired while living there and, after many failures, dies clinging to the hope that the land, when finally sold, will make his family happy and prosperous. Other characters resemble Twain's mother, his brothers Orion and Henry, and most especially, his mother's cousin, James Lampton. Indeed, the most memorable character in the book is modeled on Lampton: Colonel Beriah Sellers, an irrepressible, lovably silly, incurably optimistic, big-talking promoter of preposterous schemes that will bring untold wealth to his family and friends. "Many persons regarded Colonel Sellers as a fiction, an invention, an extravagant impossibility, and did me the honor to call him a 'creation,'" Twain wrote in his *Autobiography*, "but they were mistaken. I merely put him on paper as he was; he was not a person who could be exaggerated." Colonel Sellers was always going on about the "oceans of money" he was just on the verge of bringing in, the powerful New York businessmen who were begging him to join them in a venture worth five or six million, his secret plans for a revolutionary new eyewash or for cornering the hog market. Meanwhile, his wife and children were subsisting on turnips and cold water and, because they could not afford coal, burned candles in the potbellied stove to create the impression of warmth. Twain's half of the book tells the story of the Hawkins family, the fate of their beautiful adopted daughter Laura, and their schemes in Washington, D.C., to sell the Tennessee acres to the government.

In addition to the incomparable pages describing Colonel Sellers' bluster and big plans, the novel is most notable for the satirical scorn it heaps on numerous aspects of American life. Before the writers are done, they skewer everything from lawyers to newspapers, from jury trials to religious hypocrites, from social climbing women to ignorant rural voters, from wretched service on trains to women reformers, from sentimental opponents of the death penalty to trashy romantic novels. Principally, however, the authors have two targets directly and consistently in their sights: the ruthless, dishonest, demoralizing speculation in real estate, business, and railroads, and the unconscionable bribery and corruption at every level of American politics. At one point, a veteran in Washington politics explains how to get an appropriation bill through Congress. It costs money, he explains:

> A majority of the House committee, say $10,000 apiece—$40,000; a majority of the Senate committee, the same each—say $40,000; a little extra to one or two chairmen of one or two such committees, say $10,000 each—$20,000; and there's $100,000 of the money gone, to begin with. Then seven male lobbyists, at $3,000 each—$21,000; one female lobbyist, $3,000; a high moral Congressman or Senator here and there–the high moral ones cost more, because they give tone to a measure—say ten of these at $3,000 each, is $30,000; then a lot of small-fry country members who won't vote for anything whatever without pay–say twenty at $500 apiece, is $10,000 altogether. . . .

Two of the novel's main subplots—one, the scheme to push the land bill through Congress; the other, the effort to expose a dishonest senator which ends with the denunciation of the upright accuser rather than his corrupt target—were both based on two sensational incidents of the early 1870s. The notorious Crédit Mobilier scandal of 1872 involved the Union Pacific's offering bargain-priced company stock to dozens of well-placed politicians, including Vice President Schuyler Colfax and a future president, James Garfield. The second incident centered on the rather obvious $7,000 bribe paid by Kansas Senator Samuel Pomeroy (Senator Dilworthy in the novel) to get himself reelected in 1873. After an investigation, Congress found insufficient evidence to condemn Pomeroy.

But Twain and Warner were only using those two incidents, drawn from the day's headlines, to illustrate what they regarded as the underlying spirit of the age in which they lived. Their judgment of that age, moreover, has been echoed by numerous historians. Scholars who have studied late-nineteenth century America have portrayed a period of tremendous industrial energy, resulting in vastly increased production, great advances in transportation and communication, and remarkable improvements in the everyday lives of middle-class Americans; it was a time when "the American dream" of prosperity earned through honesty and hard work seemed to countless ambitious Americans, possible as never before. At the same time, the Gilded Age was characterized by unscrupulous speculation, questionable business practices, brutal treatment of workers and immigrants, and cutthroat efforts to stifle competition and monopolize markets. In some respects, the late nineteenth century saw the flowering of democratic governance and participatory politics, but it was also marred by instances of breathtaking corruption, big city "bosses," and political malfeasance. If it was an "age of enterprise" (as two historians called it in the 1940s), it was also an "age of excess" (as another named it in the 1960s). Twain and Warner may not have been entirely fair to the more admirable and enterprising aspects of their time, but they were relentless and fearless critics of its seamy side.

Their novel is also noteworthy for its treatment of female characters. Besides the flock of empty-headed socialites and naive reformers, three women have prominent roles. Each of them is based on a well established Victorian archetype. Ruth Bolton is a plucky New England girl who wants to be a doctor. After a curious scene in which she cannot bring herself to dissect the cadaver of an African American, she comes to her senses, abandons her professional dreams, and agrees to marry the heroic Philip. A second female character is the noble Alice Montague. She is Ruth's dear friend, but she also secretly loves Philip. In the end, she denies her own longing and steps modestly aside for her friend: "And the world never knows how many women there are like Alice, whose sweet but lonely lives of self-sacrifice, gentle, faithful, loving souls, bless it continually." Both of these stock characters were mainly the work of Warner. Twain's principal female is Laura, a woman of devastating beauty who had been adopted by the Hawkins family as a child. After she is seduced and betrayed by a married Confederate officer, she becomes an ambitious, ruthless, and coldhearted lobbyist in Washington, D.C. Her specialty is corrupting vulnerable politicians. She is, in short, that archetypal woman of dangerous sexuality (like Eve, Delilah, Jezebel, Salome, Helen of Troy), too beautiful for her own good and a grave danger to unwary males. In the end, Laura murders her former lover, is found innocent after a farcical trial, takes to the lecture circuit, and dies of shame and a broken heart. Since one of Twain and Warner's purposes in *The Gilded Age* was to burlesque the sappy popular novels of the day, it is difficult to know how seriously to take these cartoon-figure women.

Like *Roughing It*, this book was sold by subscription and did quite well for a while. Almost 60,000 copies had been sold by the end of 1874, and each author received around $18,000 for his efforts.

IV

Even before Twain and Warner were cajoled by their wives into writing their novel, Twain had started work on another book, one based on his childhood in Hannibal. Working on it in at least three spurts, he finished it in his retreat at Quarry Farm during the summer of 1875. He sent the manuscript to Howells for comments and was pleased when his friend called it "the best boy's story I ever read" and predicted that it would be "an immense success." *The Adventures of Tom Sawyer* appeared in the United States in December 1876—for copyright reasons, the book was first published in England the preceding July. Although initial sales were slow, *Tom Sawyer* was destined to become perhaps the best loved of all Twain's works; it has, since its initial publication, sold somewhere around five million copies.

The story is set in the village of St. Petersburg, but the features of that fictional town—its buildings and the cemetery, the river and its islands, the nearby cave—are all drawn from Twain's flawless memories of the place where he grew up. The main characters are based on people he knew. There is a lot of young Sam Clemens himself in Tom Sawyer (although Twain insisted that Tom "is a combination of the characteristics of three boys whom I knew"). Tom's stern but compassionate guardian, Aunt Polly, is an idealized picture of Twain's mother; Twain's brother Henry is transformed into Tom's strait-laced and annoying half-brother, Sid; Tom's girlfriend, Becky Thatcher, was a neighborhood girl named Laura Hawkins (a name Twain had already used in *The Gilded Age*); her father, Judge Thatcher, bore some resemblance to the writer's justice-of-the-peace father; and a couple of town loafers and drunkards are transformed into the hapless Muff Potter and the villainous Injun Joe. Tom's sidekick, a free-spirited lad named Huckleberry Finn (destined, ten years later, to have a book of his own), was modeled, Twain claimed, on Tom Blankenship, a boy from a large, destitute family that lived next door to the Clemenses. In his *Autobiography*, Twain describes Tom Blankenship: "ignorant, unwashed, insufficiently fed; but he had as good a heart as ever any boy had. . . . He was the only really independent person—boy or man—in the community, and by consequence he was tranquilly and continuously happy and was envied by all the rest of us. We liked him; we enjoyed his society. And as his society was forbidden us by our parents the prohibition trebled and quadrupled its value, and therefore we sought and got more of his society than of any other boy's."

Some of the episodes of *The Adventures of Tom Sawyer* are so firmly embedded in our national imagery that they have become a permanent, part of our idealized picture of small-town American life. By calling his town St. Petersburg (the town of St. Peter), Twain probably intended to associate it with happiness and freedom from care, despite the dangerous, violent, and thrilling events described in the story; he once called the book "a hymn put into prose." Even people who have never read the book know some of its best moments: Tom getting his friends to whitewash the fence; Tom showing off in front of Becky, the new girl in town; Tom suffering through the boredom of church and tyranny of school; the boys escaping to Jackson's island to become pirates; Huck teaching them how to smoke; Tom and his friends attending their own funeral; the hilarious examination-evening at school; Tom taking Becky's whipping from the insufferable schoolmaster; the murderous night in the grave-yard; the ordeal of Tom and Becky in the cave; the discovery of Injun Joe's treasure.

Twain had experimented with this sort of tale in some of his sketches—especially "The Story of the Bad Little Boy Who Didn't Come to Grief" (1865), and "The Story of the Good Little Boy Who Did Not Prosper" (1870). In the novel, Tom occupies a middle ground. On the one side are the good boys like his brother Sid and Willie Mufferson, the Model Boy, who took "as heedful care of his mother as if she were cut glass. He always brought his mother to church, and was the pride of all the matrons. The boys all hated him. . . ." On the other side stood the thoroughly disreputable Huck, a complete stranger to church and school, dirty and dressed in rags, sleeping wherever he could find a dry place, free as a bird and "continuously happy." The great tension in the novel is an echo of the great tension in the life of its author. Tom admires and envies the free-dom and independence of Huck, but he is inevitably drawn toward maturity and respectability. When he bravely steps forward to save Becky from the schoolmaster's strap, he is on the way to becoming a grownup; when he heeds his conscience and risks the murderous revenge of Injun Joe, he is practically there. By the time he and Becky get lost in the cave, and he becomes her protector and comforter, Tom Sawyer has turned his back on boyhood and his face toward responsibility, matu-rity, adulthood. Becky's father saw it. After Tom entrusted his share of the treasure to Judge Thatcher (who invested it "at six per cent") the Judge hopes "to see Tom a great lawyer or a great soldier some day. He said he meant to look to it that Tom should be admitted to the National military academy and afterwards trained in the best law school in the country, in order that he might be ready for either career or both." So much for Tom ever again sneaking off with Huck for a smoke behind the barn! Mark Twain also knew that Tom was lost to the carefree life of youthful independence. In the book's brief "Conclusion," he writes: "So endeth this chronicle. It being strictly a history of a *boy*, it must stop here; the story could not go much further without becoming the history of a *man*."

V

Between 1880 and 1883, Mark Twain published three additional books, and these are so varied in style, content, and genre that it is difficult to imagine them springing from the mind and pen of the same person. As was typical of his writing, all three had lengthy periods of gestation.

In April 1878, the family packed up and moved to Europe. They did this for several reasons, but one was the hope of both Twain and Bliss for an encore to *Innocents Abroad*, another amusing account of an American's adventures in Europe. The travelers were Mark and Livy, their two young daughters, a friend of Livy's named Clara Spaulding, and a German nursemaid who was instructed by Twain to speak German to the girls. The party settled in Heidelberg, and within a month, Twain started on the book. In July they moved to Baden-Baden. Then, on August 1, Joe Twichell arrived—Twain had sent him $300 to cover the passage and paid the minister's expenses for the next five weeks. Leaving Livy and the others behind, the two friends set out on a memorable tour—on foot, by train, by rented carriage or river boat—through the Black Forest and the Swiss Alps. When Twichell returned home on September 9, the family moved to Italy, where they lived until November in Venice, Florence, and Rome. Then it was back to Germany for three months of writing in Munich. In late February 1879, they went to Paris and stayed there until July. Then, through Belgium and the Netherlands to England where they lived (and socialized) for a month. On August 23, they embarked for home, going directly to Quarry Farm until October.

During this fifteen-month frenzy of travel, Twain filled his notebooks with observations and ideas, and, whenever settled in one place long enough to unpack, worked to convert some of those notes into literature. He had a hard time finishing the work—probably because, unlike his normal practice, he was unable to put this book aside when his tank was empty, but had to see it through to a finish. The product of this effort was called *A Tramp Abroad*. Twain sent Bliss the manuscript in January 1880, the American Publishing Company canvassed for subscriptions in the following months, and the book appeared in mid-March. It never equaled *Innocents Abroad*, but it sold well enough to fatten Twain's financial situation.

In the book, the narrator adopts much the same stance as in *Innocents Abroad*: the skeptical American realist looking unblinkingly at European scenery, manners, art, and music, immune to the idealized and romanticized delusions of so many of his fellow tourists. (Twain is particularly acerbic in describing the pretentious and pompous Americans he encounters along the way). He and "Mr. Harris" (the name he gives Twichell) march through the European countryside, struck by the natural beauty, interested in the old legends, attracted or repelled by the people they meet or the hotels at which they reside. They are frequently reminded of things American, and those memories of home lead to long digressions; some of the most often praised and remembered (and reprinted) parts of *A Tramp Abroad* are the sketches of American memories awakened in the narrator by some European encounter. These side-excursions give the book a wandering and unstructured feel—a relaxed rumination, Mark Twain chatting with his readers about whatever comes into his head. Twain himself offered a description of the book: "It is a gossipy volume of travel. . . . It talks about anything and everything, and always drops a subject the moment my interest in it begins to slacken. . . ."

Even before leaving for Europe, Twain was at work on another book and one unlike anything he had ever attempted before. He probably began writing *The Prince and the Pauper* at about the same time that he was finishing *Tom Sawyer*, put it aside while working on *A Tramp Abroad*, and resumed work on it in January 1880. The book was finished in September and finally appeared in November 1881. Unlike his previous books, *The Prince and the Pauper* was not based on Twain's own experiences. In fact, the novel was set during the 1540s in England.

In order to convey the social and political life, the manners, and (importantly) the language of Tudor England, Twain undertook extensive study, reading the plays of Shakespeare, the historical novels of Sir Walter Scott, and some sober histories of Europe and England. From the start he intended the book for children, and, as chapters were completed, he tried them out on his own girls and the children of his friends.

The unpersuasive plot centers around two young boys. One of them is Edward Tudor, the pampered son of Henry VIII, and heir to the English throne. The other is Tom Canty, a child born in the wretched poverty of Offal Court, one of the poorest and filthiest slums of London. By a strange (and preposterous) happenstance, the two boys bear so close a physical resemblance to one another that when they trade places, no one recognizes that a switch has occurred. The rest of the novel is a description of how Tom adjusts to his new role as the Crown Prince, while Edward endures the brutality and injustice of poverty. In the end, the confusion is straightened out: Edward is restored to his rightful position, though chastened and now aware of the hardships of the poor, and Tom becomes a ward of his friend Edward and goes on, we presume, to a life of happiness. The story gave Twain the opportunity to blast such extreme class differences and to evoke sympathy for those who daily suffer unfair treatment and grinding misery. Some of his descriptions of the horrifying results of English conditions and English law are presented with forcefulness and passion (as when Edward witnesses the burning at the stake of some innocent women who had shown him kindness, but who were deemed to be religiously unorthodox). Some analysts of Twain's writing have called attention to what was to become a familiar literary tool for him—the use of twins and mistaken identity in his plots. They have attempted to connect this repeated device to the author's own double life (Samuel Clemens/Mark Twain) and to his own divided nature and ambivalent attitudes and responses.

Twain hoped that *The Prince and the Pauper* might mark a departure for him. There is evidence that he was tired of being considered merely a low comedian, a cheap retailer of tall tales and jokes, that he wanted to be considered a serious writer capable of high artistry. He even thought about publishing the book anonymously, so his reputation for humor would not prejudice readers against the serious story he wanted to tell them. Livy, who was often critical of her husband's subject matter, thought this book was quite wonderful, and the girls loved it—thirteen-year-old Susy believed it "unquestionably the best book he has ever written." Others also bestowed fulsome praise on the book, noting its moral tone, its noble social conscience, the quality of the research that went into it. Twain was touched one day, when his neighbor Harriet Beecher Stowe, out for a stroll, clasped his hands and said she was reading it for the fourth time and that it was "the best book for young folk that was ever written." Not everyone felt that way. Twain's old mentor Joe Goodman, in a private letter, was brutal: "You went entirely out of your sphere," he told his friend, ". . . .[a]nd after all you don't succeed. . . . The laboriousness is apparent everywhere by which you endeavor to harmonize irreconcilable improbabilities, to manage the obsolete customs and parlance of the times, and to wrestle generally with a condition of things to which you feel yourself alien and unsuited." When we finish the book, Goodman charged, "we feel that all the pomp and pauperism has been a masquerade, and not the genuine article."

By the time the manuscript was finished, Twain and Bliss had experienced their bitter falling out, and *The Prince and the Pauper* was published by James R. Osgood, a Boston friend of Twain and the publisher of Howells's books. Unfortunately, Osgood was an amateur when it came to getting subscriptions, and Twain's book sold poorly. Over the years, however, the story has often been adapted to the stage, radio, television, and film. The book was republished many times and remains one of the sentimental favorites among all of Twain's works.

Only eighteen months after the appearance of *The Prince and the Pauper*, Twain and Osgood brought out Twain's next important book, *Life on the Mississippi*. This book too had a long history. Almost ten years earlier, in 1874, Howells had pleaded with his friend for a contribution to the *Atlantic Monthly*, which Howells edited and Osgood published. On October 24, Twain wrote Howells two letters. In the first, he said that although "Mrs. Clemens has diligently persecuted me day by day" to write something for the January issue, "I find I can't." Then a few hours later, he had gotten his inspiration and dashed off another note. "I take back the remark that I can't write for the Jan. Number. For Twichell & I have had a long walk in the woods & I got to telling him about old Mississippi days of steamboating glory & grandeur as I saw them (during 5 years) *from the pilot house*. He said, 'What a virgin subject to hurl into a magazine!'" The result was the acclaimed articles (January–August 1875) titled "Old Times on the Mississippi."

In these articles Twain described, in some of his very best writing, his boyhood dream of becoming a pilot; his days as a green apprentice under the fiery, sarcastic, and ultimately lovable Horace Bixby; the arduous effort to learn the language of the river, to memorize its every bend and landmark, to master the hidden meanings and the dire warning signs of its ever-changing face. For these articles Twain adopted the same pose as he had used so successfully in *Roughing It*——the hopeless greenhorn who suffers many humiliations, but who grows, matures, and learns his trade. By any standard, the *Atlantic* articles constitute one of the great treasures of American literature. They also awakened in Twain the desire to write an entire book on the subject, and after waiting eight years while he worked on other projects, he decided to go back and have another look at the old river.

For a month in the spring of 1882, Twain (with publisher Osgood) traveled up and down the Mississippi, from St. Paul to New Orleans. If he had hoped to make this sentimental journey as an anonymous, note-taking reporter, he had miscalculated his celebrity. He was everywhere instantly recognized and fawned over, greeted by the local dignitaries, invited to dinners, asked for a few remarks. Steamboat pilots let him take the wheel for a while; reporters gathered around for his reunion with Bixby (who was still piloting). He even had the thrill of spotting a docked steamboat bearing the name *Mark Twain*. The high point, no doubt, was the three days he spent in Hannibal, now a town of 15,000 with paved streets and strange faces and too many railroad tracks to suit him. The early apprenticeship articles from the *Atlantic Monthly* eventually became fourteen chapters near the beginning of *Life on the Mississippi*, and there is general agreement that none of the rest of the book matched those chapters for brilliant prose or interesting subject matter.

Much of the book (what Twain calls "these dry details" at the start of Chapter Seventeen) is borrowed from the works of others, and more than one critic has accused him of "padding." Like other nonfiction books that he wrote, *Life on the Mississippi* is a collection of geographical, historical, and political information presented rather randomly. The overall sentiment is regret at how the Valley has changed since the days of his youth. To his wife back home, he wrote "That world which I knew in its blossoming youth is old and bowed and melancholy now; its soft cheeks are leathery and wrinkled, the fire is gone out of its eyes." The most remarked upon aspect of the book was the author's spirited denunciation of the American South. He condemns his section's backwardness, its feudal decadence, its lynching and murdering ways—what is one to say of a region that regards cockfighting as a sport? Twain dubiously places a good part of the blame on southerners' excessive reading of romantic novels, and especially those of Walter Scott. All that ridiculous twaddle about chivalry, about noble gentlemen obsessed with defending their "honor" through acts of violence, both poisoned the southern mind into rejecting modern progress and covered over the brutality and lawlessness that was at the heart of southern culture. The transplanted Marion Ranger had come a long way.

VI

It is not possible to understand Mark Twain's writing fully without understanding the cultural and literary context in which he worked. Historians of American literature have given the name "realism" to the techniques and the subject matter that became characteristic of the best American writing at the end of the nineteenth century, but precise definitions of the movement are slippery. There is general recognition that literary realism had prominent representatives among European writers such as the Frenchman Emile Zola and that the broad impulse had echoes in journalism, painting, music, the theater, and other fields. There is also agreement that American literary realism was brought into being by a number of factors. The brutality and violence of the Civil War, with its impersonal movements of massive armies, for example, made old-fashioned depictions of chivalry and personal heroism seem naive. Advances in technology and science, including the teaching of Charles Darwin, bestowed special importance upon close and accurate observation of discrete, individual facts. The rise of so-called local color writing and of southwestern humor with their emphasis on regional peculiarities of custom, culture, and language, put a premium on precise description. The hard realities of rapidly expanding cities and rapidly multiplying factories required writers to pay attention to detail, even unpleasant detail. Also important was the rise in literacy, the increased availability of books, and a virtual explosion in popular magazines that provided ready outlets for the work of the young realists—Frank Luther Mott, the historian of American magazines, estimates that a thousand new ones were put on the market between 1885 and 1890.

In general, American literary realism can be best understood as a rebellion against the romantic and sentimental writing which had dominated antebellum America and was still present, practitioners like Twain believed, to a disheartening degree in popular novels after the Civil War. To the rising generation of American writers, the old Romantics—with their insistence on providing eternal moral lessons, their use of characters to "represent" classical virtues or vices, their inaccurate depictions of real life or even their complete indifference to it, their preposterous language and miraculous plot devices—were no longer capable of speaking to the actual world that Americans were encountering. Besides Twain, the new breed of realist writers included Howells and Henry James (the two chief theorists of the movement), Stephen Crane, Charlotte Perkins Gilman, Hamlin Garland, Kate Chopin, Charles Chesnutt, Edith Wharton, and many others. They were determined to follow Howells's dictum that modern writing should be "nothing more and nothing less than the truthful treatment of material." They thought of themselves as unwilling to shrink from harsh reality, determined to portray human nature in all its aspects, to have their characters talk and behave as they would in real life. As it happened, like many others among history's rebels, they vastly overestimated the extent of their rebellion. They were not always immune from sentimentality and propriety, they did not always refrain from moralizing, and there were limits to their boasted frankness (particularly sexual limits) beyond which they would not venture. Before very far into the next century, another generation of writers, styling themselves "naturalists," were chuckling over how tame their "realistic" predecessors had actually been.

In any case, the books that Mark Twain produced during his late thirties and forties, under the influence of this school of literary practice, were by any measure remarkable for the diversity of their subject matter. There was one novel about contemporary American politics and another about a small town boy's life a quarter of a century earlier and another about the injustices of sixteenth-century England. One of his books told the story of his life in the American West, another was about a tour of Europe, and still another was about the Mississippi and those who lived in its great valley. All of these works enjoyed large sales (although, in some cases not large enough to satisfy the author). By 1883, they had been read and loved by tens of thousands of everyday American readers and praised extravagantly by many of the most astute literary critics in the country. It was, taken all together, a singular demonstration of literary genius of a high order. Nevertheless, both the typical reader and the accomplished literary connoisseur might have been surprised to learn that America's favorite writer was about to present the public with the most stunning achievement of them all.

9

"The Best Book We've Had"

I

In 1935, twenty-five years after Twain's death, the American novelist Ernest Hemingway delivered a famous verdict about American writing: "All modern American literature," he declared, "comes from one book by Mark Twain called *Huckleberry Finn*. . . . [I]t's the best book we've had. All American writing comes from that. There was nothing before. There has been nothing as good since." Whether or not one subscribes to Hemingway's judgment about all American literature, it is certain that *Adventures of Huckleberry Finn* is Twain's greatest and most celebrated work. For a century and a quarter it has been enjoyed by millions of readers at every stage of life. It has been required reading in countless American high school and college classes and minutely analyzed and debated by scholars in dozens of books and articles. Even the notorious cynic H. L. Mencken thought that the book was "one of the great masterpieces of the world" and "the full equal of 'Don Quixote' and 'Robinson Crusoe.'" *Huckleberry Finn* "will be read by human beings of all ages," Mencken predicted, "not as a solemn duty but for the honest love of it, and over and over again. . . ."

Like many of Twain's other books, *Huckleberry Finn* also had a difficult birth. He began enthusiastically enough the moment he had finished writing *Tom Sawyer* in 1875, producing four hundred manuscript pages at Quarry Farm during the summer of 1876. He then ran out of inspiration and put the project aside for three or four years. He picked it up and set it aside several more times before finally finishing it at Quarry Farm in a spurt of energy during the summer of 1883. The book was published in the United States in February 1885 (but, once again to ensure his copyright, it appeared two months earlier in Great Britain). It was an immediate success, selling around fifty thousand copies within a few months. It has, of course, continued to be popular, having sold perhaps twenty million copies and being translated into dozens of languages.

II

Mark Twain's *Adventures of Huckleberry Finn* may be considered as consisting of three sections. The first, comprising the four opening chapters, contains material that appears to be left over from *Tom Sawyer*. "You don't know about me, without you have read a book by the name of 'The Adventures of Tom Sawyer,'" the story starts. "That book was made by Mr. Mark Twain, and he told the truth, mainly. There was things which he stretched, but mainly he told the truth." Set in St. Petersburg, and picking up from the end of the earlier novel, readers once again enter the world of Tom and his gang of "robbers"—their midnight escapades, their solemn blood oaths, their bold schemes to murder the men but to treat the women with respect while holding them for ransom, their grim resolution to ambush and annihilate every band of Arabs and Spaniards unlucky enough to be caught plotting their villainy in rural Missouri! These chapters might have been merely more of the same familiar territory: Mark Twain's amusing boyish nonsense. They are redeemed and elevated, however, by two of the author's most ingenious decisions.

First, while *Tom Sawyer* is told by an omniscient narrator, *Huckleberry Finn* comes to us in the first person, through the eyes, the ideas, and the words of fourteen-year-old Huck Finn. By this brilliant stroke Twain imparts to the novel a consistent and fascinating point of view, presenting to readers the innermost thoughts and feelings, the troubling conflicts and difficult ethical judgments of an unlettered, maltreated, and endearing youngster. We see things through Huck's eyes, but we also know more than he does; we perceive that he is not an entirely reliable narrator and that his views are sometimes distorted by his youth, his innocence, or his upbringing. In short, we judge and evaluate *him* as he struggles with complex moral decisions and grows to a kind of maturity. By the end of these four chapters, Twain has clearly distinguished Huck from Tom Sawyer. Tom is portrayed as a hopeless romantic, spellbound by his reading of silly novels with their ridiculous rituals and make-believe adventures, while Huck comes to be seen as a wonderful combination of naivete and hardheaded realism. He sees through the "lies" of Tom's band of robbers: "We hadn't robbed nobody, we hadn't killed any people, but only just pretended." At one point Tom organizes the boys for a daring raid on the Arabs and Spaniards with their camels and elephants. To Huck, the victims of this ambush look very much like the children at a Sunday school picnic. He thinks about it for a while and then pronounces his decisive conclusion on Tom's fantasy life: "I reckoned he believed in the A-rabs and the elephants, but as for me I think different. It had all the marks of a Sunday school."

The second way in which Twain saves the opening section of *Huckleberry Finn* from becoming a simpleminded story of boyish adventuring is by his introduction of one of the novel's central themes. At the end of *Tom Sawyer*, Huck is adopted by the kindly Widow Douglas and her stern sister, Miss Watson. As *Huckleberry Finn* opens we see Huck struggling under the oppressive rule of these two women. They are determined to civilize him, to make him respectable. They dress him in starched and uncomfortable clothes, insist that he come to meals punctually and sit up straight, that he give up smoking and listen to their interminable Bible readings and undergo the terrors of the spelling book. He hates it. He longs for the freedom and independence he once knew as the town derelict; he rejects their religion and their education and their puritanical morals, and he yearns for the woods. This tension between respectability and freedom (so large an element in Twain's own life, particularly after his marriage) invests the book with a philosophic and psychological depth that, together with the other issues Twain will raise, lifts this work far above the commonplace.

III

The middle section of *Huckleberry Finn* is what nearly everybody has in mind when calling the book a masterpiece. That section begins with the sudden reappearance of Pap, Huck's demented and demonic father. After suffering at the hands of this drunken sadist, the boy decides to fake his own murder and escape from the old man's tyranny. He hides out on Jackson's Island. There he meets Miss Watson's slave, Jim, who is also escaping, having learned that the pitiless old woman is about to sell him away from his wife and children. This unlikely pair, the white boy and the black man, join together in their quests for freedom. They plan to raft down the Mississippi until they come to Cairo, Illinois, and then sell the raft and take a steamboat up the Ohio River and into the free territory of the North. That plan is doomed, however, when they drift by Cairo in the fog and head deeper and deeper into slave territory. Their journey down the river is punctuated by Huck's various adventures ashore—some of them brief, others quite lengthy; some of them hilarious, others harrowing. At one point, as we have seen, the raft is destroyed by the onrushing steamboat; later, when it is repaired, it is invaded and occupied by two rascally con-men who pretend to be the Duke of Bridgewater and the Dauphin, the forlorn son of King Louis XVI and lawful heir to the throne of France. Huck and Jim serve these two frauds as they make their way from one ragged Arkansas village to the next, cheating the helpless (and stupid) inhabitants before fleeing back to the raft and moving to the next unlucky town. This section of the book ends with Chapter 31, when the treacherous Dauphin sells poor Jim to a plantation owner named Silas Phelps.

A sensitive reading of this part of *Huckleberry Finn* brings to the surface several of Twain's deepest beliefs and most pressing concerns. Perhaps most apparent is the contrast he draws between the idyllic world of nature aboard the raft—its harmony and beauty, its quiet serenity and brotherhood—with what Huck encounters whenever he ventures into "civilized" society on shore. Every place the boy goes he encounters humanity disporting itself with raw and reckless abandon. He witnesses a murderous and senseless feud between two warring families, a harmless drunk gunned down in the street, the conscienceless depredations of the Duke and the Dauphin, including their nefarious scheme to steal the inheritance of the vulnerable Wilks family. In every aspect of their journey—except for their life on the raft—there is tawdriness, vulgarity, brutality, greed, and corruption. This contrast, of course, was not a new one for Mark Twain, and we have seen it emerge in many places before this. But he rarely expressed it with such grace and artistry, with such depth of feeling, as in these remarkable chapters of *Huckleberry Finn*.

It is also hard to miss in these chapters the fact that Twain is ruminating about race and the place of blacks in American society. Over the years since its publication, the greatest controversies about *Huckleberry Finn* have centered on his handling of that burning late nineteenth-century issue. On the matter of the immorality of slavery, the feelings of this son of a slave owner are perfectly clear; but on the related matters of the nature of African Americans and their equality with whites, the writer's attitudes have been the subject of lively debate. Those arguing that Twain held relatively enlightened views on these questions point to several passages in this section of his novel. For example, in Chapter 15, Huck plays a cruel and thoughtless trick on Jim, and Jim indignantly rebukes his white friend. "Then he got up slow," Huck tells us, ". . . without saying anything but that. But that was enough. It made me feel so mean I could almost kissed his foot to get him to take it back. It was fifteen minutes before I could work myself up to go and humble myself to a nigger—but I done it, and I warn't ever sorry for it afterwards, neither. I didn't do him no more mean tricks, and I wouldn't done that one if I'd a knowed it would make him feel that way." Then, in the next chapter, we learn that Jim is planning to work hard in the North and save his money and buy his wife and children from their owner. In Chapter 23, Jim tells Huck the heartbreaking story of how he once struck his little daughter for her disobedience, not realizing that she was deaf and dumb. "Oh, Huck, I bust out a-cryin' en grab her up in my arms, en say, 'Oh, de po' little thing! De Lord God Amighty forgive po' ole Jim, kaze he never gwyne to forgive hisself as long's he live." These episodes, and others, bestow upon Jim a dignity, a depth of feeling, a kind of wise common sense and kindly humanity that was rare in white depictions of African Americans in the 1870s and 1880s, and Twain's defenders point to them as evidence of the distance he had traveled from his boyhood in Missouri. His leaving the South and then criticizing it, his marriage into a family of committed abolitionists, his friendship with such vocal defenders of civil rights as Frederick Douglass, James Redpath, Petroleum Nasby, and the Beechers, they argue, had brought him around to a general belief in the equality of the two races.

Those taking the opposite view often admit that Twain had come a long way from his youth, but they insist that he still had a distance to travel before he could be regarded as a true champion of racial equality. Some of his critics, especially some African Americans, are understandably uneasy with his use of the word "nigger"—and Twain uses that word around two hundred times in this book. Even those who acknowledge that the word now carries a much more pernicious, openly racist, and insulting meaning than it did, even among southern whites like Huck Finn in the 1840s, point out that modern young African Americans who are required to read the book in high school and college classes find the constant use of the word demeaning. But the criticism extends beyond the use of that offensive word. Some claim that Twain's treatment of blacks, while sympathetic, is nonetheless condescending and somewhat patronizing. Jim is often portrayed, even in these chapters, as childlike and hopelessly naive, the eager pupil of an unschooled fourteen-year-old white boy. As will be seen, when it came to the third section of the book, the critics of Twain's racial views have been able to mount an even stronger case.

The difficulty in getting to the bottom of Twain's attitude about race can be illustrated by a passage that occurs later in the book. In Chapter 31, Huck describes a (fictitious) steamboat accident to Mrs. Phelps. "Good gracious!," she says, "anybody hurt?" Huck replies: "No'm. Killed a nigger." "Well, it's lucky," Mrs. Phelps replies, "because sometimes people do get hurt." Critics charge that an exchange like that one demonstrates Twain's insensitivity and racism. Defenders argue that he was satirizing the insensitivity and racism of so many southern whites, attempting to point up their ignorance, blindness, and ingrained bigotry. No doubt the debate about Twain's views on race will continue for a long time.

Finally, Twain presents, in this middle part of *Huckleberry Finn*, another theme that had considerable importance for him: the conflict between a culture's conventions, its traditions, assumptions, and teachings, and the relentless demands of an individual conscience. For the whole of his life, Huck (like young Sam Clemens) had been taught that slavery was sanctioned by God and endorsed in His holy Word. The abolitionists, who set themselves against that sanctified institution, were the agents of evil, sinners who deserved punishment in this life and the next. When Jim confesses to Huck that he intends to buy his wife and children and, if the master refuses to sell them, to get an abolitionist to go and steal them, Huck, under the influence of southern orthodoxy, is thunderstruck: "It most froze me to hear such talk. . . . Here was this nigger which I had as good as helped to run away, coming right out flat-footed and saying he would steal his children—children that belonged to a man I didn't even know; a man that hadn't ever done me no harm. I was sorry to hear Jim say that, it was such a lowering of him." And yet, despite his upbringing, there is something in Huck's innermost being, something in his heart, that leads him in another direction; he can never quite bring himself to turn over his friend to the authorities. The moral climax of this struggle—and one of the most memorable moments in all of American literature—occurs in Chapter 31. Huck, learning that Jim was being held at the Phelps plantation, dutifully scribbles a note to Miss Watson informing her of the whereabouts of her escaped slave so that she can arrange to recover her lost property. He composes his one-sentence letter and begins to reflect on it:

> I felt good and all washed clean of sin for the first time I had ever felt so in my life, and I knowed I could pray now. But I didn't do it straight off, but laid the paper down and set there thinking—thinking how good it was all this happened so, and how near I come to being lost and going to hell. And went on thinking. And got to thinking over our trip down the river; and I see Jim before me . . . and we a floating along, talking, and singing, and laughing. But somehow I couldn't seem to strike no places to harden me against him, but only the other kind. I'd see him standing my watch on top of his'n, stead of calling me, so I could go on sleeping. . . .

Huck recalls other incidents of their journey together. Then his eye falls upon his letter to Miss Watson. "I took it up, and held it in my hand. I was a trembling, because I'd got to decide, forever, betwixt two things, and I knowed it. I studied a minute, sort of holding my breath, and then says to myself: 'All right, then, I'll go to hell'—and tore it up."

IV

If the middle section of *Huckleberry Finn* has received (and deserved) much praise for the author's skill in combining captivating storytelling, marvelous writing, and thoughtful consideration of large social and psychological questions, the third section of the book has very often been criticized. The final dozen chapters of the novel begin with Huck making his way to the Phelps plantation, determined to help Jim escape from slavery. Upon his arrival, he is miraculously mistaken for Tom Sawyer by the matronly Sally Phelps, Tom's Arkansas aunt (yet another instance of Twain's propensity for building a tale on the basis of mistaken identity). In case readers fail to find this development sufficiently implausible, Twain then has Tom himself unexpectedly show up for a visit. In order to protect Huck's cover, Tom pretends to be his own half-brother Sid. Tom not only agrees to help Huck free Jim, he soon takes over complete command of the operation. He insists that Jim's escape be undertaken in accord with the requirements of the romantic adventure stories that have always shaped Tom's approach to life. Huck has some reservations about this, but meekly agrees, becoming again—as in the book's early chapters—Tom's willing subordinate. For the next few weeks, the two boys put Jim through hell—making him write a journal in his own blood, scratch messages with a nail onto tin plates that he then throws out the window of the one-story shack where he is confined, take in all manner of snakes, spiders, and rats. In short, Jim is reduced in these chapters to a helpless buffoon, a mindless minstrel-show figure for the amusement of Tom and Huck. All the while, moreover, Tom knows that Jim is already free, that he had been released from bondage by Miss Watson on her deathbed. After a midnight escape from the Phelps farm, Tom is wounded and Jim recaptured. Tom then confesses all, his Aunt Polly suddenly appears, Jim is freed, and Huck is taken in to be civilized by Aunt Sally.

It is not merely that these final chapters are silly and exaggerated—a slapstick throwback to that raucous western humor that had been Twain's specialty twenty years before. It is that this crude burlesque of Tom's devotion to romantic fiction turns its back on the rest of the book. The perceptive historian of American culture Leo Marx believes that "the ending of *Huckleberry Finn* makes so many readers uneasy because they rightly sense that it jeopardizes the significance of the entire novel. To take seriously what happens at the Phelps farm is to take lightly the entire downstream journey." If the rest of the book is about Huck's growth to maturity, his easy capitulation to Tom's foolishness makes no sense. If the rest of the book intends to convey the dignity and humanity of an African American, the treatment of Jim as a childish clown who willingly puts his fate in the hands of a couple of teenage pranksters seems strangely out of place. If the rest of the book is about a friendship that crossed racial lines, the willingness of Huck to put Jim through a heartless and unnecessary ordeal seems especially cruel. If the rest of the book is about the nobility of the quest for freedom, the end appears to belittle that quest by reducing it to low comedy. Even Bernard DeVoto, Twain's devoted defender and literary executor, is unwilling to defend the ending of *Huckleberry Finn*: "[I]n the whole reach of the English novel," he lamented, "there is no more abrupt or more chilling descent."

What can explain this unfortunate ending to Mark Twain's greatest novel? Some critics, including the eminent poet T. S. Eliot, have justified Twain's decision to end the book as he does, arguing that there is a certain formal appropriateness in bringing the novel full circle—returning Huck and Tom to where they were at the start, rambunctious practitioners of boyish hijinks, with Huck again reduced to Tom's pliant lieutenant. But, as Leo Marx points out, this decision, if Twain consciously made it, sacrifices the moral meaning of the novel to the demands of a formal symmetry. Marx and others find this an unsatisfactory resolution. Other analysts attempt an explanation more sympathetic to Twain's central problem in constructing the novel. He decided to have the raft drift by Cairo in the fog, to let it float into the hostile slave territory of the deep South; he probably did this so he could continue to write about the Mississippi

Valley that he knew so well rather than trying to write about life along the Ohio River, which he did not know at all. But once he made that critical decision, it is difficult to see how Twain could have brought the novel to a satisfying conclusion, and almost impossible to see how he could have produced a happy ending. Perhaps when faced with this difficulty, and having returned to working on the novel several times already, Twain resorted to these unconvincing contrivances—mistaken identity, the miraculous reappearance of Tom and his aunt, the absurd clowning, the reduction of Jim to a minstrel character, and the remarkable conversion of Miss Watson at the end of her life—to bring the story to some sort of a conclusion.

V

There is, however, another way to look at the problem of the final section of *Huckleberry Finn*, a way that goes both to the heart of one of the central tensions in Mark Twain's own life and to the tortured ambivalence he felt about his country. In the end, Twain decides to bring about Jim's freedom, not by virtue of Jim's own action, nor as a result of any radical measure taken by Huck. Rather, Jim is freed by that stern symbol of conventional midwestern morality and orthodox behavior, Miss Watson, the woman who makes Huck sit up straight and wear decent clothes and listen to Bible readings and give up smoking. "She pronounces the polite lies of civilization that suffocate Huck's spirit," says Leo Marx. One of Huck's main motives in undertaking his journey, after all, is to get away from the likes of her. And yet, even though nothing we know about Miss Watson prepares us for her generous gesture, Twain has this representative of respectability bring about the happy ending of Jim's freedom. Twain, who has demonstrated throughout the book a very keen awareness of the weakness, the injustice, the greed and corruption and hypocrisy of America, cannot quite bring himself to a full and radical rejection of his country's underlying values. His friend William Dean Howells saw many of the same evils in American society, and he became a Socialist. This was not a possible course of action for Twain; his spirit was too deeply divided. He was solicited, on the one side, by his outrage at injustice and corruption and materialism, and he possessed perhaps the sharpest eye in America for what was wrong with the country and the sharpest tongue for denouncing it. He was solicited, on the other side, by so strong an attraction to the conventional and the respectable that he could never bring himself to boldly renounce the possibility that those values might somehow redeem the nation.

A dozen years before, in *The Gilded Age*, Twain and Warner exhibited the same ambivalence. Most of that book, as we have seen, is a spirited condemnation of prevailing American values. The authors are unmerciful critics of American greed, the blind pursuit of wealth, and the wild schemes and political dishonesty that accompany that pursuit. No book ever written by Twain better shone the spotlight on the follies and the dangers of Americans' mad scramble after wealth following the Civil War. Other observers who might have made the same diagnosis of the American disease might have been led to recommend a program of thoroughgoing reform, even one that stopped short of socialism. Instead, at the very end of the book, the authors have the heroic Philip Sterling, after unstinting study and arduous labor, strike it rich, discovering coal on the land of his future father-in-law. In an outcome that might have been written by that faithful oracle of hard work and monetary success, Horatio Alger, Twain and Warner again vindicate conventional American faiths. While it is true that, through Philip, they insist that the wealth and respectability must come honestly and on the basis of effort, they show no willingness to question that definition of what constitutes a happy ending.

There is a similar conclusion at the end of *Tom Sawyer*. After the boys' great adventure, the free-spirited Huck is taken in by a grateful Widow Douglas. She "introduced him into society—no, dragged him into it, hurled him into it—and his sufferings were almost more than he could bear." He was kept "clean and neat, combed and brushed," and he slept in an actual bed. "He had to eat with knife and fork; he had to use napkin, cup, and plate; he had to learn his book, he had to go to church; he had to talk so properly that speech was become insipid in his mouth." Twain sums up poor Huck's situation: "the bars and shackles of civilization shut him in and bound him hand and foot." After three weeks of this torture, Huck escapes from the Widow's grasp. Tom goes hunting for him and eventually finds him living happily in a hogshead barrel out behind the slaughterhouse, smoking his pipe. It is a crucial moment. What will his friend Tom say to him? Tom tells him to go back to the Widow, back to the life of respectability. Huck resists: "Don't talk about it, Tom. I've tried it, and it don't work; it don't work, Tom. It ain't for me. . . . I can't stand them ways. . . . It's awful to be tied up so."

Huck even admits a hatred for the wealth he and Tom have acquired as a result of discovering Injun Joe's treasure, and it is not difficult to see Mark Twain meditating about his own situation as he puts words into Huck's mouth: "Looky-here, Tom, being rich ain't what its cracked up to be. It's just worry and worry, and sweat and sweat, and a-wishing you was dead all the time. . . . No, Tom, I won't be rich, and I won't live in them cussed smothery houses. I like the woods, and the river, and hogsheads, and I'll stick to 'em too." But then Tom, that devious spokesman for civilization, "saw his opportunity." He tells Huck that he is about to revive his gang of make-believe robbers. Huck is overjoyed until Tom delivers his crushing verdict: "But, Huck, we can't let you into the gang if you ain't respectable, you know." Huck is reduced to begging for admission: "Now, Tom, hain't you always ben friendly to me? You wouldn't shet me out, would you, Tom? You wouldn't do that, now, *would* you, Tom?" Tom is adamant. "Huck was silent for some time, engaged in a mental struggle. Finally he said: 'Well, I'll go back to the widder for a month and tackle it and see if I can come to stand it, if you'll let me b'long to the gang, Tom." Thus do Tom and Huck and their creator agonize over the choice between the pleasures of affluent respectability and the satisfactions of joyous freedom, and thus, at the close of *The Adventures of Tom Sawyer*, is the conflict temporarily resolved, reluctantly, in favor of respectability.

Ten years later in *Huckleberry Finn* the old dilemma persists. Huck has found a new caretaker in kindly Sally Phelps, and this incarnation of the Widow Douglas and Miss Watson has her own ambitions in the direction of making the boy respectable. But Mark Twain chooses to end his great book by having Huck restate the tension in a couple of immortal sentences: "But I reckon I got to light out for the Territory ahead of the rest," says Huck, "because Aunt Sally she's going to adopt me and sivilize me and I can't stand it. I been there before."

Despair

All say, "How hard it is that we have to die"—a strange complaint to come from the mouths of people who have had to live.

> *Mark Twain,* The Tragedy of Pudd'nhead Wilson *(1894)*

What a man sees in the human race is merely himself in the deep and honest privacy of his own heart. Byron despised the human race because he despised himself. I feel as Byron did, and for the same reason.

> *Mark Twain, marginal notation in a book*

10

A Writer Who Thought
He Was a Businessman

I

In addition to pouring out books and articles at a prodigious pace, Mark Twain, perhaps unfortunately, involved himself in a range of other activities. Some of these were connected to the publishing industry, some not; and while some of them were pleasant enough, others were quite the opposite. All of them diverted him from his true calling as a literary artist.

Among the distractions that he found most enjoyable (and most seductive) were those that sprang from his phenomenal celebrity. Probably no American writer, while still living, has ever enjoyed the universal renown that Twain knew from the early 1870s until his death in 1910. The fame that came to him because of his books was augmented by the fame he won by virtue of his personality. His lively conversation and irrepressible wit were legendary, and his running and often devastating commentaries on every aspect of national and world affairs were regularly quoted and endlessly repeated. Twain's distinctive appearance—that fantastic head of gleaming white hair, that great mustache, those shaggy eyebrows—made him instantly identifiable wherever he went. From his earliest days he paid careful attention to his clothes and to the impression they made—from what Van Wyck Brooks calls "the barbaric magnificence of the pilot's costume" to the wild get-up of his mining days, to a sealskin overcoat by which he was easily noticed, to those famous white suits he wore constantly in his last years. When he was an old man he wrote his daughter Clara, "I go out frequently & exhibit my clothes."

He loved being recognized. Albert Bigelow Paine, Twain's earliest biographer and, for the last five years of the writer's life, his constant companion, tells a revealing story. When Twain was in his early seventies, he and Paine checked in at the fashionable Willard Hotel in Washington, D.C. Soon it came time for dinner. "I did not realize then the fullness of his love for theatrical effect," Paine confessed. He innocently guided the elderly Twain to a remote elevator that would carry them directly down to the dining room without having to pass through "Peacock Alley," the hotel's long corridor where fashionable Washingtonians gathered to parade themselves. "When we reached the entrance of the dining-room, he said: 'Isn't there another entrance to this place?' I said there was, but that it was very conspicuous. We should have to go down the long corridor. 'Oh, well,' he said, 'I don't mind that. Let's go back and try it over.' So we went back up the elevator, walked to the other end of the hotel," and descended the magnificent staircase. "Of course he was seized upon at once by a lot of feminine admirers, and the passage along the corridor was a perpetual gauntlet. . . . I did not again make the mistake of taking him around to the more secluded elevator. I aided and abetted him every evening in making that spectacular descent of the royal stairway. . . . " When he was in New York City, Twain sometimes took a Sunday morning stroll. These walks, Paine reports, "would be timed for about the hour that the churches would be dismissed." One Sunday, Paine "thoughtlessly suggested" that they take a route that would avoid the staring and admiring throng. Twain quietly told his friend, "I like the throng." An editorial in a New York newspaper summed it up: "Things have reached the point where, if Mark Twain is not at a public meeting or banquet, he is expected to console it with one of his inimitable letters of advice and encouragement. If he deigns to make a public appearance there is a throng at the doors which overtaxes the energy and ability of the police."

Everywhere he went, famous people wanted to meet him, entertain him, hold dinners in his honor, invite him into their homes or be invited into his, for his beguiling grace as an attentive host was equaled by his beguiling charm as a house guest. He came to know—sometimes casually, sometimes intimately— nearly every important figure of the age. He gravitated toward men of wealth and authority. He called Carnegie "Saint Andrew," and that august personage sent him tokens of esteem: "the whiskey arrived in due course," Twain reported, and "last week one bottle of it was extracted . . . and inserted into me, on the installment plan." He liked playing poker with Thomas Brackett Reed, Speaker of the House of Representatives. Secretary of State John Hay was a close friend; so was Chauncey Depew, president of the New York Central, and George Harvey, the electric-railroad magnate and owner of magazines and newspapers. During his several trips to England he met and mingled with Charles Darwin, Anthony Trollope, Lewis Carroll, Charles Kingsley, Robert Browning, Herbert Spencer, George Bernard Shaw, Bram Stoker, and many others; in June 1907, he enjoyed a pleasant chat with the King and Queen. The young English writer Rudyard Kipling sought Twain out at Quarry Farm in 1889, and that encounter blossomed into a lifelong friendship. His experiences with leading intellectual and political notables in other countries were similar; in 1892, for example, he listened with pleasure as Kaiser Wilhelm praised several of his books at a private dinner.

His fabled reputation as a public speaker resulted in countless requests for after-dinner talks. Normally, these little humorous performances were hugely successful, his remarks being reprinted in the local papers and praised enthusiastically for their marvelous humor and delivery. On one occasion, however, he managed to produce a humiliating disaster. In December 1877, the *Atlantic Monthly* arranged a gala dinner at a Boston hotel to celebrate the seventieth birthday of the venerated New England poet and essayist, John Greenleaf Whittier. William Dean Howells arranged for Twain to address the dozens of distinguished Boston intellectuals who had come to honor Whittier. When it was his turn, Twain rose to his feet and told his listeners that once, back in California, an unkempt old miner told him about the time that three ragged tramps appeared at his cabin door and introduced themselves as Ralph Waldo Emerson, Oliver Wendell Holmes, and Henry Wadsworth Longfellow. (All three of these worshipped New England sages were sitting in the audience as Twain drawled on.) The old miner described the three in decidedly uncomplimentary terms: the one who called himself Holmes, for example, "was fat as a balloon; he weighed as much as three hundred and had double chins all the way down to his stomach." The three invaded the miner's cabin, proceeded to drink all his whiskey, cheat him at cards, and steal his boots. Well! Boston's literary elite, who regarded the three with reverence, were *not* amused. They sat in stony silence; Twain remembered that their faces turned into "a sort of black frost." For once in his life, the joke fell flat. He was deeply embarrassed by the incident and wrote agonized notes to the three saints, abjectly begging for forgiveness. Despite their generous replies, asserting that no offense had been taken and that he should not give the incident any further thought, Twain was haunted by the episode for the rest of his life.

If the seductions of celebrity were one source of distraction from his writing, another was his incessant travel. To the end of his days, he was to remain that "insatiable sight-seer," the man for whom "the very name of a new point of interest filled him with an eager enthusiasm to be off." He would always be the same restless creature who had written to his family while waiting for the departure of the *Quaker City*, "I am wild with impatience to move–move–*Move*!" His travels were to take him to every part of the globe: England and New Zealand, India and Italy, Ceylon and Australia, Germany and South Africa. Sometimes he went on business (as on his several trips to Canada and England to secure his copyrights); sometimes he went to pick up some quick cash (as on his several lecture tours in the United States and around the world); sometimes he went to gather material for one of his five travel books; sometimes he went in pursuit of better health for himself or Livy or the girls. In June 1891, in an attempt to save money, he and Livy closed up the Hartford house and moved to Europe, where they wandered from country to country for nine years. Between June 1892 and May 1894, Twain sailed across the Atlantic Ocean eight times. He traveled around America to see friends or make speeches or visit members of the family. He fell in love with the beauty of Bermuda and visited that island half a dozen times. Many summers were spent with the family in quiet vacation spots. On some of these jaunts, when he was able to get settled somewhere for a time, he could actually do some work. And occasionally his travels provided raw materials or inspiration for his pen. But it is hard to believe that, in general, this constant nomadic life did not interfere with his ability to write.

II

The greatest distractions and the most serious obstacles to Twain's creative life, however, resulted from his devotion to business affairs. His determination to earn the large sums of money necessary to the kind of life he envisioned for himself and Livy and his daughters led him to spend countless hours pondering the monetary opportunities and pitfalls of his trade. Most immediately, he took an extraordinary interest in peddling his own product for the highest possible return. The spirit which he had demonstrated in those earliest negotiations with Elisha Bliss ("But I had my mind made up to *one* thing—I wasn't going to touch a book unless there was *money* in it, & a good deal of it") stayed with him to the end. When he finished *Tom Sawyer*, for example, Howells wanted to serialize it in the prestigious *Atlantic Monthly*. Twain's reply was typical: "I would dearly like to see it in the Atlantic," he told his friend in July 1875. But then he explained at length why it would not pay him to sell the publication rights. "You see I take a vile mercenary view of things—but then my household expenses are something almost ghastly." He studied the literary marketplace, knew what other writers and lecturers were getting, and never let mere sentiment or prestige get in the way of business.

Twain's obsession with selling his work drew him directly into the intricacies of the publishing business. He was never satisfied with the efforts that his various publishers were expending on his work—they were always behind schedule and delaying publication for some reason or other; they never gave the new book sufficient publicity or pushed it hard enough to suit him; they never enlisted a large enough army of door-to-door subscription salesmen. Above all, he very often suspected that they were cheating him blind. Elisha Bliss, for example, had sworn a solemn oath that seven and a half percent royalties would amount to half the profits on his books, once the cost of producing them had been subtracted. Thirty-five years later, Twain was still bitter about it: "It took me nine or ten years to find out that that was a false oath and that seven and a half per cent did not represent one-fourth of the profits. But in the meantime I had published several books with Bliss . . . and of course had been handsomely swindled on all of them." In an unpublished fulmination in February 1906, Twain passed his final verdict on the publisher, describing him as "a tall, lean, skinny, yellow, toothless bald-headed, rat-eyed professional liar and scoundrel. . . . I have had contact with several conspicuously mean men, but they were noble compared to this bastard monkey." Next he went to James Osgood, "one of the dearest and sweetest and loveliest human beings to be found on the planet anywhere," Twain acknowledged, "but he knew nothing about subscription publishing and he made a mighty botch of it." Osgood published *The Prince and the Pauper* (1882) and *Life on the Mississippi* (1883). Twain liked him well enough, and the two spent countless hours bent over the billiard table. Nevertheless, by the end of 1883, Twain was accusing Osgood of mishandling "the only books of mine which have ever failed." The "failure," in the case of *Life on the Mississippi*, consisted of an initial sale amounting to only 30,000 copies (which would have thrilled almost any other author), when Twain expected 80,000. "[I]t is not a calming subject for me to talk upon," Twain complained to poor Osgood. "I am out $50,000 on this last book. . . . [T]here were things about the publishing of *my* books which you did not understand. You understand them now, but it is I who have paid the costs of the apprenticeship." By mutual agreement, the two ended their business arrangements.

The unhappy relations with Bliss and Osgood led Twain to one of the most ill-advised decisions of his life: he would start his own company, which would publish his books and those of other writers. To manage this enterprise, Twain chose a relative. Annie Moffett, the daughter of Twain's sister Pamela, had married, in 1875, an eager civil engineer named Charles Webster. After testing him out in some of his other business affairs, Twain made him a partner and manager of "Charles L. Webster and Company." During the mid-1880s, the business enjoyed a couple of notable successes—one of them being *Adventures of Huckleberry Finn*. But the successes were vastly outnumbered by disappointing failures. Soon Twain was shoveling his own royalties into the company to keep it afloat. His relations with young Webster quickly soured. He came to regard his niece's husband as stupid, incompetent, and lazy; Webster increasingly resented

Twain's tyrannical demands and insulting tone. In 1888, with Webster's health deteriorating, Twain forced him out. With all of the understatement typical of Twain when money was involved, he told his brother Orion, in July 1889, "I have never hated any creature with a hundred thousandth fraction of the hatred which I bear that human louse, Webster." Charles Webster died three years later at the age of forty. The company struggled on for a few more years, but finally succumbed during the general American depression of the early 1890s.

If Twain's commercial ventures had been confined only to the publishing business, they would have been sufficiently troubling and diverting. Unfortunately, his preoccupation with getting rich fast was never limited to the trade he knew something about. He was an inveterate gambler, a high-stakes investor in numerous get-rich-quick schemes. He threw entire fortunes into these ventures and always suffered disappointment. He put more than $20,000 into a new Hartford insurance company. He bet another $50,000 on a new way to produce illustrations for magazines and books. This miraculous process, called Kaolatype, he confidently assured Orion, "will utterly annihilate & sweep out of existence one of the minor industries of civilization & take its place." He threw his money into a New York watch company, and then into a proposal to produce a steam generator. After that, he put $32,000 into an idea to produce a steam pulley and, after that, $25,000 to promote a new way to flash telegraph messages across the ocean. He wanted to sink $1.5 million into purchasing the American rights to a carpet-pattern machine, but, luckily for him, cooler heads prevailed and he was talked out of it. In short, just as he had contracted the silver mining fever back in Nevada in the early 1860s, he now surrendered to the Gilded Age mania of speculation and gambling. All of these harebrained adventures failed miserably, but the most costly and catastrophic of Mark Twain's investments still lay ahead.

Many of these business failures reveal not only Twain's financial incompetence but also his fascination with new technology, his Gilded Age faith in the latest gadgetry, the limitless possibilities of machinery. The same openness to new inventions that led him to install one of the first telephones in his home or experiment with the typewriter and the phonograph and the bicycle, the same impulse that led him to describe the inventor as "a true poet," made him vulnerable to those who came to see him about some dubious new mechanical possibility. It also led him, from time to time, to put aside his pen and work on some invention of his own. On several of these he took out patents. He came up with an elastic strap to keep men's trousers from slipping, a bed clamp to hold a baby's sheets and blankets in place, a new kind of garter, a perpetual calendar, a scrapbook which did not need paste and which, under the title *Mark Twain's Self-Pasting Scrapbook*, actually earned him a few dollars. For his daughters he invented a "memory-improving" history game, where children would move along an outdoor track by naming historical battles, kings, and presidents; this game he thought about patenting and mass-producing.

What is especially interesting (and revealing) about Twain's mad career of speculation, invention, and gambling is that he was not unaware of the recklessness, the folly, the sheer ineptitude of his activities. "All through my life," he confessed in his *Autobiography*, "I have been the easy prey of the cheap adventurer. He came, he lied, he robbed and went his way, and the next one arrived by the next train and began to scrape up what was left." In one of his later books, he gave a definition of the month of October: "This is one of the peculiarly dangerous months to speculate in stocks in," he wrote. "The others are July, January, September, April, November, May, March, June, December, August, and February." He was simply too intelligent, too thoughtful, too keen and honest an observer both of his culture and of his own proclivities to have been blind to what it all meant to his country, to its values and to his, and to his art.

Twain's multifaceted business activities of the 1880s were punctuated by one enormous success and one devastating failure. Sadly, the success was very quickly eclipsed by the disaster.

III

Ironically, Mark Twain's greatest commercial success came at the hands of the Union officer who had chased the Marion Rangers all over Missouri a quarter of a century earlier. Both that intrepid Colonel, then aged thirty-nine, and the prudently retreating twenty-five-year-old Ranger had come a long way since 1861.

On the strength of a string of victories, culminating in the battle of Vicksburg in 1863, Ulysses S. Grant had become the head of the Union armies in 1864. His defeat of Robert E. Lee elevated him into one of the transcendent heroes of the Civil War, and in 1868, he was elected president of the United States. One measure of his popularity is the fact that he was only the second president since Andrew Jackson, four decades before, to win reelection to a second term. While Grant is usually ranked among the worst of American presidents, the widespread corruption that tainted his administration was never connected to him directly; he was justly charged with naivete, unwarranted loyalty to men who did not deserve his confidence, and inadequate supervision of his subordinates, but not with personal dishonesty. After leaving the White House and enjoying a triumphal world tour, Grant tried his hand at business. Through no fault of his own, but as a result of a dishonest associate, he was in terrible financial difficulty by 1884 (this was a day before retired presidents received pensions, and Grant had surrendered his military pension to become president). If his financial situation was not troubling enough to the old soldier, he learned, at the same time, that he was suffering from cancer of the throat and that he had not much longer to live. He agonized about the fate of his wife and family.

Perhaps it was inevitable that the most famous military and political figure of his age should become acquainted with the most famous literary figure, and the paths of Twain and Grant crossed several times before the mid-1880s. The most memorable of their encounters occurred in November 1879. Grant was completing his world tour, the last leg of which took him from California to Chicago—a journey, Twain recalled, that was "one continuous ovation." In Chicago, a magnificent banquet was prepared in his honor by veterans of the Army of Tennessee, his first command as a general. (Skeptics believed that the whole thing was an attempt to test the waters for a possible try for an unprecedented third term in 1880.) Twain, who was asked to come to Chicago and deliver the evening's final toast, left a memorable description. "I sat near him on the stage of a theatre which was packed to the ceiling with surviving heroes of that army and their wives. When General Grant, attended by other illustrious generals of the war, came forward and took his seat, the house rose and a deafening storm of welcome burst forth which continued during two or three minutes. There wasn't a soldier on that stage who wasn't visibly affected, except the man who was being welcomed, Grant. No change of expression crossed his face." Twain was deeply impressed by the man's iron stoicism. The evening's many orators (by the time Twain rose to deliver the last toast it was 2 A.M.!) poured "Niagaras of glory" not only upon Grant, but upon other Union generals in the auditorium: Sheridan, Sherman, Logan, and others. All the others "writhed and fidgeted and squirmed and suffered. . . . Not one of them was able to sit still under the fiery deluge of praise except that one man, Grant. He got his Niagara every quarter of an hour for two hours and a half, and yet when the ordeal was over he was still sitting in precisely the same attitude which he had assumed when he first took that chair. He had never moved a hand or foot, head, or anything." It was, Twain thought, "an achievement which I should not have believed if I had not seen it with my own eyes."

After that, Twain encountered Grant several times and visited him regularly in New York, and firm friendship based on mutual admiration developed between the two. In November 1884, Twain learned that Grant, facing death and desperate for money for his wife and family, had agreed to write his memoirs. He rushed to see him. As he entered the room, Grant was about to fix his signature to a contract with the Century Company that would have paid him ten percent royalties. The company had recently paid Grant $500 for each of four articles on Civil War battles ("The offer came to the despairing old hero like the fabled straw to the drowning man," Twain wrote, and Grant had grasped at it although those articles "were easily worth ten thousand dollars apeice but he didn't know it."). Twain listened to the details of the Century contract and begged Grant to reconsider. "I explained that these terms would never do; that they were all wrong, unfair, unjust. I said, 'Strike out the ten per cent and put twenty per cent in its place. Better still, put seventy-five per cent of the net returns in its place.'" Twain claimed that he had originally hoped to place Grant's book with the American Publishing Company "and enrich that den of reptiles." But "the sober second thought came then. I reflected that the company had been robbing me for years . . . and that now was my chance to feed fat the ancient grudge I bore them." In the end, Twain persuaded Grant to publish his memoirs with the Charles L. Webster publishing company. Twain agreed to pay Grant seventy percent of the sales and to absorb all expenses for producing the book out of his own thirty percent share.

Despite his rapidly collapsing health and the awful pain caused by his spreading cancer, Grant set about writing his book. Twain, who read the sections of the work as Grant produced them, was impressed with the quality of the writing. It was characterized, he thought, by "clarity of statement, directness, simplicity, uunpretentiousness, manifest truthfulness, fairness and justice toward friend and foe alike, soldierly candor and frankness and soldierly avoidance of flowery speech." He thought Grant's work would rank with the *Commentaries* of Julius Caesar and he said so. (Over the years other readers have shared Twain's admiration for the quality of Grant's prose.) Meanwhile, many Americans were caught up in the drama, well publicized by the newspapers, of the brave soldier racing against death to complete his final mission. For some weeks before his death, Grant was unable to speak but communicated with pencil and paper. "I went to see him once toward the end," Twain recalls in his *Autobiography*, "and he asked me with his pencil, and evidently with anxious solicitude, if there was a prospect that his book would make something for his family." Twain had the satisfaction of telling him that the early sales were splendid, the money was coming in rapidly, and the subscription solicitation effort was only about half finished. Twain told him that even if the effort "should stop where it was there would be two hundred thousand dollars coming to his family. He expressed his gratification, with his pencil."

Grant's memoirs, which appeared in two handsome volumes, sold extremely well. The General died on July 23, 1885, five days after he had handed over the second volume to Webster. A few months later, Twain presented Julia Grant a check for $200,000, the largest royalty payment in American history to that point. Before it was over, the Grant family received around $450,000. Twain himself earned around $200,000 for his part in the enterprise. As it happened, he needed the money badly. Unfortunately, it wasn't enough.

IV

At the same time that he was involved with the hugely successful Grant project, Mark Twain was also mired in the greatest financial disaster of his life. It all began with a visionary scheme hatched in the mind of an inventor named James W. Paige. Convinced that he could produce a machine that would automatically set type, Paige took out his first patent in 1872 and moved to Hartford three years later. He was lured by the town's prosperity, its reputation for mechanical expertise, and the potential he saw for raising investment capital there. He rented a workshop in the Colt Arms Factory and set about the twin tasks of tinkering his machine into reality and rounding up investors to finance the costly operation. Since the fifteenth century, type had been set by human beings laboriously placing one letter at a time into a composing stick, justifying the right-hand margin of each line by hand, and then breaking up and redistributing the used letters into their proper boxes so they could be used again. Paige's ambition was to duplicate these steps mechanically, to invent a device that would enable an operator at a keyboard to convert type into printed pages at breathtaking speed, justify lines, and distribute the used type. He kept adding new functions to the original conception, and by the time it was at the height of its complexity, the Paige typesetter required more than 18,000 separate parts.

Paige's vision had a natural appeal to Twain. After all, Twain had earned his living setting type as a youngster and knew very well the arduous and time-consuming labor involved in the procedure. He had seen the process from other perspectives as a reporter in the West and a newspaper owner in Buffalo. As an author, he had been regularly frustrated by the inevitable delays in converting his manuscripts into finished books. When someone in town told him about a device that could set type mechanically, Twain immediately invested $2,000. Shortly after that, he walked over to the Colt Factory to see for himself. He found Paige to be intelligent, experienced, and persuasive. ("What a talker he is!" said Twain. "He could persuade a fish to come out and take a walk with him. When he is present I always believe him; I can't help it.") He added an additional $3,000. That was in 1880, and he was hooked. Twain was dead certain that the machine, once perfected, would revolutionize the business of publication, that every publisher and every newspaper in the world would leap at the chance to own or rent Paige's machines. He thought 100,000 typesetters was not an unreasonable number to produce.

For fourteen disappointing years, Twain poured vast sums into Paige's project. There was always some new wrinkle that postponed completion, and Paige was nothing if not a perfectionist. He kept dismantling the thing and starting over. Some of the early test runs were promising, but the device could never operate for very long without breaking down and needing repair. Twain persisted. Before long he was sinking $3,000 a month into Paige's enterprise, including the royalties he was getting from *Huckleberry Finn* and the operating capital of his publishing company. He tried to persuade his friends to invest, and he constantly predicted that when the thing was finally finished, he would be fabulously wealthy and could give up writing forever. (The very same hope that his father had placed in *land* a generation earlier, he was now placing in *machinery*—a revealing symbol of the country's transformation from an agrarian to an industrial economy.) Twain negotiated for half ownership of the machine; then, in 1889, he agreed to put Paige on a salary and own the full rights himself. By the time it was all over, he had sunk at least $200,000 into that wild dream with nothing ever coming of it. Part of the reason for the failure was Paige's incurable perfectionism, his insistence on adding new features and functions, the impossible complexity of the machine. But the failure was also partly attributable to a rival machine being constructed on an entirely different principle and rapidly being brought to completion. While Paige's machine tried to duplicate the work of a human typesetter, the eventually successful typesetter made no such attempt—for example, instead of resorting used type the way people had been doing for centuries, the new version automatically melted down the metal and reproduced new type. Even before Twain gave up on Paige, the new "linotype" was being widely adopted by leading American newspapers.

The failure of the Paige typesetter affected Mark Twain in at least two important ways. He had always harbored some doubts about machinery, of course—the steamboat, after all, was quite capable of plowing heedlessly through the raft. But in general, as his other reckless investments showed, Twain believed in the miracles of the Gilded Age—a Colonel Sellers in his own way, buoyantly hopeful about the improvements he saw being brought forth all around him. He had always had faith in the wonders of modern mechanical invention and a boyish eagerness to try out the latest gadget. At the very least, the typesetter modified that optimism. The episode accentuated the doubts about mechanical improvements and about the age and the culture that pinned such extravagant hopes on them. The venture with James Paige, many critics believe, tilted the balance in his mind toward the negative and cautionary aspects of those nineteenth-century faiths. His writing was henceforth to reflect these doubts, this pessimism.

Even more immediate was a second result of the Paige debacle: Mark Twain was wiped out. The publishing company enjoyed few successes after the publication of Grant's memoirs, and some bad business decisions were made. Whatever cash came in Twain siphoned off into the typesetter. He ultimately resorted to accepting $60,000 in loans out of Livy's own money, something he had vowed never to do. Thus even before America entered the Depression of 1893, the worst economic crisis in its history to that point, Mark Twain was in serious trouble.

CHAPTER 11

Writing His Way Out of Debt

I

Faced with overwhelming financial difficulties, and no longer able to maintain the Hartford mansion, Mark and Livy found other employment for the servants, closed down that much-loved house, and moved to Europe in June 1891. They hoped to find a place where they might enjoy something like their customary lifestyle, but to do so more cheaply than was possible in their own country. Twain and his wife also hoped that a sojourn abroad would bring improvements to their health; he was suffering from rheumatism that made writing by hand painful, and she was starting to show symptoms of the heart disease that was to make her an invalid during her final years. Abandoning Hartford was an obvious defeat for the ambitious man who harbored such an extravagant belief that the typesetter would mean vast wealth and a comfortable retirement. Forty years later, in a book about her father, Clara recalled the family's feelings: "We adored our home and friends. We had to leave so much treasured beauty behind that we could not look forward with any pleasure to life abroad. We all regarded this break in a hitherto smooth flow of harmonious existence as something resembling a tragedy."

Over the next years, the family wandered the Continent, living for short periods in France, Switzerland, Germany, and Italy. Wherever they went they were greeted and entertained by prominent political and intellectual figures. Americans traveling in Europe inevitably called to pay their respects—the Twichells came

176

over to see their friends and Mark and Joe took another jaunt together. Driven by necessity, Twain worked intermittently on his writing. Before leaving America, he had contracted with *McClure's Magazine* for letters from Europe, and he was actually able to concentrate on some longer projects after he and Livy settled in a handsome villa near Florence, a place where they were, for once, relatively contented. These years were punctuated by frequent trips back to the United States that Twain made without Livy, who was usually too weak or ill to travel. He undertook those journeys back home in increasingly desperate and generally unsuccessful attempts to raise capital for the typesetter or to borrow money to keep the publishing company afloat. While back in America, he visited friends, checked on the progress of the typesetter, gave public readings, and made some of those legendary after dinner talks. Every place he traveled, during these returns to America, he was greeted with enthusiasm and affection and treated like royalty. But nobody was quite ready to lend him money.

II

On one of those trips, in September 1893, Twain met Henry Huttleston Rogers, a man who was to play a crucial part in his affairs for the rest of his life. Five years younger than Twain, Rogers had worked his way up from a modest boyhood to become one of the richest and most powerful men in the United States. He had entered the oil business early, and at thirty-four helped to form the Standard Oil Company; in 1890, he became a vice president. By virtue of shrewd investments in various enterprises, Henry Rogers amassed a huge fortune. He also earned a reputation, and it was not a very good one. Most observers saw him as a man of exceptional ruthlessness and a contempt for basic morality. Known as "the Hell Hound of Wall Street," Rogers was regarded as one of the most unscrupulous and merciless of the "robber barons." Many historians agree with Ron Powers' view that he was a man with "a Visigoth's disdain for fair play. . . . a butcher, a shark, a man without remorse."

Twain did not see him that way. After a chance encounter in the lobby of a New York hotel, introductions by a mutual friend, and a few drinks, the two had laid the foundation for a long and affectionate companionship. "We were strangers when we met and friends when we parted, half an hour afterward," Twain said at Rogers' death in 1909. Of course it did not hurt that Rogers confessed to being an admirer of Twain's work, that he read his books aloud to his children, that years ago he had attended one of those early lectures about Hawaii. But it was much more than that. Twain was attracted by Rogers' keen intelligence, his conversational dexterity, a wit almost equal to his own, a handsome and masculine appearance and imposing self-confidence, a generosity to his friends that might have surprised some of his critics. During that first encounter Twain made known his financial problems, and Rogers suggested a Saturday meeting at his office. While the dispirited writer sat there, his new friend took out his checkbook and "in six minutes" solved the immediate credit crisis. "When I arrived in September," Twain reported to Livy, "lord how black the prospect was—how desperate, how incurably desperate! . . . I flew to Hartford—to my friends—but they were not moved, not strongly interested, and I was ashamed that I went. It was from Mr. Rogers, a stranger, that I got the money and was by it saved." The two men were soon constant companions. They spent hours on Rogers' yacht, playing cards, smoking cigars, drinking whiskey; they were constantly busy at billiards and went to the theater together and to boxing matches. Twain felt free to drop in at Rogers' office whenever he pleased.

Above all, the astute businessman started taking a friendly interest in Twain's financial situation. He became the author's financial adviser. "I did hate to burden his good heart and overworked head with it," Twain told his wife, "but he took hold with avidity and said it was no burden to work for his friends, but a pleasure." Twain was grateful not only for the help Rogers rendered, but also for the spirit in which he rendered it: he did these things, Twain later wrote, "at no cost to my self-love, no hurt to my pride; indeed, he did them with so delicate an art that I almost seemed to have done them myself. By no sign, no hint, no word did he ever betray any consciousness that I was under obligations to him." In this kindly way, Rogers helped put Twain's financial affairs in order. One of the busiest men in America traveled twice to Chicago on Twain's behalf, examining Paige's typesetter for himself and then trying to bargain that venture onto a more advantageous basis for its chief investor. Rogers even entered into

Twain's publishing enterprises, supervising an arrangement in April 1894 that let the American Publishing Company round up subscribers for Twain's new book, while the respected company of Harper and Brothers would retail the volume to the bookstores. Ten years later, Rogers negotiated with Harper's an agreement giving the company exclusive rights to Twain's work in exchange for a yearly payment. Twain readily signed over his power of attorney to Rogers and returned to Europe and Livy.

Not even the magic of Henry Rogers, however, could forestall the inevitable disaster. No one could make the typesetter actually work, no matter how advantageous were the financial arrangements in place for the day when it was to reach perfection. And no one could save the Charles Webster publishing house in the face of the severe economic downturn that began at the start of 1893. That depression, one of the most calamitous in American history, lasted for almost three years. It caused widespread suffering across the country, in agricultural and urban regions alike. The banking and credit system was particularly hard-hit, and one of Twain's creditors mercilessly called in one of the writer's loans. Twain hastened back to America in April 1894, and consulted with Rogers. Then, on April 18, America's most beloved writer reluctantly made a declaration of voluntary bankruptcy.

Even in that grim moment, Henry Rogers was able to work a minor miracle. On the basis of Livy's $60,000 "loan" to the Webster Company, he arranged for her to be declared a "preferred creditor," entitled to having her debt satisfied first. By this ploy Twain was able to hang on to the Hartford property and the copyrights to his books. Rogers then muscled the other creditors into settling for half of what they were owed—for every dollar that Twain was to have paid, they agreed to take fifty cents. Still, Livy took the bankruptcy hard. "I cannot get away from the feeling that business failure means disgrace," she wrote to her adopted sister, Susan Crane. "Most of the time I want to lie down and cry. Everything seems to me so impossible . . . I feel that my life is an absolute and irretrievable failure."

But Twain, at Livy's urging and with Rogers' wholehearted approval, solemnly vowed to ignore the agreement to pay creditors only half of what they were owed—he publicly pledged to repay every last penny. He was now almost sixty and not in good health. He had harbored a profound hope that his days of writing and lecturing were over at last and that prosperity and blessed leisure were just around the corner. There was, therefore, a kind of admirable courage in his resolution. He must have known that keeping his word was not going to be easy.

III

It was inevitable that Twain's writing would reflect some of his troubles and give expression to some of his feelings, and no book reveals more about the direction of his thought than *A Connecticut Yankee in King Arthur's Court*. Although he had shown interest in the legend of King Arthur earlier, he probably first seriously considered the idea for a book in late 1884, when, while on a lecture tour, he came upon Thomas Malory's fifteenth-century work, *Mort D'Arthur*. That old book, which told the stories of Arthur and the knights of his Round Table, gave him the notion of contrasting sixth-century England with modern America. When he began work on the project, in February 1886, things were going particularly well: the lecture tour had been a financial success, both Grant's memoir and *Huckleberry Finn* were selling well, and his optimism about the Paige typesetter was at its height. His general satisfaction with life can be seen in the lively humor and philosophic optimism of the first part of the book. By the time he finished writing it in 1889, however, his affairs were much less satisfactory; the publishing company desperately needed cash, and Paige's never-finished machine was causing him increasing doubt and anxiety.

In *Connecticut Yankee*, Twain once again uses the device of the "frame story," a contrivance that had served him well since the "Jumping Frog" tale. In this case, a narrator touring England's Warwick castle meets a talkative stranger who then hands him a manuscript containing a curious story. It centers on Hank Morgan, a skilled and resourceful mechanic at Hartford's Colt Arms Factory, the very place where James Paige began work on his invention. During a brawl ("a misunderstanding conducted with crowbars") one of his employees knocks Hank unconscious, and when he awakens, he miraculously finds himself in King Arthur's England. He uses his nineteenth-century knowledge and technological expertise to defeat the evil magician Merlin, win the confidence of the King, and become second only to Arthur himself in managing the affairs of England. He is soon known throughout the realm as "the Boss." Over the next few years, Hank secretly prepares to supply ancient England with all the innovations and conveniences of the modern world. He starts newspapers and a patent office, introduces telephones and the telegraph, electricity and bicycles, scientific mining and photography, a fair system of taxation and advertising and schools. Before he is finished, he plans to give the country railroads, power plants, and a stock exchange. "Unsuspected by this dark land," says the Boss, "I had the civilization of the nineteenth century booming under its very nose!" He hopes to introduce democratic measures someday— separation of church and state, a free press, even the abolition of slavery. He must act cautiously, however, because of the twin forces of oppression: the English aristocracy and the Roman Catholic Church. These powerful and privileged few have enslaved and impoverished the masses and turned everyday lives into ordeals of bitter suffering. Everywhere the Boss travels he witnesses disease and death, terrible punishments arbitrarily meted out by unfeeling aristocrats, grinding poverty, merciless torture, heartbreaking misery and desperation. He is determined to uproot this system and bestow upon the wretched population his technological and political advances.

Interspersed in this tale of hopeful industrial and democratic progress are Twain's entertaining, sometimes hilarious episodes and subplots. The Boss falls in love and marries, goes on a knightly mission to rescue captive virgins (who turn out to be barnyard pigs), and participates in a jousting tournament where he uses a lasso and a pistol to defeat his bewildered opponents. With the aid of some plumbing equipment and explosives, he performs a "miracle" at a sacred fountain that had gone dry. He is always blowing up things. He accompanies the King, both of them in disguise, on a tour of the country where Arthur sees the suffering of his people and the daily injustices they endure. When the two are captured, sold into slavery, and condemned to death, the Boss sends a telegram and five hundred knights ride in on bicycles to save the day. There is a memorable chapter where poor Hank squirms and sweats and cannot scratch himself in his suit of armor (and, like Huck Finn, comes to equate confining clothing with misery and oppression). There are wonderful and witty asides—former noblemen working as conductors on the new railroad or wandering the countryside advertising toothpaste; some of these little intrusions are on the naughty side—as when Twain places a monastery on one side of the Valley of Holiness, a nunnery on the other, and halfway between them, a home for abandoned babies. He sprinkles the work with wisecracks, sly digs at modern institutions and practices, jokes that readers of the time would have quickly recognized. But underneath all the marvelous storytelling and fun, it is clear that Twain approves of the Boss's modern innovations and that he disapproves of the feudal institutions of England, its despotic aristocrats and uncompassionate priests.

Given the optimism of the book's beginning, therefore, its ending,—written as Twain's own fortunes were declining and the prospect of being saved by Paige's machine seemed ever more remote—seems especially gruesome and grotesque. The Church and the nobility, determined to regain their power, mount a gigantic military offensive against the Boss. Together with only fifty-two loyal boys, the Boss takes refuge in a cave surrounded by a broad belt of sand. Using his mechanical skills, he prepares his little band for their desperate defense against the gathering forces of reaction. The thirty-thousand armored knights charge across the sand. Suddenly there is a terrible eruption—the Boss had planted explosives—and the front ranks of the enemy "shot into the sky with a thunder-crash, and became a whirling tempest of rags and fragments." When the smoke clears, the defenders see the results: "Of course we could not *count* the dead, because they did not exist as individuals, but merely as homogeneous protoplasm, with alloys of iron and buttons." (In an early draft of the book, Twain has Hank estimate the number of the dead mathematically by weighing the jellied protoplasm—it came to 1,069,362 pounds—and then subtracting for horses, dry-goods, and iron. One of the author's friends, who read the book in manuscript, persuaded Twain to drop that particular horror.) Then, in order to deny the enemy the benefits of his innovations, the Boss "touched a button and shook the bones of England loose from her spine!" All his factories "went up in the air, and disappeared from the earth" (more previously planted explosives!).

In case all this mayhem was not jarring enough, Twain had more nightmares in store. The Boss diverts a stream and electrifies fences surrounding the cave. Night falls, and one by one the knights creep forward in the darkness and touch the fence with their swords; the defenders see "a blue spark" and know that a knight has been electrocuted. They keep coming, and the Boss watches "the silent lightning do its awful work upon that swarming host. . . . [A] black mass was piling itself up beyond the second fence. That swelling bulk was dead men! Our camp was enclosed with a solid wall of the dead—a bulwark, a breastwork, of corpses, you may say." The Boss touches another button and the spotlights flash on like "fifty electric suns aflame." He electrifies the rest of the fences and strikes "the whole host dead in their tracks! *There* was a groan you could *hear*! It voiced the death-pang of eleven thousand men." Enough? No, not for Mark Twain. He still had to dispose of the remaining ten thousand knights. The Boss fires his revolver—the signal to "Turn on the water!" Within sixty seconds the diverted brook becomes a rushing river, drowning countless armored knights. Then the Boss orders his thirteen machine guns to open fire and they "began to vomit death into the fated ten thousand." The slaughter was measureless. But Twain is still not finished with the reader. After a few days, the dead bodies surrounding the cave in an impenetrable wall begin to decay, releasing their poisonous fumes. "We were in a trap, you see—a trap of our own making. If we stayed where we were, our dead would kill us; if we moved out of our defenses we should no longer be invincible. We had conquered; in turn we were conquered." One by one the Boss and his young friends succumb to the poison gas wafting into their fortress.

Of all of Twain's books, except for *Huckleberry Finn*, this one has called forth the widest range of critical interpretation. Some have noted Twain's pioneering use of an element of modern science fiction, time-travel; some earlier authors had created characters who awoke into the future, but this book is among the first where the travel is backwards into history. Some analysts point out the similarities between the Boss and the inventor James Paige, but others see, in the character and attitudes of Hank Morgan, elements of Twain himself, while still others detect a little of Twain's hero, Ulysses Grant. Much of the scholarly debate surrounding *Connecticut Yankee* centers on figuring out what was the principal target of the book's social criticism. Some reviewers were satisfied that Twain was simply aiming at the cruel and backward institutions of medieval England, particularly the Church and nobility. Others see him mounting a general attack on the rank stupidities of romantic ideas of chivalry (echoing his ridicule of Tom Sawyer's convoluted plan to rescue Jim according to his zany adventure books). From there it was a small step for some scholars to interpret *Connecticut Yankee* as an attack on the antebellum American South, with its rigid class distinctions, human slavery, and delusional beliefs about chivalry, aristocracy, and honor. There were British reviewers who were sure that Twain was criticizing not medieval England, but the England of the nineteenth century and its entrenched class structure and aristocratic pretensions. Finally, some saw Twain's book as an assault on modern America's conscienceless robber barons exploiting a downtrodden working class—a suggestion strengthened by the fact that one of the illustrations that Twain approved for the book depicted "The Slave Driver" with the unmistakable face of that ruthless villain of American business, Jay Gould.

Whichever interpretation (or combination of them) one accepts, however, it is hard to miss in this book Twain's uncertainty about the modern world. Did its science, its technological pride, its faith in the machine, portend resistance to old injustices and elevation out of ignorance and poverty? Most of Twain's contemporaries certainly thought so. Or did that confidence in steam and electricity and factories carry more dangerous possibilities, a more ominous message? Could these modern things also cause dashed hopes, devastation on unprecedented scales, and the release of forces that mere human beings could never fully control—forces that, like Frankenstein's monster or the Boss's electrified fences, might destroy even those proud mortals who invented them? Maybe that uncertainty was the lesson that James Paige reinforced for Mark Twain.

IV

Between December 1889, when he published *Connecticut Yankee*, and 1898, when he at last succeeded in paying his creditors everything he owed them and won the applause of the world for his fortitude and honesty in doing so, Mark Twain rushed out six new books. They were all produced while the family lived in Europe, and all but one were serialized in newspapers and magazines before appearing as books. At least three of them were written only under the lash of economic necessity and are never mentioned as being among Twain's lasting contributions to American literature. These three resurrect characters that had earlier won fame for Twain. He had long recognized the appeal of Colonel Beriah Sellers, that loveable rascal whose wild schemes and boundless dreams had provided the most memorable passages of *The Gilded Age* twenty years earlier. In fact, Twain had twice put Colonel Sellers on the stage, once in 1874 (a dramatization of the novel) and once, collaborating with Howells in 1883, in a comedy called *Colonel Sellers as a Scientist*. Now, facing financial disaster, Twain brought the Colonel back in *The American Claimant*. He dashed the novel off in ten weeks in 1891, serialized it in several newspapers, and had the still afloat Webster Company publish it in April 1892. In the novel, the Colonel is now elderly but still high-spirited and enterprising; he is hot on a scheme to manage the world's weather by controlling the sunspots—there would be *millions* in it! He thinks he is the rightful heir of an English earldom. Twain wove into the plot a love story, a radical Englishman who becomes disillusioned with democracy (not unlike the Boss in *Connecticut Yankee* two years before), and some satirical jabs at American business and politics.

For the other two potboilers, Twain resurrected Tom and Huck. In 1894, the Webster Company (on the very day it went bankrupt!) copyrighted *Tom Sawyer Abroad*, a short and pointless story of Tom, Huck, and the former slave, Jim, getting aboard a hot-air balloon, disposing of the balloon's villainous owner, and floating across the Atlantic Ocean where they visit the Sahara Desert and Egypt. The tale, told by Huck, consists largely of exasperated conversations between the pompously romantic Tom and the practical and realistic Huck, with now and then Jim putting in a comment or two. Some critics also fault the book for being too derivative of Jules Verne's popular *Five Weeks in a Balloon*, which had been published five years before. Then, two years after *Tom Sawyer Abroad*, Twain produced another flimsy attempt, *Tom Sawyer, Detective*. This one he wrote in less than a month. It was based on a crime that had occurred in Denmark during the previous century, but Twain moved the action to the Phelps plantation (where Jim had been held captive at the end of *Huckleberry Finn*). In the story, also narrated by

Huck, Uncle Silas confesses to committing a murder, but Tom, by shrewd observation and a flair for courtroom histrionics, proves his uncle innocent. Twain hoped to capitalize on the popularity of detective stories, particularly those of Arthur Conan Doyle's Sherlock Holmes. Since the Webster Company no longer existed, he sold it to Harper's, which serialized it in *Harper's Monthly Magazine* before bringing it out as a book.

These three hasty and ill-considered books were obviously the work of a man desperate for money. He could hardly have taken much satisfaction in them, and they added nothing to his reputation as a writer. The other three books written during these troubled years, while not among his best work, are not so easily dismissed.

V

Probably the strangest book that Mark Twain ever wrote was originally called *The Tragedy of Pudd'nhead Wilson and the Comedy of Those Extraordinary Twins*. It too was written in great haste, Twain putting in a prodigious effort to complete a saleable manuscript. First serialized in *Century Magazine,* the book finally appeared in November 1894, seven months after his declaring bankruptcy. Unfortunately, the work suffers from changed and ultimately divided purposes, from several revisions undertaken—not entirely successfully—to unify the novel, from the author's wrestling with some difficult philosophic questions, and from a complexity that leaves many readers befuddled.

The story is set in Dawson's Landing, another of Twain's villages that bear resemblances to Hannibal. Into town comes Dave Wilson, a sophisticated and reclusive Easterner with unorthodox opinions and a curious hobby, fingerprinting. (Twain had just read Francis Galton's book, *Finger Prints*, published two years earlier and revealing that no two prints are identical.) Shortly after Wilson's arrival, two children are born in town. One is the son of the local aristocrat; the other, although only one thirty-second black, is destined to be a slave. Wilson routinely fingerprints them. Then Roxy, the mother of the slave child and nurse of the other, switches the babies in their cradles. Her true son is raised in luxury and grows up to be arrogant, cruel, and dishonest—he ends up a thief and murderer; he even knowingly sells his mother. The wealthy child, now raised as a slave, soon adopts the mannerisms, the shuffle, the dialect of the other slaves. Into this core plot, Twain introduces a set of Italian twins who also move to town and whose doings and past lives, Twain, somewhat irrelevantly, details. This is because the book was originally intended to be a farce on a set of conjoined twins and their bizarre lives together; Twain separated them into two independent individuals but kept them in his book, although they are rather tangential to the central plot. After various twists and turns, there is a murder. One of the twins is accused. But in one of his trademarked courtroom dramas, Twain has Wilson show by means of fingerprints both that Roxy's now-pampered son is the killer and that the two young men are not who everyone thought they were.

Changing a farce about Siamese twins into a dark tragedy was done partly for financial reasons—Twain hoped to sell the book by subscription and realized that he had to make it bigger. But that conversion, with the Italian twins worked awkwardly into the story, was not quite successful, as many critics have pointed out. The book is also filled with standard Twain devices: twinning; mistaken identity; the horrors of slavery; village intrigue; a mystery unraveled in a dramatic courtroom showdown. In recent years scholars have given Twain some credit for grappling, in *Pudd'nhead Wilson*, with such serious themes as human nature, race, the influence of environment on personality, and the possibility of real freedom in a largely determined world. He has also been praised for his powerful portrayal of Roxy, one of the most interesting and complicated females in any of Twain's work. The book also features terse aphorisms that Twain affixed to the start of each chapter. Twain labels these witty epigrams as excerpts from "Pudd'nhead Wilson's Calendar," and they reveal the writer's cynical and sarcastic views on many topics. Some of them are notably dark and indicate where Twain's views were heading: "Whoever has lived long enough to find out what life is, knows how deep a debt of gratitude we owe to Adam, the first great benefactor of our race. He brought death into the world." "Why is it that we rejoice at birth and grieve at a funeral? It is because we are not the person involved." "All say, 'How hard it is that we have to die'—a strange complaint to come from the mouths of people who have had to live."

Pudd'nhead Wilson is certainly a cut above the two Tom Sawyer sequels of 1894 and 1896, but it is hard to escape the conclusion that its driving force was the same—quick money. Nor did Twain attempt to disguise it. At the end of July 1893, during the negotiations leading to the novel's publication, Twain made his motivation perfectly clear: "Now then," he wrote, "what is she worth? The amount of matter is but 3,000 words short of the American Claimant, for which the syndicate paid $12,500. There was nothing new in that story, but the fingerprints in this one is virgin ground—absolutely *fresh* and mighty curious and interesting to everybody."

Five months after the publication of *Pudd'nhead Wilson*, chapters of Twain's next book began to appear in *Harper's Magazine*. It was unlike anything he had ever attempted, and he knew it and wanted it that way. *Personal Recollections of Joan of Arc* purported to be the reminiscence of an eighty-year-old man who had been a youthful friend and companion of Joan; now, sixty years after the martyred maid was burned at the stake in 1431, he wants to share his memories of her. Twain had been fascinated by Joan for a long time. He claimed that he could recall a day, as a teenager in Hannibal, when the wind blew across his path a single loose page that told part of her story. To write this book, he devoted himself to research in English and French sources (scholars have found more than a dozen books devoted to the topic in Twain's library). He started writing in Florence in August 1892 but, as usual, put it aside in favor of other undertakings, finally completing it in Paris in March 1895. He believed that there was something quite special about this particular book. "I have never done any work before that cost so much thinking and weighing and measuring and planning and cramming, or so much cautious and painstaking execution . . . ," he wrote Henry Rogers as he was finishing it. "Possibly the book may not sell, but that is nothing—it was written for love." He wanted this one to constitute his bid for enduring fame as a great writer. He even tried to publish it anonymously so that his reputation as a comedian would not get in the way of having it taken seriously—but after the first few installments in *Harper's*, it was clear to everyone who the author was.

Twain probably went to his grave believing that *Personal Recollections of Joan of Arc* was his finest work. He was sustained in this view, moreover, by members of his family who were enthralled by the story as he read finished portions of it to them in the evenings. Genteel observers such as Mother Fairbanks also admired its moral tone and the unashamed idealism of the tale's heroine. On the other hand, numerous critics, both in the 1890s and since, have not seen it that way. Some complain about historical anachronisms or that Twain somehow invested Joan with the traits of a modern American girl; others object to the book's excessive sentimentality. Most agree, however, that in this, his only book in which a female occupies the central place, Twain embodies his view of the ideal woman. Some of her chief attributes were those generally applauded in Victorian society; Twain sees her as highly moral, modest, and virginal—a pure and innocent spirit surrounded by a hypocritical and depraved world. But Twain also portrays her as individualistic, courageous, and wise—a foe of injustice, a defender of the downtrodden who does not shrink before authority. She was, he thought, "perhaps the only entirely unselfish person whose name has a place in profane history." There are many who think that Twain's Joan was modeled on his daughter Susy, just turned twenty as he began to write Joan's story. Her father poured into his picture of his heroine not only Susy's physical attributes, but also the intelligence and independence, the ideals and eloquence and large sympathies that he saw and loved in his favorite child. (By this time, he had abandoned his earlier hesitations about granting women the right to vote and had moved to the view that their presence in political life would refine and purify a process that males had made sordid.)

Twain's final work of this period was the one most directly the result of his bankruptcy. With the utmost reluctance, he resorted to the detested old standby that had always been there when he needed money, a lecture tour. This time he agreed to a schedule that would carry him around the globe and that would produce another travel book based on the trip. Leaving Susy and Jean with Livy's sister Susan Crane, he, Livy, and Clara started their year-long journey in mid-July, 1895. The speaking began with daily appearances across the northern United States and Canada. The party boarded ship on August 23 and sailed west. Twain had hoped to revisit Hawaii, the paradise he remembered so fondly, but it was under a cholera quarantine when they arrived and they proceeded to Fiji. Then it was on to Australia, New Zealand, Ceylon (Sri Lanka), India, and southern Africa.

From South Africa the family sailed to England, arriving on July 31, 1896. At every stop, he packed the auditoriums and was accorded the enthusiastic reception of the celebrity that he was—a fame enhanced by the attention given to his brave struggle against debt. Despite bouts of bad health (painful carbuncles, rheumatism, a nagging cough, occasional exhaustion), and despite spending around eighty-five days at sea, Twain managed to give at least a hundred readings and lectures. As the fees came in, he dutifully sent them to Henry Rogers, who invested the money and began paying off his friend's debts. When the tour ended, the family rented a house in London and Twain sat down to write his book about the experience.

The manuscript, eventually titled *Following the Equator: A Journey Around the World*, was finished in May 1897, and the book appeared in November. Writing it was a joyless ordeal. He was tired, unwell, and in a bleak mood. "I wrote my last travel-book in hell," he told Howells, "but I let on, the best I could, that it was an excursion through heaven." He vowed that someday he would read it again, and if "its lying cheerfulness" fooled *him*, he would suppose that it fooled his readers. "How I did loathe that journey around the world!—except for the sea part and India." (He was quite enchanted by India, where he spent more than five months and saw much—thirty-three of the book's sixty-nine chapters were devoted to that part of the trip.) No doubt he had hoped to recapture the verve, the audacious humor, the captivating charm and fun of his earlier travel-books, *Innocents Abroad*, *Roughing It*, and *A Tramp Abroad*. But this time he proved incapable, for the most part, of bringing it off. "It seems halfhearted and tired," Philip Beidler has written, "because he was halfhearted and tired." Anecdotal, derivative, sometimes a little tedious, and too long (it was the longest book he ever wrote), *Following the Equator* was the least engaging of Twain's travel books. Nevertheless, both the reviews and the early sales were respectable, and the money went a long way toward helping Rogers pay the creditors.

In *Following the Equator*, Twain also used short aphorisms at the head of each chapter; these he labeled as coming from "Pudd'nhead Wilson's New Calendar." As before, some of these were deliciously sarcastic: "It takes your enemy and your friend, working together, to hurt you to the heart; the one to slander you and the other to get the news to you." "It could probably be shown by facts and figures that there is no distinctly native American criminal class except Congress." And, as before, some of them were darkly reflective of a pessimism and contempt for human nature that was becoming ever more common in Twain's pronouncements: "Pity is for the living, envy is for the dead." "Man is the only animal that blushes. Or needs to." "Each person is born with one possession which outvalues all his others—his last breath." Perhaps the bitter mood that these aphorisms reveal was partly attributable to the route of Twain's journey. The trip took him through large parts of the British Empire, and he saw firsthand some of the results of European imperialism. During the last third of the nineteenth century, all of Europe seemed intent on conquering or controlling vast areas of the earth's surface and of governing native peoples regardless of those peoples' traditions, cultures, or languages. In general, Twain held his tongue about this—partly because of all the empires in the world, the British was among the least pernicious, and partly because he hoped to sell some books in England and did not want to sour the possibility by a too strident criticism of imperial practices. But he did not like what he saw, and occasionally his displeasure shone through. "There are many humorous things in the world," he wrote in Chapter 21, "among them the white man's notion that he is less savage than the other savages." It was not necessarily that Twain admired pre-industrial cultures and peoples; it was just that he had come to the conclusion that those who governed them were no better. This was a theme to which he would shortly return, and when his own country got infected with imperial ambitions, he was to be unrestrained in his criticism.

By January 1898, Mark Twain—by virtue of his own super-human effort and the wise management of Henry Rogers—had paid off the last of his debts and was widely praised for the courage and sense of honor he had demonstrated in accomplishing that feat. He was still living in Europe and would not be ready to return to America for another two and a half years. He was now sixty-two years old and had a dozen years of life left to him. They would not be happy ones.

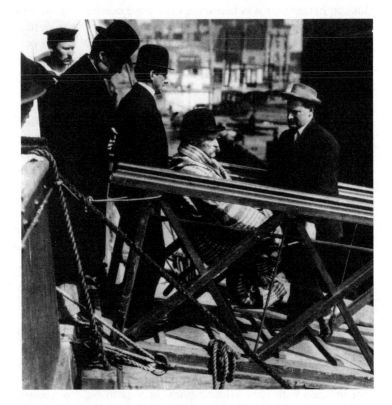

An aged and ailing Mark Twain is carried off a ship from Bermuda to
New York in April 1910. (Courtesy of The Bancroft Library.
University of California, Berkeley.)

At the End, Dark Despair

I

Ten years after the writer's death, Van Wyck Brooks began his book, *The Ordeal of Mark Twain*, with this sentence: "To those who are interested in American life and letters there has been no question of greater significance, during the last few years, than the pessimism of Mark Twain." That pessimism encompassed ideas and attitudes that absorbed Twain in his later years, but that were not always smoothly integrated or entirely consistent. Some of those beliefs had been present in his outlook for a long time and can be detected in his earlier fiction and essays. By the late 1890s, however, these dark views were no longer merely elements that complicated his writing; by the last decade of his life they dominated it.

Among the grim thoughts that contributed to his gloom was his conviction that free will was a delusion. He came to believe that each person's behavior was attributable either to a string of causes-and-effects that stretched back to the beginning of time, or to an inherited temperament over which no person had control, or to an oppressive "training" that determined each man and woman's every act and every belief. Added to his philosophic determinism was a withering contempt for human beings, an undisguised scorn for "the damned human race." At the same time, nevertheless, he could not stop accusing himself of terrible failures, delinquencies, and misdeeds. (Some analysts of his later ideas suggest that his determinism was a way for him to excuse his own imagined shortcomings—if we are merely machines acting out our predetermined destinies, then I am not to blame for the awful things I have done.) Into this jumble of ideas, Twain also sometimes speculated about whether life itself were real—perhaps all existence, which seems so tangible (and often so painful) was, in actuality, merely a dream. Nevertheless, despite his belief that all human actions are determined and that individuals are, therefore, not responsible for what they do, he still found considerable fault in the way things were going in America and the world, and he regularly erupted in furious anger at the individuals whose (supposedly foreordained) acts were bringing about this unhappiness.

Of course he had never been that much of an admirer of humans—particularly humans in groups. From the slack-jawed yokels duped by the fast-talking Colonel Sellers and the ignorant jurors who acquit Laura of murder in *The Gilded Age*, his view of men and women (but especially of men) was never starry-eyed. As time passed, however, denunciations of humanity became one of his stocks in trade. In an 1883 talk entitled "What is Happiness?" he presented his notion that men and women are machines directed entirely by outside forces beyond their control. In *Huckleberry Finn*, two years later, Twain included a scene where a village mob is ridiculed by the murderous Colonel Sherburn, its intended target; he tells them they are cowards pretending at bravery and advises them to "droop your tails and go home and crawl into a hole." The crowd quickly disperses. By the time Twain got to *Connecticut Yankee*, in 1889, he was a confirmed believer in the inability of people to overcome their "training." At one point in that novel, the evil queen Morgan I Fay blithely stabs to death a young page who accidentally brushed her while serving the wine. When the Boss suggests that this was a crime, she protests that it was not a crime because she intends to pay for the boy. The Boss, in a famous passage, explodes: "Oh, it was no use to waste sense on her. Training—training is everything; training is all there is *to* a person. . . . We have no thoughts of our own, no opinions of our own: they are transmitted to us, trained into us." Our characters, our actions, our ideas are all "atoms contributed by and inherited from, a procession of ancestors that stretches back a billion years. . . ."

If these depressing thoughts had been building up in Twain for some time, by the late 1890s, as he entered his sixties, his attacks on humanity grew increasingly bitter, unrestrained, and frequent.

His daughter Clara remembered the days in London in 1896, when her father indulged "the habit of vituperating the human race. . . . What started as formless criticism grew into a sinister doctrine. There was no hope for the human race because no appreciable improvement was possible in any individual." In his great short story, "The Man Who Corrupted Hadleyburg" (1899), Twain describes how the leading citizens of a town that had been boastful of its morality, are easily exposed as greedy liars. Twain attempted a systematic discussion of these views in "What Is Man?" a series of dialogues between a wise "Old Man" and an idealistic but naive "Young Man." He labored over these "conversations" for at least eight years, publishing a final version in 1906. In the first dialogue, Old Man explains about "Man the machine—man, the impersonal engine. Whatever a man is, is due to his *make*, and to the *influences* brought to bear upon it by his heredities, his habitat, his associations. He is moved, directed, COMMANDED, by *exterior* influences—*solely*. He *originates* nothing, himself—not even an opinion, not even a thought." Twain returned to these bleak themes obsessively in dozens of his late pieces, many of them so raw and desolate that he would not permit their publication while he was alive. In such works as "Corn Pone Opinions" (written in 1901, but not published until 1923), "The Five Boons of Life" (1902), "Was the World Made for Man?" (1903), "In the Animal's Court" (1905), "No. 44, The Mysterious Stranger" (written over a nine-year period culminating in 1908, and eventually appearing in a questionable version in 1916), "Letters from the Earth" (written in 1908, but not published until 1962), "The Turning Point of My Life" (1910), and many others, Mark Twain, the world-famous humorist, poured out his cynicism and anger, his despair and contempt, his pessimism.

Van Wyck Brooks, who wrote when American intellectuals were first encountering the teachings of Sigmund Freud, believed there was a psychological reason for Twain's gloom. Brooks argued that Twain possessed a raw elemental power, an enormous potential for creating enduring works of genius. But instead of using that gift, Twain squandered it. He was handicapped in his youth by the sterile atmosphere of small-town Missouri and the West, but hurt even more gravely by the pressure from his mother and then his wife to be respectable, genteel, and successful. Brooks believed that by the end of his life Twain had come to feel, perhaps unconsciously, that he had wasted his genius, that he had allowed his wife and friends like Howells to tame his innate power. He had spent his life timidly producing second-rate books for money, striving for shallow applause and middle-class gentility. This realization led to profound regret, bitterness, and melancholy, to a "deep malady of the soul. . . ." John Milton had long ago observed that some talents were "death to hide," and Brooks shared this belief: "Mark Twain's 'talent' was just so hidden. That bitterness of his was the effect of a certain miscarriage in his creative life, a balked personality, an arrested development of which he was himself almost totally unaware, but which for him destroyed the meaning of life."

Whatever one thinks of Brooks's explanation of Twain's gloomy final years (and numerous critics have disputed his thesis at several points), it is possible to theorize that other causes were also at work to produce the pessimism and hopelessness. No doubt his brush with financial disaster in the 1890s left its mark on his psyche. By 1900, thanks to Henry Rogers, his monetary affairs seemed to be once again on a healthy footing. In 1902, he probably earned around $100,000 in book sales, and his contract with Harper and Brothers, finalized the next year, guaranteed him at least $25,000 a year, for exclusive rights to his work. Livy's investments were also making a comeback after the depression of the 1890s, and she was probably worth close to $200,000. Nonetheless, the family felt the need to economize. In May 1903, they finally sold the Hartford place (where they had not lived for a dozen years) and tried to live frugally. On the other hand, Twain's calamitous experience with the typesetter had not ended his passion for speculation. In 1900, he jumped into a new investment called "Plasmon," a food supplement made from milk—he was sure it would cure indigestion, make people healthier, and end famines. He tried to interest Andrew Carnegie and Henry Rogers in the company. They thought not. Before it was over, Twain lost between $30,000 and $50,000 in the enterprise. He then invested $6,000 in the Spiral Pin Company, but that was also wasted money.

Twain's feelings of regret and his financial troubles may have been possible sources of his sour views, but they were probably not the most important reasons for his gloom. Two other causes loomed much larger in accounting for the darkness that characterized and clouded the author's final years.

II

His family was a source of constant anxiety. In August 1890, he got news that his mother, who was eighty-seven and living with Orion in Keokuk, had suffered a stroke. Twain hurried to Iowa. After rallying briefly, she died in late October, and her son boarded a train for the funeral in Hannibal. Then, less than a month later, Livy's mother, of whom Twain was very fond, died in Elmira. While at her bedside, he received the terrible word that his youngest daughter, Jean, age ten, was dreadfully ill. Leaving Livy with her failing mother, he rushed back to Hartford; it was the beginning of Jean's lifelong struggle against epilepsy. "I have fed so full on sorrows, these last weeks," Twain wrote Howells, "that I seem to have become hardened to them—benumbed." Half a dozen years later, in 1897, when the family was living in Venice, Twain's brother Orion died. "Notwithstanding his forever-recurring caprices and changes," Twain wrote in his *Autobiography*, "his principles were high, always high, and absolutely unshakable." In 1904, death came to Orion's widow Mollie, and a few months later, his sister Pamela—the last of the Clemens siblings—died in a Massachusetts sanitarium. Although Twain loved all of these family members and their loss touched him, their passing could not have been unexpected; Mollie was sixty-nine, Orion and Pamela were both in their seventies. But two other deaths in the family struck Twain with devastating force. He never got over them, and they contributed greatly to the despair he knew until the end of his own life.

On July 31, 1896, Twain, Livy, and their daughter Clara arrived in England, having completed at last that arduous year-long lecture tour undertaken to pay off the creditors. Susy and Jean, who had been left at Quarry Farm with Susan Crane, prepared to cross the ocean and join their parents. On August 4, a day before the girls were to depart, Twain and his wife received a cable from Livy's sister. There would be a small delay—the trip would have to be postponed for a week. A couple of days later another cable informed them that Susy, now at the Hartford house where she had gone to pack, was slightly ill. The family rushed to Southampton to return to the United States, but a third cable assured them that their daughter's recovery would be "long but certain." On the strength of that news, Twain stayed in England while Livy and Clara sailed home to look after Susy. By the time they were halfway across the ocean, Susy's condition was hopeless. In the last stages of incurable meningitis, she was fevered and delirious, wandering around the old Hartford house, scribbling irrational notes, unresponsive to any treatment. The Twichells hurried to the bedside, and Susan and Theodore Crane came with Jean from Elmira. Susy became blind, then lapsed into a coma, and on August 18, she died. She was twenty-four. Twain received the news before his wife. A cable, phrased as comfortingly as possible, came from Susan Crane (for whom Susy had been named): "Susy could not stand brain congestion and meningitis and was peacefully released to-day." Ten years later, dictating his *Autobiography*, he recalled, in a remarkable sentence, getting the news: "It is one of the mysteries of our nature that a man, all unprepared, can receive a thunder-stroke like that and live." Friends hastened to New York to break the news to Livy and Clara, but they already knew. Two days before landing, the captain had called Clara to his quarters and handed her a news dispatch. In his *Autobiography*, Twain, in more unforgettable words, wrote: "On the 23rd her mother and her sisters saw her laid to rest—she that had been our wonder and our worship."

He never fully recovered from the Susy's death. He had invested in her such pride, such admiration and hope, so much love. It was a love, he knew, she had returned in boundless measure. They had delighted in each other's company, played games and told stories together; she had written a juvenile "biography" of "papa" when she was fourteen. Naturally, he found a way to blame himself—if he had not so foolishly, so irresponsibly, fallen into bankruptcy, he and Livy would never have been separated from her and could have watched over her and prevented this calamity. Three days after her death, he wrote Livy, "I eat—because you wish it; I go on living—because you wish it; I play billiards, and billiards, & billiards, till I am ready to drop—to keep from going mad with grief & with resentful thinkings." From now on Christmas and Thanksgiving, her birthdays and the anniversaries of her death, were to be days of solemnity, mourning, and silence. And just as bad was to follow.

Of course Livy's health had been precarious for years, but her condition now began to deteriorate markedly. For a few years, the family wandered around Europe—England, Switzerland, Austria, Hungary, Sweden. They frequented various spas, hoping for relief from both Livy's heart disease and Jean's worsening epilepsy. In October 1900, they returned to America, first to a house in New York City, then to a mansion overlooking the Hudson River in Riverdale, New York. For the next two years, Twain endured the double misery of seeing Livy's inability to recover her health and Jean's ever-worsening attacks. Then, starting in August 1902, Livy suffered a series of horrifying onslaughts—struggling to breathe, heart beating wildly. The doctors, fearing that her husband's presence would overexcite her, ordered that he be with her for only a few minutes each day, but he sneaked occasional extra visits and slipped love notes under her door.

She fluctuated between life and death until the middle of 1903. Then she improved enough to want to return to Italy, where they had once been exquisitely happy. The doctors felt that a warmer climate might help her, and in October, she and her husband, together with Clara and Jean and a collection of secretaries and nurses, made the trip. The experience was not a happy repetition of the former stay—their first landlady was terrible and unfeeling, the weather was dreary, Twain was now restricted to daily visits of two minutes. At last, on June 5, 1904, Livy's long agony came quietly to an end. The next day Twain described the final moments and his own desolation in a message to Howells. "Last night at 9.20 I entered Mrs. Clemens's room to say the usual good-night—& she was dead! tho' no one knew it. She had been cheerfully talking, a moment before. She was sitting up in bed—she had not lain down for months. . . . They supposed she had fainted, & they were holding the oxygen pipe to her mouth, expecting to revive her. I bent over her & looked in her face, & I think I spoke—I was surprised and troubled that she did not notice me. Then we understood, & our hearts broke. How poor we are to-day! But how thankful I am that her persecutions are ended. I would not call her back if I could." And before closing the letter to his friend, one last thought: "I am tired & old; I wish I were with Livy."

III

For some people, such heartbreaking tragedies might have been cushioned somewhat by the consolations and hopes offered by religious faith. For Mark Twain this was not a possibility. He had traveled a long way from his mother's stern Presbyterian beliefs. His brief flirtation with Christianity, during his courtship of Livy and for the first few months of their marriage, while probably sincere, had not been permanent—indeed, instead of his piety increasing, hers went into decline. Nonetheless, throughout his life Twain was obsessed with religion. At every stage it enters his published work, his unpublished manuscripts, his notebook jottings, his private letters. He is far from consistent in these myriad statements, but some of his views emerge with fair clarity, and they are not friendly toward religion.

"I believe in God the Almighty," he wrote in his notebook in 1887. But he quickly followed that declaration with sentiments that would have given little comfort to the faithful: "I do not believe He ever sent a message to man by anybody, or delivered one to him by word of mouth, or made Himself visible to mortal eyes at any time in any place. I believe that the Old and New Testaments were imagined and written by man, and that no line in them was authorized by God, much less inspired by Him. I do not believe in special providences." He goes on to ridicule the sadistic notion of eternal suffering in hell, the idea that good and evil will be rewarded or punished after death, and the idea that God is the author of morality: "It needed no God to come down out of heaven to tell men that murder and theft and the other immoralities were bad. . . ."

Twain alternated between two depictions of God. Sometimes He was portrayed as the majestic Creator of the immense universe, hurling out vast galaxies by the power of his imperial Will—and entirely indifferent to the petty doings of puny mankind. In the first of his *Letters from the Earth*, Satan offers as evidence of the "insanity" of human beings the fact that Man "blandly and in all sincerity calls himself the 'noblest work of God'. . . . Moreover—if I may put another strain upon you—he thinks he is the Creator's pet. He believes the Creator is proud of him; he even believes the Creator loves him; has a passion for him; sits up nights to admire him. . . . He prays to Him, and thinks He listens. . . . I must put one more strain upon you," Satan tells his fellow-angels, "he thinks he is going to heaven!" At other times, however, Twain depicts the God of the Old Testament as a vindictive and cruel tyrant, all *too* concerned with mankind. This is the God who made Man with all his crippling weaknesses and then decided to punish those weaknesses with terrible penalties. He curses humanity with terrible diseases for no good reason. He commands the slaughter of innocents and even, as in Noah's flood, murders the innocents Himself. Twain describes the terrifying scene as the waters rise, the lamentations "of the multitude of weeping fathers and mothers and frightened little children who were clinging to the wave-washed rocks in the pouring rain and lifting imploring prayers to an All-Just and All-Forgiving and All-Pitying Being. . . ." Twain offers, as more evidence of human insanity, that while making God responsible for all those diseases and miseries "which he could have prevented," the Christian "blandly calls him Our Father!" The human being "equips the Creator with every trait that goes to the making of a fiend, and then arrives at the conclusion that a fiend and a father are the same thing! . . . What do you think of the human mind? I mean, in case you think there is a human mind."

But Twain's denunciation of the God of the Bible was only the start of his heresy. He knew the Bible well and mocked it constantly. In many of his later essays such as "Little Bessie," "Papers of the Adam Family," "Bible Teaching and Religious Practice," he denounced the "upward of a thousand lies," the preposterous stories, the terrible punishments meted out for trivial crimes or for innocently acting out the natural impulses (including the sexual impulses) of human nature. Twain rejected the notion of the divinity of Christ ("It is all just a fairy tale like the idea of Santa Claus"), and ridiculed the idea that God would kill Himself on the Cross, calling it a suicide. As far as the message of Jesus was concerned, Twain was inconsistent.

He sometimes thought that Christ's teachings were "just, merciful, charitable, benevolent, forgiving, and full of sympathy for the suffering of mankind." At other times, however, he argued that Jesus "invented hell" and condemned to eternal torture those who did not believe in Him, including those born before He came to earth; for this, Twain wrote, the "palm for malignity must be granted to Jesus."

When it came to organized religion, he was (despite his friendship with several ministers) unequivocally denunciatory. In book after book, he treated with derision the hypocrisies of the church, the dishonesty of sanctimonious clergymen, the duplicity of Bible-thumping politicians, the pathetic gullibility of simple, everyday believers, the boredom of church, and the horrors of Sunday school. No denomination escaped his scorn, but he was particularly harsh toward two of them. From his youth upward, he bore a distinct animosity against Roman Catholicism. Like many other nineteenth-century American Protestants, Twain saw Rome as the center of decadence, corruption, and luxury extracted at the expense of the ignorant poor. From *Innocents Abroad*, with its ridicule of the follies and injustices of Catholic Europe, through *Connecticut Yankee*, where the Church is the resolute enemy of the Boss's schemes for progress, Twain saw Catholicism as a pernicious force in history. Whether his portrayal of the Catholic saint, Joan of Arc, was, in reality, the portrayal of a modern Protestant (as some critics have suggested), he insisted that Joan's bitterest enemies were the entrenched and evil Church hierarchy. And if he denounced an ancient European faith, he also trained his guns on a young American one. In 1907, he published *Christian Science*—partly a humorous attack on that faith's central belief that the pain and sickness of the physical world were somehow unreal and that only the spirit was real. Mostly, however, the book was a devastating and detailed polemic against Mary Baker Eddy, the denomination's founder and head, whom Twain portrayed as dishonest, greedy, unintellectual, and tyrannical. Although he himself had some sympathy toward faith-healing and had experimented with it on himself and members of his family, he expressed the fear in his book that Mrs. Eddy's religion was spreading its pernicious influence and endangering the nation.

IV

If the cataclysms that befell his family—unalloyed as they were by any comforting belief in a kindly Deity or a sympathetic religious community—were an additional source of Twain's slide into pessimism and melancholy, they were not the only one. He was also drawn increasingly to the conviction that his country, and much of the world along with it, was going straight to hell. "I have been reading the morning paper," he wrote to Howells in April 1899. "I do it every morning—well knowing that I shall find in it the usual depravities and basenesses & hypocrisies & cruelties that make up Civilization, & cause me to put in the rest of the day pleading for the damnation of the human race. I cannot seem to get my prayers answered, yet I do not despair."

The evils that he and Warner had decried in *The Gilded Age* a quarter century earlier had not disappeared; indeed, they had intensified. By the start of the new century, it was apparent to nearly every observer that industrial conditions in the United States had grown more troubling. As the depression of the 1890s receded, American business entered upon an orgy of mergers, trust-building, and high finance. These developments greatly expanded the power of corporate executives and leading bankers. Before long, large parts of the American economy were in the hands of a few gigantic trusts and their leaders. Meanwhile, as factories became larger, machinery grew more complex and dangerous, and work itself more impersonal, repetitive, and unrewarding, labor conditions worsened faster than labor unions could effectively ameliorate them. Almost every week, one of those reporters whom Theodore Roosevelt, in 1906, had labeled "muckrakers" revealed some new corrupt business practice or some fresh and sinister collusion between government and business. When Twain moved to New York City in 1900, he saw with his own eyes the work of the notorious Tammany political machine.

It was not merely the old evils of business and politics that bothered him. He was also appalled by the treatment of African Americans. The post-Reconstruction explosion of vicious exploitation, disenfranchisement, and segregation was bad enough (and some think that these practices were one of his chief targets in *Pudd'nhead Wilson*), but the wave of brutal lynchings that took place, especially after the mid-1880s, convinced Twain, that the white South was hopelessly barbaric and backward. He was also angered by the turn that American foreign policy took after 1898. He had initially favored the Spanish-American War, seeing it as a noble attempt to rescue the people of Cuba from Spanish tyranny. But when, in the war's aftermath, the country embarked upon an imperial policy, acquiring overseas territories and imposing its authority over native populations, Twain was outraged. The subjugation of the Philippine Islands seemed to him a particularly flagrant and inexcusable exercise of national arrogance. Of course Mark Twain was far from being the only old man who thought that the world was in decline, but the list of his grievances against modern practices must surely have contributed to his gloom.

Although he did not remain silent about these evils, Twain never subscribed to a particular philosophy of social reform; he never became a disciple of Karl Marx or Eugene Debs, never joined hands with the followers of Henry George or Edward Bellamy, two extremely popular contemporary advocates of reform schemes. He lived long enough to see the start of what became American Progressivism, but remained unpersuaded that human beings were capable of reforming either their society or themselves. He had little but derision for that gaudy symbol of both American imperialism and American reform, Theodore Roosevelt. "Mr. Roosevelt is the Tom Sawyer of the political world. . . ," he remarked to Andrew Carnegie; "always showing off; always hunting for a chance to show off . . . he would go to Halifax for half a chance to show off, and he would go to hell for a whole one." To Joe Twichell he was not so restrained: "[I]n fairness we ought to keep in mind that Theodore, as a statesman and politician, is insane and irresponsible."

Instead of enlisting with others, Twain confined his displeasure with the direction of affairs to what he did best—pointed barbs, spoken and written, aimed at what he regarded as the follies and injustices of the modern world. He sharpened his attack on certain business tycoons. He may have liked Carnegie and loved Henry Rogers, but he had no use for Rogers' employer: "Satan twaddling sentimental silliness to a Sunday-school would be no burlesque upon John D. Rockefeller," he wrote. Every time that avaricious man steps before his Bible class, "he strikes the utmost limit of grotesqueness." The department store pioneer John Wanamaker was "a butter-mouthed hypocrite"; Jay Gould was "the mightiest disaster which has ever befallen this country"; Cornelius Vanderbilt should "go surprise the whole country by doing something right." Nor did Twain's long animosity toward politics and politicians slacken. He supported the reform candidate for mayor of New York City in 1901, made anti-Tammany speeches, and published a letter in the *New York Times* in 1903: "I should think that any humane and honest person would rather be convicted of one robbery and one murder than become a cold and deliberate confederate in wholesale robbery and wholesale murder by voting a Tammany ticket."

Regarding the treatment of African Americans, Twain was, by the end of his life, fully committed to more just relations between the races. In addition to his obvious arguments against slavery and discrimination in *Huckleberry Finn, Connecticut Yankee*, and *Pudd'nhead Wilson*, he spoke out against the evils of race hatred and mob violence. On the other hand, while his most forthright statement against the horrors of lynching, "The United States of Lyncherdom," was written in 1901, he did not allow its publication; it did not appear until a dozen years after his death. He had considered writing a whole book on lynching, but backed off when he thought it might hurt his reputation (and sales) in the South.

It was in his statements against American imperialism that Twain's outrage reached its fullest expression. He fulminated against the claims of the expansionists that they were motivated by a desire to bestow civilization and Christianity upon native peoples. Such claims, he charged, were flimsy and hypocritical rationalizations for the traditional motives of power, territory, and greed. He had seen, on his world tour, that imperialism was designed to capture valuable raw materials and provide markets for the sale of industrial goods. And now, Americans were behaving like Europeans in their grasping exploitation. His fullest indictment, directed at European as well as American imperialism, was "To the Person Sitting in Darkness," an essay published in early 1901, and read widely when the Anti-Imperialist League distributed more than 100,000 copies. After some missionaries objected to his allegation that they were willing agents of the imperialist enterprise, he struck back in a second article, "To My Missionary Critics." These essays, and other statements against imperialism, have given Twain the status of a prophet among modern foes of American expansionist policies. On the related issue of war, Twain was not always consistent. Sometimes he argued that wars fought for freedom and against tyranny were justifiable (like those waged by Joan of Arc or to free the enslaved Cubans). Yet in "The Mysterious Stranger," Satan explains that all wars, without exception, have been unjust and unnecessary. Twain's best known work on war is "The War Prayer," written in 1905, but not published until 1923. "It was a time of great and exalting excitement," Twain begins. "The country was up in arms, the war was on, in every breast burned the holy fire of patriotism. . . ." At a solemn church service, the minister was offering a fervent prayer for victory when suddenly an aged stranger in a white robe approached the altar. He tells the shocked congregation that he comes from the throne of God to inform them of *everything* they had just asked for, the unspoken half of their plea for victory: "O Lord our God, help us to tear their soldiers to bloody shreds with our shells; help us to cover their smiling fields with the pale forms of their patriot dead; help us to drown the thunder of the guns with the shrieks of their wounded writhing in pain. . . . help us to wring the hearts of their unoffending widows with unavailing grief; help us to turn them out roofless with their little children to wander unfriended the wastes of their desolated land in rags and hunger. . . ."

V

Mark Twain's life, after Livy's death, was a mixture of public adulation and private unhappiness, of endless billiards (sometimes until 2 or 3 A.M.) and ceaseless movement, of bitter polemical writing, loneliness, and steadily declining health. After returning from Italy and seeing Livy buried in Elmira next to her infant son and Susy, he spent that summer in a cottage in the Berkshires. He then leased an ornate house on Fifth Avenue in New York City and installed some of his old Hartford furniture—including the big bed in which he was to spend much of his time writing, smoking, talking to visitors, and being endlessly photographed. During the three years that this was his official residence, the restless Twain spent two summers in New Hampshire, six weeks in England, and a good deal of time on Henry Rogers' yacht; he also made three trips to Bermuda. In late 1906, he asked Howells' architect son to design him a new home near Albert Bigelow Paine's place in Redding, Connecticut. In June 1908, he moved into that spacious and comfortable house (which he had never actually seen until he arrived) and named it "Stormfield," after the colorful sailor whose "Visit to Heaven" Twain labored on for almost half a century. Mrs. Rogers surprised him with a housewarming gift: a new billiard table. Stormfield was to be the nomad's last home.

His family now consisted only of Clara and Jean. Both suffered mental and physical problems, and both spent time in sanitariums and rest homes. Clara, who underwent a mental collapse after Livy's death and did not see her father for an entire year, recovered but spent little time with him. She was soon absorbed in her vocal career, studying in Europe and then performing professionally. Jean, meanwhile, fell deeper and deeper into epilepsy, depression, and mental instability. After attempting to find a cure in Germany, she joined her father at Stormfield in April 1909. For companionship, Twain relied on Paine, frequent visits with Rogers until the magnate died in May 1909, and a few with Howells. In a development both touching and sad, he started, in 1906, when he was seventy-two, to "collect" a dozen little girls, aged ten to sixteen. He formed them into his "Aquarium Club" and called them his "angelfish." He wrote some mock membership rules and over the next years wrote hundreds of playful letters to these girls. He enjoyed it when they and their mothers came for visits, went with him to concerts, listened to his talk, took walks, played cards. It is a measure of his nostalgia for the time when his own girls were young, and an indication of how lonely he was that in 1908 he called the Club his "life's chief delight."

He was able to do some literary work during these last years, some of it published, but most of it not. There appeared a tribute to Howells, some more comedy about Adam and Eve, that denunciation of Mary Baker Eddy. In 1909, he published his last book, a half-comic, half-serious entry in the ongoing argument about who "actually" wrote the plays credited to Shakespeare; Twain's contribution, *Is Shakespeare Dead?*, took the now discredited position that those works were really written by Francis Bacon. Mostly he labored on works that would not appear until long after his death, when, he said, he would at last be free to say what was really on his mind. He worked on "Letters from the Earth" and "The Mysterious Stranger," but his main concern was his *Autobiography*. He had been putting down random reminiscences since the 1880s, but when Paine received his permission to write a biography, Twain started to dictate episodes from his life. He produced these reminiscences in wildly disconnected order, talking to Paine and a stenographer about whatever occurred to him: one day it might be some memory of walking in Austria with Twichell; the next day it might be an episode in Virginia City; the day after that, a boyhood memory of Hannibal. He made more than 250 such dictations between 1906 and 1909, and scholars have made several attempts to put them together in a more or less coherent fashion.

There were certainly some gratifying moments in Mark Twain's last years. He continued to revel in the attention of much of the world. His every move, his every clever remark, every aspect of his personal life was devoured by the press. He was photographed constantly, and countless cartoons, caricaturing his striking face, his luxuriant hair, appeared in dozens of newspapers. His face was among the most universally and immediately recognizable on the planet. He had the satisfaction of seeing the success of his lobbying efforts on behalf of the reform of copyright law. He was still deluged with requests for one of his famous talks, and he occasionally agreed; but now he did it only for good causes and free of charge. In 1907, Oxford University awarded him an honorary doctorate, and he crossed the Atlantic one last time to receive it. It was his fourth honorary degree; he already held two from Yale and a third, in 1902, from the University of Missouri. When he went to receive the Missouri degree, he paid a visit to Hannibal that he knew would be his last and, uncharacteristically, broke down as he bid farewell to the townspeople who had gathered to see their most famous son. But the degree from Oxford was quite special. It was, he thought, "a loftier distinction than is conferrable by any other university on either side of the ocean, and is worth twenty-five of any other, whether foreign or domestic." During the weeks he spent in England he was greeted and dined and interviewed and praised extravagantly everywhere he went. Best of all, the Oxford honor came with a splendid red academic robe. Twain loved wearing that robe, and when Clara got married in October 1909, he appeared at the ceremony wearing it. This recognition, these honors and moments of satisfaction, were welcome counterpoints to the general unhappiness that typified the old man's final years.

Fate had one more cruelty waiting for him. On Christmas Eve, 1909, eight months after she had come to live with her father at Stormfield, Jean suffered an epileptic fit and died in her bathtub. She was twenty-nine. The next day Twain went to her bedroom and saw that it was filled with the presents she had wrapped for the servants and friends. They were not labeled. "The hands are forever idle that would have labeled them today." Then he went to his own room and wrote a moving and beautiful few pages about her and about how, after her long absence "shut up in sanitariums," he had been getting reacquainted with her. And then, heartbreaking lines that reveal his feelings about life and death: "Would I bring her back to life if I could do it? I would not. If a word would do it, I would beg for strength to withhold the word. And I would have the strength; I am sure of it. In her loss I am almost bankrupt, and my life is a bitterness, but I am content: for she has been enriched with the most precious of all gifts—that gift which makes all other gifts mean and poor—death." When he had finished writing, he carried the pages to Paine and told him that he was finished with writing and that the words about Jean should be the final chapter of his *Autobiography*.

His health had been bothersome for years and growing worse, but at the start of 1910, it was evident that his days were few. He had joked about his own death for years and planned elaborate pretended obituaries and elaborate funerals. He was still joking about it now, even as the chest pains came more frequently and the weakness grew more debilitating. "While I am not ruggedly well, I am not ill enough to excite the undertaker." He went to Bermuda one final time in January, but three months later he arranged to go home, telling Paine that he did not want to end his life there. Paine hurried down to help him get home. He was in tremendous pain by the time they lifted him off the boat and carried him into his house on April 12. Clara and her husband rushed home; she sang songs to him as he slipped in and out of coherency. He died on April 21. His body was taken to a church in New York City where Joe Twichell waited on the altar and choked through the appropriate words; then it was carried to Elmira and laid beside Livy and Langdon and Susy and Jean. Everywhere in the world where men and women knew books, there was heartfelt mourning. Halley's comet flashed serenely across the night sky, apparently indifferent to the passing of an esteemed and unique spirit.

Epilogue

I

When it came to guessing about how long his fame would endure, Mark Twain was (as usual) ambivalent. Sometimes, he was capable of a boisterous, if jocular, confidence. In September 1906, for example, he decided to let the *North American Review* publish some chapters from his *Autobiography*. He told readers of the magazine that "I intend that this autobiography shall become a model for all future autobiographies when it is published, after my death, and I also intend that it shall be read and admired a good many centuries because of its form and method. . . ." He reported that his old friend Howells had come for a visit the day before and that he had told Howells that "this autobiography of mine would live a couple of thousand years without any effort and would then take a fresh start and live the rest of the time." On other occasions, however, he was not quite so sure. "Fame is a vapor; popularity an accident," he wrote in his notebook. "The only earthly certainty is oblivion." In a fragment called "The Secret History of Eddypus," begun in 1901 but never finished, he wrote: "We struggle, we rise, we tower in the zenith a brief and gorgeous moment, with the adoring eyes of the nations upon us, then the lights go out, oblivion closes around us, our glory fades and vanishes, a few generations drift by, and naught remains but a mystery and a name."

It is, of course, not possible to determine which of these estimates represented Twain's actual view. Perhaps the first was his hope speaking and the second his fear. Perhaps he sometimes truly believed that his fame would endure and, at other times, truly believed that his reputation would fade and vanish once a few generations had drifted by. But it has now been a full century since Mark Twain's death, and it appears—at least for now—that his fame is in no danger of disappearing.

II

While the other celebrated American authors of his generation have tended to float off into deepening obscurity, Mark Twain has somehow retained his enormous popularity. Those writers with whom he shared the stage and who have been most highly regarded by critics and literary historians—William Dean Howells, Henry James, Jack London, Edith Wharton, Stephen Crane, Walt Whitman, Louisa May Alcott, Bret Harte, Herman Melville—are today read mostly by specialists or college students in literature courses. The names of the most popular writers of the late nineteenth century, the writers of that day's "best sellers," are now largely forgotten. Yet Twain manages to keep his hold on the imaginations and affections of readers around the world. This fact is especially noteworthy because he has not been, for a long while now, that visible and charismatic presence whose daily doings and pointed comments on current events attracted and enthralled so many of his contemporaries.

By any measure, Mark Twain's abiding popularity sets him quite apart from virtually all other American writers. Since 2000 there have been at least fifty books published with his name in their titles; they have ranged from superb full-length biographies to intense studies of some aspect of his work or some part of his life. There are now at least half a dozen sizable "encyclopedias" or "companions" or "handbooks" devoted entirely to him. In the last decade alone there have appeared hundreds of articles, master's theses, and dissertations on some aspect of Twain's life or work, and three scholarly journals—the *Mark Twain Journal*, the *Twainian*, and *The Mark Twain Annual*—are devoted exclusively to studies related to him. But it is not only the scholars who exhibit continuing interest. *Bowker's Books in Print* lists around 250 editions of one or another part of his work, a sure indication that there remains a lively market for his writing among everyday Americans. *Tom Sawyer*, *Huckleberry Finn*, *Connecticut Yankee*, *Pudd'nhead Wilson*, and *The Prince and the Pauper* were all presented as silent movies and have been remade regularly over the years—including in cartoon form. Some of Twain's short stories have also been transformed into film. There have been musical adaptations of *Huckleberry Finn* and *Connecticut Yankee*, and an operetta based on "The Jumping Frog of Calavaras County." His books and stories have been regular features on radio and television, and today there are numerous audiotapes available. Entering "Mark Twain" on YouTube results in hundreds of entries. For years there have been Twain "impersonators," the best known and most enduring of them being Hal Holbrook, whose one-man show, "Mark Twain Tonight," began in 1959 and resulted in a popular recording. In 2001, the famous filmmaker Ken Burns released a widely watched documentary covering Twain's life. In short, there seems to be little danger of Mark Twain's fame vanishing—or even fading—in the foreseeable future.

III

It is relatively simple to document Twain's enduring popularity, but somewhat more challenging to account for it. How much weight, for example, should be given to his striking physical appearance? It is certain that people who could never identify a portrait of Howells or James or Harte can instantly recognize him; indeed, his face is more familiar to Americans than those of most of our presidents. Does that moustache, that wild hair, that white suit bestow upon him a permanent presence, an illusion of acquaintanceship, a familiarity that contributes to his durability in the American psyche? (People who know very few details about the life or actual policies of Abraham Lincoln can nonetheless feel an admiration and an affection for him based largely on the familiarity of his face. This is not exactly what Howells meant when he called his friend "the Lincoln of our literature," but the parallel is worth considering.)

Surely, part of Mark Twain's continuing renown is due to the fact that he has always appealed to different sorts of readers. He has, for a century, commanded the regard and loyalty of at least three groups of devotees—three communities of readers who, in the end, love him for different reasons (and may not have much in common besides their affection for him). One group consists of those who have responded to his portrayals of a youthful and more innocent America. Many of them, one supposes, were first introduced to Tom and Huck when they were children. They see Twain as the chief chronicler, not only of the antics of boys, but also of a simpler, happier, more congenial nation—a nation of rural settings, neighborly villages, and a closeness to nature. He brings into consciousness the picture of an America before big cities with their smoke and their factories and their wretched tenements, and he lets us recall the spaciousness of the country, the freedom, the possibility of rafting down the great river, hiding out on some island, heading out for the Territory. He helps us remember a time in our history when an unschooled lad could pilot a steamboat or head west on a stagecoach to look for silver. To some extent, such readers are able to preserve the nostalgia only by being willing to minimize—to regard as being somehow alien to the "real" America—the violence, the feuding, the chicanery and villainy, the hypocritical religion and human slavery that Twain also included in his portrayals of that earlier time.

A second set of admirers is made up of those who see Twain as one of America's greatest humorists, the man who, by virtue of his flashing wit, regaled in laughter generations around the globe. He was the comic genius who produced those priceless sketches of jumping frogs, tourists pillaging the Holy Land, knights in armor riding in on bicycles, Beriah Sellers hatching some preposterous scheme. He told about sitting on the clothes of bathing Hawaiian maidens in order to guard against theft and about his military service in an outfit whose specialty was retreating; he showed how a couple of con-men befuddled the Arkansas yokels and how a sly youngster got a fence whitewashed. He skewered James Fenimore Cooper and John D. Rockefeller and Michelangelo and Mary Baker Eddy and romantic novels and sentimental poetry and recitation-day at school and the German language. He was forever flinging off those hilarious one-liners that put the nation into uproarious laughter: "golf is a good walk spoiled"; "the report of my death was an exaggeration"; "we all grumble about the weather, but nothing is done about it"; "France has neither winter nor summer nor morals"; "it is by the goodness of God that in our country we have those three unspeakably precious things: freedom of speech, freedom of conscience, and the prudence never to practice either of them." Nothing was out of bounds for his relentless joking—the ignorance of the rube, the pretensions of the sophisticate, the foibles of the author himself. And for some of his admirers, it is this irrepressible humor that is Mark Twain's most precious trait and the chief reason for their devotion to him.

Twain has also gathered a third set of admirers among those who have been drawn to the boldness and honesty of his social philosophy, his aesthetic judgments, his political barbs. True, sometimes worry about future book sales or sometimes the inhibitions of Livy or Howells led him to hold his tongue. As his views grew more radical and cynical, moreover, he increasingly decided to postpone publication of some outrageous piece of social commentary until he was safely dead. ("I speak from the grave rather than with my living tongue for a good reason," he began his *Autobiography*, "I can speak thence freely.") It was not his prudence that was particularly remarkable, however; it was his willingness, on so many occasions, to defy public opinion and to give fearless expression to what was on his mind. In any case, as time has passed the distinction between what he said while alive and what was revealed after his death has largely evaporated, and his assaults on conventional opinion have endeared him to numerous readers—especially, one suspects, those who tend to agree with his views. He ventured where many others were too timid to go. He withheld his awe from those paintings of the Old Masters and scorned those pious pilgrims to the Holy Land. He did not hesitate to lampoon the Holy Bible or to criticize the Almighty Creator or to belittle organized religion. He had no illusions about the nobility of the human race. He assailed injustice when he saw it—injustice toward the poor, toward the working class, toward the Chinese in California and African Americans in the South, toward the native victims of imperialist greed. To him the aroused patriotism of a belligerent populace was an instrument of moral blindness and reckless cruelty, something to be feared. Politicians could expect no mercy from him, either individually or as a class, and their policies, domestic or foreign, were for him just so many ready targets. And this irreverence, this sharp-eyed, sharp-tongued criticism, this merciless ridicule of human folly have also drawn to him a community of loyal followers.

The common denominator for all these devotees, of course, is Mark Twain's masterful way with words. Whether his readers are attracted to him primarily for his capacity to stir nostalgia or out of a love of his wit or a sympathy with his unorthodoxy, they are drawn by his incomparable talent for expression. Whether he was writing lyrical descriptions of nature, suspenseful episodes in fiction, raucous comedy, or vitriolic polemic, he had a talent for striking precisely the right tone. He knew exactly the right word and was not shy about inventing a new one if he had to. He fearlessly transformed adjectives into adverbs and nouns into verbs—in the late 1930s, two scholars found around 4,000 words that Twain was the first to introduce in print. He was endowed with an uncanny ear for the English language, especially as that language was spoken and heard by Americans. For someone whose formal schooling ended when he was twelve years old, this is the great unexplainable miracle of his genius. No doubt part of it is attributable to his intelligence, his endless curiosity, that legendary memory he honed as a young pilot on the Mississippi. Some of it, surely, is attributable to his long career as a journalist: the habits of close observation, the constant need to convert observations and ideas into words by means of writing, the daily practice in composition required by that profession. But even after the possible causes for his literary wizardry are duly proposed and enumerated, so unique and monumental a gift remains essentially mysterious, never entirely explicable.

IV

Finally, there was something about Mark Twain's humanity that touched people throughout the country and gained him their affection. And it was *not* his certitude, the unfailing usefulness of his teaching, any sort of reputation he had as a moral guide to the society in which Americans found themselves after the Civil War. It was, just as much, his loveable fallibility, his uncertainty, his inconsistency and ambivalence. In common with many thousands of his contemporaries, there were crucial questions he could never quite decide. Like them, he loved the natural world, but spent large parts of his mature life in big cities. Like them, he was fascinated by the potential ability of science and technology to bestow conveniences and enhance life, but he had his doubts—and serious ones—about what the rush to machinery implied for valued traditional ways of life. Like them, he indulged himself in his luxuries (his good cigars, his expensive clothes and big houses and up-to-date gadgets, his elaborate vacations and endless travel), and at the same time there was always something in him that remembered small town life fondly and longed for the simplicity of Hannibal. He loved the crowds and wanted his privacy. He was inexorably drawn to business ventures and always knew that such ventures were filled with peril. He ridiculed religion and hung around with clergymen; he ridiculed businessmen and liked to spend time with Henry Rogers. He was hypnotized by money and went to extraordinary lengths to get it, and he always understood the dangers that its pursuit posed to individuals and to civilizations. In short, he could never quite decide about the modern world, never quite resolve whether it was better to be on the raft or up in the pilot house.

It would be a mistake, however, to think that it was only to the Americans of the late nineteenth and early twentieth century that he spoke. Are those of us alive a hundred years after his death any less troubled by the things that troubled him? Are we too not torn by our addiction to modern technologies and an anxiety about what those technologies mean to the world of nature, to the future of our planet? Are we any less devoted than he and his Gilded Age contemporaries to the pursuit of private wealth? Are we any less nervous about how that single-minded quest shapes our characters, stunts our feelings of community, affects our national politics and policies? To whatever extent Mark Twain himself navigated through these enduring tensions and put these difficult questions into lasting words, he will remain one of America's most treasured writers. In his life and in his writing he revealed important truths about his age—and also about ours.

Study and Discussion Questions

Chapter 1

1. In what ways did growing up in small, rural settings favorably influence Mark Twain's career? What attributes of this upbringing presented obstacles to potential success?

2. In what positive and negative ways did John Marshall Clemens influence his son during their brief acquaintance?

3. Twain's first contact with African Americans came under the harsh conditions of American slavery. How might a person's initial observations of African Americans in that unjust condition shape his or her views of race?

4. What were Mark Twain's first experiences of the world of nature? How did they contrast with the bustling world of village life?

Chapter 2

1. What can we learn about American society during this period from the fact that an uneducated lad in his early twenties could rise to the prestigious position of a steamboat pilot?

2. What were the principal legacies gained by Twain as a result of his training and experiences as a pilot?

3. In Twain's best-known writing, the Mississippi River occupies an important role. What did the great river mean to Twain— both as a boy growing up on its banks and as the master of a riverboat?

4. What can we learn about American ideals of equality and informality from the strange career of the Marion Rangers in the opening days of the Civil War?

Chapter 3

1. The American West has sometimes been depicted as the hatching place for the most important and lasting values in the American character. What values did Twain encounter on the frontier and how did he respond to them?

2. What were the chief characteristics of Twain's writing as a Nevada newspaperman? Why did these traits emerge? What do they tell us about the cultural values and tastes of the mining regions of the American West?

3. How did Twain's encounters with Artemus Ward and Bret Harte affect him?

Chapter 4

1. What does Twain's experience tell us about the cultural relations between the settled and urbanized East and the frontier American West?

2. Why did Twain's story of the jumping frog receive such a sensational reception? What can we infer from its popularity about the state of American literature at the time of its publication?

3. Describe the contrast that Twain saw between life in San Francisco and life in Hawaii.

4. What factors account for Twain's enormous success as a lecturer?

Chapter 5

1. What does the ambitious plan to mount the very first tourist expedition to Europe and the Middle East tell us about the state of American culture and of American cultural aspirations after the Civil War?

2. How did Twain and his friends differ from the typical "pilgrim" on board the *Quaker City*? What larger class, educational, and generational divisions within American society do these differences reflect?

3. What can we learn about Twain's character from observing his relationship to fellow-passenger Mary Mason Fairbanks?

4. Why did average Americans reading Twain's letters from abroad find them so admirable and delightful? What does their reaction tell us about the attitudes of Americans toward the rest of the world?

Chapter 6

1. What can we learn about Twain's view of women from his infatuation with Livy Langdon? In what ways do her attitudes and behavior exemplify the ideal of Victorian womanhood?

2. What does Twain's arduous attempt to win over Livy and her family reveal about nineteenth-century patterns of upper-middle-class courtship?

3. How did Twain's experience in Washington, D.C., shape and reinforce his view of American politics? Did the fact that he came to the nation's capital at the moment when he did shape his attitudes?

4. What does Twain's sharp bargaining for the publication of his travel letters indicate both about American publishing and about his own character?

Chapter 7

1. What did Twain find so attractive about Hartford? How did it contrast to Buffalo?

2. How did the house that Twain and his wife built reflect their characters, their ambitions, and their values? What does that mansion reveal about American values and tastes in general?

3. Given his own religious views, how can you explain Twain's warm friendships with ministers Beecher and Twichell?

4. Describe Twain's writing process.

Chapter 8

1. What are the principal themes that appear in Twain's writing between 1870 and 1885? How do these themes reflect his view of American political and economic life?

2. How does Twain exploit his remarkable fund of personal experiences in his various and varied books in this period of his life?

3. What does an industrializing and urbanizing country's love affair with *Tom Sawyer* tell us about the concerns and anxieties of late nineteenth-century Americans?

Chapter 9

1. If you agree with the many others who believe that *Huckleberry Finn* was Twain's masterpiece, what do you think makes it so? If you disagree with those who think that the book was his best work or that it is one of the great novels written in the United States, what do you find to be its faults?

2. What can we detect about Twain's view of race from the way he draws the character of Jim? How might white Southerners react to his portrayal?

3. Besides his thinking about race, what do other themes of *Huckleberry Finn* reveal about Mark Twain's own attitudes and beliefs? How do his own views compare with those of most of his contemporaries?

Chapter 10

1. What, if anything, can one deduce about Twain's character from his constant preoccupation with business and speculation? What does this preoccupation tell us about general American attitudes after the Civil War?

2. Why did both Twain and the American people idolize Ulysses Grant? Does American culture have a special regard for illustrious soldiers?

3. How did Twain's experience with the Paige typesetter affect his view of progress, machinery, and technology?

Chapter 11

1. What does Twain's relationship with Henry Huddleston Rogers indicate about the author's attitudes toward capitalism, wealth, and friendship?

2. How does the ending of *The Connecticut Yankee in King Arthur's Court* reveal Twain's complex attitudes toward the modern world? Is his view unusual in America or does it reveal unspoken anxieties that might be found more commonly among the American people?

3. What does *Connecticut Yankee* tell us about Twain's attitudes toward organized religion? Does his view of the Catholic church reflect more widespread anti-Catholic feelings in the United States during this period?

4. Why did Twain invest so much emotional capital in his portrayal of Joan of Arc? What did he see in Joan's life and character and why was telling her story so important to him?

Chapter 12

1. How does the literary critic Van Wyck Brooks account for Twain's growing pessimism? Does Brooks explanation seem plausible or are there other factors in American life and culture that troubled Twain, but that Brooks ignores or underrates?

2. How, during the last years of his life, was Twain able to retain his great popularity despite his attacks on things most Americans hold dear: optimism about social improvement, a high view of human nature, organized religion, and American foreign policy?

A Note on the Sources

H. Wayne Morgan, a leading historian of the Gilded Age, once wrote that "the literature on Mark Twain is almost endless and nearly every week sees a new study of some phase of his career." Morgan wrote that sentence in 1965, and in the forty-five years since then, the pace of writing on Samuel Langhorne Clemens/Mark Twain has increased rather than abated. He has been the subject of countless books, articles, theses, and dissertations. Those wishing to do additional research or reading on some aspect of his life or work should probably begin by consulting one of the encyclopedias, handbooks, or companion volumes devoted to him. Especially valuable is J. R. LeMaster and James D. Wilson, eds., *The Mark Twain Encyclopedia* (New York: Garland, 1993); each of its 740 entries, moreover, includes its own list of bibliographical references. Other helpful starting places are Gregg Camfield, ed., *The Oxford Companion to Mark Twain* (New York: Oxford University Press, 2003), and R. Kent Rasmussen, *A Critical Companion to Mark Twain: A Literary Reference to His Life and Work* (2 vols.; New York: Facts on File, 2006). Less comprehensive overviews include David E. E. Sloane, *Student Companion to Mark Twain* (Westport, CT: Greenwood Press, 2001), and John C. Gerber, *Mark Twain* (Boston: G. K. Hall, 1988). There are several fine collections of recent scholarly articles on aspects of Twain's work. These include Peter Messent and Louis J. Budd, eds., *A Companion to Mark Twain* (Oxford, England: Blackwell, 2005); Shelley Fisher Fishkin, ed., *A Historical Guide to Mark Twain* (New York: Oxford University Press, 2002); Laura E. Skandera Trombley and Michael J. Kiskis, eds., *Constructing Mark Twain: New Directions in Scholarship* (Columbia, MO: University of Missouri Press, 2001); and Forrest G. Robinson, ed., *The Cambridge Companion to Mark Twain* (New York: Cambridge University Press, 1995).

There are thousands of editions of individual Twain works or collections of them. These now include works published during his lifetime, pieces published after his death, and writing never intended for publication, such as his letters and notebooks. Robert M. Rodney's exhaustive compilation, *Mark Twain International: A Bibliography and Interpretation of His Worldwide Popularity* (Westport, CT: Greenwood, 1982), lists more than five thousand separate editions of Twain's works published here and abroad before 1980. A pioneering attempt at a complete listing of Twain's published work can be found in Merle Johnson, *A Bibliography of the Works of Mark Twain* (New York: Harper, 1935); of course that listing does not include works first published after 1935. Very useful is the chronological listing of 800 of Twain's publications, "A Bibliography of Works by Samuel L. Clemens," an appendix to Camfield's *Oxford Companion* (pp. 675–721); but that compilation ends at 1910 and does not claim to be complete. Over the years, Harper published several "complete editions" of Twain's work—the last being a thirty-seven volume collection, *The Writings of Mark Twain*, in 1929. All previous editions of his writings, however, are eclipsed by the magnificent work being done by the Mark Twain Project at the University of California. This ambitious and ongoing effort, employing the finest Twain scholars as editors and advisers, is publishing a series of *The Works of Mark Twain* (scholarly and authoritative editions of his published writings undertaken in cooperation with an earlier project at the University of Iowa) and a series of *The Mark Twain Papers* (expertly edited and annotated collections of his letters, notebooks, and unpublished manuscripts).

Several collections of Twain's wise and witty short remarks are available. Among the most thorough and usable are Caroline Thomas Harnsberger, comp., *Everyone's Mark Twain* (South Brunswick and New York: A. S. Barnes, 1948, 1972), which contains 700 pages of Twain quotes organized by subject; R. Kent Rasmussen, *The Quotable Mark Twain* (New York: McGraw Hill, 1998), which gives 1,800 quotations; and Alex Ayres, comp., *The Wit and Wisdom of Mark Twain* (New York: Harper Perennial, 2005). An encompassing online collection can be found at http//www.twainquotes.com/quotesatoz.html.

Full biographies of Mark Twain start with the authorized and perhaps overly friendly account undertaken with the subject's help, Albert Bigelow Paine, *Mark Twain: A Biography* (3 vols; New York: Harper, 1912). Many of the later biographies rely on Paine, even though they may disagree with some of his interpretations. Readers should not ignore the beautiful and perceptive tribute, William Dean Howells, *My Mark Twain: Reminiscences and Criticisms* (New York: Harper, 1910). Ten years after the writer's death, the literary critic Van Wyck Brooks published *The Ordeal of Mark Twain* (New York: E. P. Dutton, 1920), a strenuously argued psychological study that portrayed Twain as a "wounded" genius—a traitor to his literary power, tamed into mediocrity, frustration, and despair, first by his culturally impoverished western upbringing and later by his wife's gentility and his own financial ambition. There were many answers to Brooks, the principal one being Bernard DeVoto, *Mark Twain's America* (Boston: Little Brown, 1932). Lewis Leary has compiled a collection centering on this controversy—*A Casebook on Mark Twain's Wound* (New York: Crowell, 1962). Biographical studies took an important turn with Justin Kaplan, *Mr. Clemens and Mark Twain* (New York: Simon and Schuster, 1966), a brilliant analysis, based on fine scholarship, that pioneered the speculations about Twain's divided self. Unfortunately, Kaplan's book does not take up the story until Twain leaves California at the age of thirty-one. Three recent additions to Twain biography are especially noteworthy, and readers who want a more substantial one-volume survey of his entire life based on rigorous scholarship and fine writing, will be well rewarded by Andrew Jay Hoffman, *Inventing Mark Twain: The Lives of Samuel Langhorne Clemens* (New York: William Morrow, 1997); Fred Kaplan, *The Singular Mark Twain: A Biography* (New York: Doubleday, 2003); and especially Ron Powers, *Mark Twain: A Life* (New York: Free Press, 2005).

Those who wish to delve more deeply into Twain's early life are directed to Minnie Brashear, *Mark Twain: Son of Missouri* (Chapel Hill: University of North Carolina Press, 1934); Dixon Wecter, *Sam Clemens of Hannibal* (Boston: Houghton Mifflin, 1952); Walter Blair, "Introduction," to *Mark Twain's Hannibal, Huck and Tom* (Berkeley: University of California Press, 1969); Ron Powers, *Dangerous Water: A Biography of the Boy Who Became Mark Twain* (New York: Basic Books, 1999); Edgar M. Branch, *The Literary Apprenticeship of Mark Twain* (Urbana: University of Illinois Press, 1950); John Lauber, *The Making of Mark Twain: A Biography* (New York: American Heritage Press, 1985); Margaret Sanborn, *Mark Twain: The Bachelor Years* (New York: Doubleday, 1990); Jeffrey Steinbrink, *Getting to Be Mark Twain* (Berkeley: University of California Press, 1991); Effie Mona Mack, *Mark Twain in Nevada* (New York: Scribner, 1947); Nigey Lennon, *Sagebrush Bohemian: Mark Twain in California* (New York: Paragon House, 1990); Joseph L. Coulombe, *Mark Twain and the American West* (Columbia, MO: University of Missouri Press, 2003); Dixon Wecter, ed., *The Love Letters of Mark Twain* (New York: Harper, 1949); Susan K. Harris, *The Courtship of Olivia Langdon and Mark Twain* (New York: Cambridge University Press, 1996); and Resa Willis, *Mark and Livy: The Love Story of Mark Twain and the Woman Who Almost Tamed Him* (New York: Routledge, 2004).

The middle years of Twain's life, including his development as a literary artist, are covered in Kenneth R. Andrews, *Nook Farm: Mark Twain's Hartford Circle* (Cambridge, MA: Harvard University Press, 1950); Henry Nash Smith, William M. Gibson, and Frederick Anderson, eds., *Mark Twain–Howells Letters: The Correspondence of Samuel L. Clemens and William D. Howells, 1872–1910* (2 vols.; Cambridge, MA: Harvard University Press, 1960); Hamlin Hill, ed., *Mark Twain's Letters to His Publishers, 1867–1894* (Berkeley: University of California Press, 1967); and Mark Perry, *Grant and Twain: The Story of a Friendship That Changed America* (New York: Random House, 2004). Superb studies of Twain as a literary artist include Henry Nash Smith, *Mark Twain: The Development of a Writer* (Cambridge, MA: Harvard University Press, 1962); Larzer Ziff, *Mark Twain* (New York: Oxford University Press, 2004); and Everett Emerson, *Mark Twain: A Literary Life* (Philadelphia: University of Pennsylvania Press, 1999).

The end of the story can be explored in Charles H. Gold, *"Hatching Ruin" or Mark Twain's Road to Bankruptcy* (Columbia, MO: University of Missouri Press, 2003); Michael Shelden, *Mark Twain: Man in White: The Grand Adventure of His Final Years* (New York: Random House, 2010); Karen Lystra, *Dangerous Intimacy: The Untold Story of Mark Twain's Final Years* (Berkeley: University of California Press, 2004); Laura Skandera Trombley, *Mark Twain's Other Woman: The Hidden Story of His Final Years* (New York: Knopf, 2010); John Cooley, ed., *Mark Twain's Aquarium: The Samuel Clemens–Angelfish Correspondence, 1904–1910* (Athens: University of Georgia Press, 1991); Hamlin Hill, *Mark Twain: God's Fool* (New York: Harper and Row, 1973); William R. Macnaughton, *Mark Twain's Last Years as a Writer* (Columbia, MO: University of Missouri Press, 1979); Louis J. Budd, *Mark Twain: Social Philosopher* (Bloomington, IN: Indiana University Press, 1962); Philip Foner, *Mark Twain: Social Critic* (New York: International Publishers, 1958); Frederick Anderson, ed., *A Pen Warmed-up in Hell: Mark Twain in Protest* (New York: Harper and Row, 1972); Bernard DeVoto, ed., *Mark Twain in Eruption: Hitherto Unpublished Pages about Men and Events by Mark Twain* (New York: Harper, 1940); Jim Zwick, ed., *Mark Twain's Weapons of Satire: Anti-Imperialist Writings on the Philippine-American War* (Syracuse, NY: Syracuse University Press, 1992); Paul F. Boller, "Mark Twain's Mechanistic Determinism," in Boller, *Freedom and Fate in American Thought: From Edwards to Dewey* (Dallas: SMU Press, 1978), 188–216; and Tom Quirk, *Mark Twain and Human Nature* (Columbia, MO: University of Missouri Press, 2007).

Among the numerous books dealing with particular aspects of Twain's life and work, the following are especially worthwhile: Sherwood Cummings, *Mark Twain and Science: Adventures of a Mind* (Baton Rouge: Louisiana State University Press, 1988); Arthur G. Pettit, *Mark Twain and the South* (Lexington: University of Kentucky Press, 1986); Howard G. Baetzhold, *Mark Twain and John Bull: The British Connections* (Bloomington: Indiana University Press, 1970); Robert L. Gale, *Plots and Characters in the Works of Mark Twain* (2 vols.; Hamden, CT: Archon Books, 1973); Dan Vogel, *Mark Twain's Jews* (Jersey City,

NJ: KTAV Publishing House, 2006), Mary Ellen Goad, *The Image and the Woman in the Life and Writings of Mark Twain* (Emporia: Kansas State Teachers College, 1971); Laura E. Skandera Trombley, *Mark Twain in the Company of Women* (Philadelphia: University of Pennsylvania Press, 1994); Kenneth S. Lynn, *Mark Twain and Southwestern Humor* (Boston: Little Brown, 1959); Pascal Covici, Jr., *Mark Twain's Humor: The Image of a World* (Dallas: Southern Methodist University Press, 1962); David E. E. Sloane, *Mark Twain as a Literary Comedian* (Baton Rouge: Louisiana State University Press, 1979); Frederick W. Lorch, *The Trouble Begins at Eight: Mark Twain's Lecture Tours* (Ames: Iowa State University Press, 1968); Margaret Duckett, *Mark Twain and Bret Harte* (Norman: University of Oklahoma Press, 1964); and Allison Ensor, *Mark Twain and the Bible* (Lexington: University of Kentucky Press, 1969).

Of course, the general history of America during Twain's life has been the subject of innumerable fine studies, and it is possible to list here only a few of those that deepen the context of Twain's career. Both George Rogers Taylor, *The Transportation Revolution, 1815–1860* (New York: Rinehart, 1951) and Charles G. Sellers, *The Market Revolution: Jacksonian America, 1815–1846* (New York: Oxford University Press, 1991) explore American economic development as Twain was growing up. The former gives fascinating details about steamboating, but in that connection, see also Louis C. Hunter, *Steamboats on the Western Rivers* (New York: Octagon Books, 1969 edition). A good place to start learning about antebellum America and the Civil War is James M. McPherson, *The Battle Cry of Freedom: The Civil War Era* (New York: Oxford University Press, 1988). The situation in Twain's area is explored in Bruce Nichols, *Guerilla Warfare in Civil War Missouri* (Jefferson, NC: McFarland, 2004) and in William E. Parrish, *Turbulent Partnership: Missouri and the Union, 1861–1865* (Columbia, MO: University of Missouri Press, 1963). For the Reconstruction era, students should start with Eric Foner, *Reconstruction: America's Unfinished Revolution* (New York: HarperCollins, 1988). A compact introduction to the Gilded Age is Rebecca Edwards, *New Spirits: Americans in the Gilded Age, 1865–1905* (New York: Oxford University Press, 2006). A fine collection of scholarly articles are brought together in Charles Calhoun, ed., *The Gilded Age: Perspectives on the Origins of Modern America* (Wilmington, DE: Scholarly Resources, 1996); an older, but still valuable collection is H. Wayne Morgan, ed., *The Gilded Age* (Syracuse, NY: Syracuse University Press, 1970 edition).

For economic life at the end of the nineteenth century, see Walter Licht, *Industrializing America: The Nineteenth Century* (Baltimore: Johns Hopkins University Press, 1995); Naomi Lamoreaux, *The Great Merger Movement in American Business, 1895–1904* (New York: Cambridge University Press, 1985); and David Montgomery, *The Fall of the House of Labor: The Workplace the State and American Labor Activism, 1865–1925*

(New York: Cambridge University Press, 1987). On politics: H. Wayne Morgan, *From Hayes to McKinley: National Party Politics, 1877–1896* (Syracuse, NY: Syracuse University Press, 1969), or Morton Keller, *Affairs of State: Public Life in Late Nineteenth Century America* (Cambridge, MA: Harvard University Press, 1977). On domestic life and gender relations: Rebecca Edwards, *Angels in the Machinery: Gender in American Party Politics from the Civil War to the Progressive Era* (New York: Oxford University Press, 1997); Christopher Lasch, *Haven in a Heartless World: The Family Besieged* (New York: Basic Books, 1979); and Carroll Smith-Rosenberg, *Disorderly Conduct: Visions of Gender in Victorian America* (New York: Knopf, 1985). On imperialism and American foreign policy: Robert L. Beisner, *From the Old Diplomacy to the New, 1865–1900* (Arlington Heights, IL: Harlan Davidson, 1986 edition), Walter LaFeber, *The New Empire: An Interpretation of American Expansion, 1860–1898* (Ithaca, NY: Cornell University Press, 1963); and David Healy, *U.S. Expansionism: The Imperialist Urge in the 1890s* (Madison, WI: University of Wisconsin Press, 1970). On race relations, the classic study is C. Vann Woodward, *The Strange Career of Jim Crow* (New York: Oxford University Press, 1974 edition), but see also George M. Fredrickson, *The Black Image in the White Mind: The Debate on Afro-American Character and Destiny, 1817–1914* (New York: Harper and Row, 1971); Rayford Logan, *The Negro in American Life and Thought: The Nadir, 1877–1901* (New York: Dial Press, 1954), Joel Williamson, *The Crucible of Race: Black-White Relations in the American South since Emancipation* (New York: Oxford University Press, 1984); and Leon Litwack, *Trouble in Mind: Black Southerners in the Age of Jim Crow* (New York: Knopf, 1998). Many of these studies contain impressive bibliographical references that can guide curious students to numerous additional sources.

Exploring the intellectual context of Twain's life and thought should begin with George M. Fredrickson, *The Inner Civil War: Northern Intellectuals and the Crisis of the Union* (New York: Harper and Row, 1968). Other helpful introductions include Alan Trachtenberg, *The Incorporation of America: Culture and Society in the Gilded Age* (New York: Hill and Wang, 2007 edition); David Shi, *Facing Facts: Realism in American Thought and Culture, 1850–1920* (New York: Oxford University Press, 1995); Louis Menand, *The Metaphysical Club: A Story of Ideas in America* (New York: Farrar, Straus and Giroux, 2001); T. J. Jackson Lears, *No Place of Grace: Antimodernism and the Transformation of American Culture, 1880–1920* (Chicago: University of Chicago Press, 1994 edition); R. Jackson Wilson, *In Quest of Community: Social Philosophy in the United States, 1860–1920* (New York: Oxford University Press, 1970); and H. Wayne Morgan, *Unity and Culture: The United States, 1877–1900* (London: Penguin Press, 1971).

Index